Selling Solar

Damian Miller is a leading expert on solar energy in emerging markets. He was born and raised in New York City, before moving to Britain where he completed his schooling. He holds a PhD from the University of Cambridge (Trinity College), where he was based at the Judge Business School, and his dissertation addressed the role of entrepreneurs in the diffusion of solar photo-voltaic technology in Asia. After finishing his PhD in 1998 he put his research findings into practice, becoming Shell Solar's Director of Rural Operations and establishing solar subsidiaries in India, Sri Lanka, the Philippines and Indonesia. He also implemented a large-scale solar project in China and managed joint ventures in Morocco and South Africa. During this time he worked closely with multilateral and bilateral development agencies and emerging market governments to help grow local solar markets, overseeing the connection of more than 125,000 solar homes. At the end of 2006 he set up Orb Energy in India. In just two years, Orb has become one of India's leading providers of solar energy solutions. Orb sells, installs and services solar systems across multiple states in India, with plans for further expansion. He has lived, worked and traveled extensively throughout Europe, Asia and Africa, and currently resides in Bangalore, India.

Selling Solar

The Diffusion of Renewable Energy in Emerging Markets

Damian Miller

publishing for a sustainable future

London • Sterling, VA

First published by Earthscan in the UK and USA in 2009

ISBN: 978-1-84407-518-8

Typeset by FiSH Books, Enfield
Printed and bound in the UK by TJ International, Padstow
Cover design by Lani Fried

For a full list of publications please contact:

Earthscan
Dunstan House
14a St Cross St
London, EC1N 8XA, UK
Tel: +44 (0)20 7841 1930
Fax: +44 (0)20 7242 1474
Email: earthinfo@earthscan.co.uk
Web: **www.earthscan.co.uk**

22883 Quicksilver Drive, Sterling, VA 20166-2012, USA

Earthscan publishes in association with the International Institute for
Environment and Development

A catalogue record for this book is available from the British Library

Library of Congress Cataloging-in-Publication Data

Miller, Damian.
    Selling solar : the diffusion of renewable energy in emerging markets / Damian
    Miller.
        p. cm.
    Includes bibliographical references.
    ISBN 978-1-84407-518-8 (hardback)
    1. Solar energy. I. Title.
    TJ810.M5275 2008
    381'.4562147—dc22

                                                                2008035683

Contents

List of Figures and Tables

Figures

List of Acronyms
and Abbreviations

AC	alternating current
ASTAE	Asian Alternative Energy Unit (World Bank)
AU	administering unit
BOI	Board of Investments (Sri Lanka)
CER	Certified Emission Reduction
CFL	compact fluorescent lights
CDM	Clean Development Mechanism
DC	direct current
DGM	deputy general manager
DM	Deutsche mark
DME	Department of Minerals and Energy (South Africa)
DoE	Department of Energy (Philippines)
EB	Executive Board (of the CDM)
ESD	Energy Services Delivery Project (Sri Lanka)
FT	*Financial Times*
GEF	Global Environment Facility
GVEP	Global Village Energy Partnership
HCFC	hydrochlorofluorocarbon
IBRD	International Bank for Reconstruction and Development
IDA	International Development Association
IDCOL	Infrastructure Development Company Limited (Bangladesh)
IEA	International Energy Agency
IFC	International Finance Corporation
IPCC	Intergovernmental Panel on Climate Change
IREDA	Indian Renewable Energy Development Agency
kW	kilowatt
kWh	kilowatt hour
LED	light-emitting diode
LPG	liquefied petroleum gas
MFI	microfinance institution

MNES	Ministry of Non-Conventional Energy Sources (India)
MNRE	Ministry of New and Renewable Energy (India)
MW	megawatt
MSHI	Million Solar Homes Initiative
NGO	non-governmental organization
OECD	Organisation for Economic Co-operation and Development
PCI	participating credit institution
PDD	project design document
PoA	programme of activities (pertains to CDM projects)
PV	photovoltaic
PVMTI	Photovoltaic Market Transformation Initiative
R&D	research and development
REDP	Renewable Energy Development Project (China)
REEF	Renewable Energy and Energy Efficiency Fund
RERED	Renewable Energy for Rural Economic Development Project (Sri Lanka)
R	rand (South African currency)
RMB	rimimbi/renminbi (Chinese currency)
Rp	rupiah (Indonesian)
Rs	rupee (Indian)
SHS	solar home system
SDC	Solar Development Corporation
SDF	Solar Development Foundation
SDG	Solar Development Group
SEEDS	Sarvodya Economic Enterprises Development Services
SLR	Sri Lankan rupee
TW	terawatt
UNDP	United Nations Development Programme
UNEP	United Nations Environment Programme
UNFCCC	United Nations Framework Convention on Climate Change
USD	United States dollar
V	volt
VC	venture capital
VER	Verified Emission Reduction
W	watt
Wp	watt-peak

Prologue

The windows were down and I was travelling along a single-lane road between the small towns of Bible and Ampara on the eastern side of Sri Lanka. It was a sunny day and the breeze felt good. This was March 2005, three months after the tsunami had laid waste to much of the country's southern and eastern coasts, and it was the first time I had been back in Sri Lanka since the tsunami had struck.

I was then working for Shell – the oil and gas company – which at the time was engaged in the global solar business. As part of this work, I had helped set up, and was now responsible for managing, several subsidiary solar businesses in Asia, including Sri Lanka. On this particular trip our final destination was Batticaloa, on the northeast coast, where some of our staff, as well as many of our customers, had been personally affected by the tsunami.

It was a long trip from the capital, Colombo, and we were taking a circuitous route in order to visit other branches. Because we were running late, my colleagues and I had opted for some warm soft drinks and potato chips instead of lunch, and we were chatting about the business as we drove. Before setting off, I had heard that quite a few houses along this particular stretch of road had bought solar power systems, but I had no idea how many.

As we passed a house on our left, our General Manager shouted, 'There's one!', and we all turned to look. No sooner had we turned back than someone else said, 'there's another'. We were late, and driving quickly, so I asked the driver to slow down. We slowed to a crawl as we passed homes on our left, mostly brick homes with tiled roofs. It was early in the afternoon, and hot, so not too many people were out. But on each home we could see a single solar panel poking through the roof, and, as we drove, all of us joined in, pointing out 'there's another', 'and another', 'and another!' . . .

I had never seen such an extensive adoption of solar systems. This is what large-scale diffusion of solar looks like, I thought to myself, when every home in sight is using the technology. When one house buys it and has light at night, then neighbours come to see it, talk about it, get convinced and then buy it themselves.

Just five years earlier in Sri Lanka, this was not the case. You may have found one solar system in every four to five villages. But now in villages like this, it seemed you could not find a single house without a solar system. And this showed in the statistics. In 1999, barely 500 solar systems were sold by the entire solar industry in Sri Lanka. But about 18,500 solar systems were sold in 2003 alone, and by the end of 2006, more than 100,000 systems had been sold to more than 7 per cent of Sri Lanka's formerly unelectrified households. What changed? How did this happen? Understanding this story in Sri Lanka, and other emerging markets, is what this book is about. It will, I hope, shed light on what will be one of the single most challenging issues facing the world in the 21st century – the diffusion of renewable energy in emerging markets.

ॐ

I remember the day my interest in renewable energy was piqued. I was an undergraduate in London in the early 1990s, interning for Friends of the Earth a few days a week. It was one of those really grey, cloudy days you get in London in the winter, and I was asked to read through a pile of articles to help my team prepare for the Rio conference. It was kind of quiet, and despite several strong cups of tea, it was all going a bit slow. But when I picked up an article about renewable energy technology and its 'transfer' to emerging markets, something resonated with me.

It was clear from the article that emerging markets would need to consume much more energy to grow their economies and fulfil the aspirations of their surging populations. Of this there was, and remains, no doubt. But an energy future tied to fossil fuels was a scary scenario. Scary for the world as a whole, given the unprecedented levels of consumption to come. And scary for the emerging markets themselves, partly because they were likely to feel the impact of climate change disproportionately, and partly because without renewable energy, they were forging an intimate dependency on a finite resource that would become increasingly scarce.

But at this time, renewable energy technologies were simply not taken seriously. Despite their elegance, and enormous potential, they were marginalized. So I remember asking myself, 'If renewable energy technologies are such an attractive solution, why aren't they already being used more widely?'. It was a question that would stay with me from then on, and would, eventually, lead to this book.

Renewable energy technologies are today broadly referred to as 'renewables'. Sources of renewable energy we typically read about are hydro (from running water), tidal (from tidal currents), geothermal (from heat inside the

Earth), wind (from the prevailing winds), biomass (from plants) and solar (from the sun). I didn't know it then, but from the menu of renewable energy options, solar has a truly enormous potential.

To put this in perspective, today the world uses energy at a rate of 4.1×10^{20} joules per year. This is equivalent to continuous power consumption of 13 trillion watts, or 13 terawatts (TW). But with continuing economic growth and a global population growing from 6 to 9 billion, this is projected to increase from 13 TW to 30 TW by 2050, and to more than triple to 46 TW by the end of the century.[1] In terms of the range of renewables that can contribute to this surging need for energy, further hydro-electric dams could contribute only 0.5 TW, tidal currents up to 2 TW, geothermal up to 12 TW (of which only a small fraction can be tapped) and wind in the range of only 2–4 TW. Solar, however, can contribute an incredible total of 120,000 TW. Indeed, in just one hour the Earth receives enough energy from the sun to power all its needs for an entire year. Put another way, if just 0.16 per cent of the world's land mass (equivalent to the land used by the US federal highway system) was covered with solar panels of 10 per cent efficiency (less than today's commercially available panels) this would provide 20 TW of power – two-thirds of our global needs in 2050.[2]

When it comes to accelerating the deployment of solar and other renewables, many people feel that industrialized countries should lead. For some, this is a political issue: if the industrialized world caused climate change, then it should also lead in solving it. For others, it is a more practical issue: the infrastructure, financing, markets and policies are all more conducive to renewables in industrialized countries:

> It's hard to see how alternative energy technologies could succeed in developing countries. Alternative technologies are tremendously expensive and uncertain, even in the developed countries. … It is very hard to imagine a technically backward country such as China or India successfully embracing solar technology or rolling out a production-ready fuel cell model before Detroit does.[3]

But this reasoning is flawed on several counts. First, in the absence of fully formed energy infrastructures in many emerging markets, renewables might actually have a competitive advantage over fossil fuels in certain segments. Second, because emerging markets have not yet made the same infrastructure commitments as industrialized countries, there are less fixed costs to consider when transitioning to renewable energy. Third, renewable energy is a source of technological innovation, wealth-creation and jobs, as well as energy independence – so self-interest can dictate an early turn to renewables. Finally, without an early and accelerated diffusion of renewables in the emerging markets (in addition to early action in the industrialized countries), the world simply will not head off climatic disaster.

Emerging markets already account for half of the world's energy demand and since 2000 have been responsible for 85 per cent of the increase. Moreover, since 2000, world energy consumption has increased at twice the rate of the previous decade.[4] This surge in consumption is driven by a legitimate demand for the same sorts of goods and services that are taken for granted in industrialized countries – air-conditioners, computers, ovens, TVs, fridges, cars, roads, trains, communication and so on. But current increases in consumption are trivial compared to what will come. Take cars, for example. The total number of cars in China and India is projected to rise from roughly 30 million today to 750 million by 2040. This is more than all the cars presently on the world's roads, and even then it will represent only half the current per capita car ownership in the US.

Now consider where we are already in terms of environmental consequences. Start with local pollution. As *Time* reported in a special issue on pollution in Asia, all but one of the 25 most polluted cities in the world are in that continent. Of these, 17 are in China and 5 are in India. This pollution invariably has huge implications for people's health, notably respiratory illnesses such as chronic obstructive pulmonary disease (COPD), a condition:

> that begins by making it uncomfortable for you to breathe, and eventually catches your throat in a steel grip so tight that you must lie on a hospital bed with a mask over your face, gasping for oxygen.[5]

There is no question that many emerging markets, and their local populations, are already, literally and tragically, choking on growth.

But there is also a global environmental dimension to the story of unfolding energy consumption: climate change. Sometimes it is hard to comprehend the magnitude of the disaster that faces us. But I think this journalist summed it up better than most when he wrote:

> Sea levels will rise over the century by around half a metre; snow will disappear from all but the highest mountains; deserts will spread; oceans will become acidic, leading to the destruction of coral reefs and atolls; and deadly heat waves will become more prevalent. The impact will be catastrophic, forcing hundreds of millions of people to flee their devastated homelands, particularly in tropical low lying areas, while creating waves of immigrants whose movements will strain the economies of even the most affluent countries.[6]

Although China consumes only 2 barrels of oil per person per year compared to the 28 barrels per person consumed in the US,[7] it is expected to pass the US as the largest emitter of greenhouse gases in 2008.[8] And if we look a little further ahead, the share of carbon dioxide emitted by emerging markets is projected to increase to 70 per cent by 2025, much of this from the growth in fossil fuel power plants in Asia.[9]

Such projections are no longer lost on the populations and policymakers of the industrialized world. As *The New York Times* reported, the climate change spotlight is shifting to emerging markets such as China and India, 'representing a combined population of 2.3 billion and both economies growing at a pace about 9 per cent a year', where it has become clear that 'allowing them to pollute as much as Western countries would have catastrophic effects on the environment'.[10]

For emerging markets, this concern with the environment, and climate change, comes at just the wrong time. Just when technology and capital has started to flow like never before – enabling them to develop their economies and lift their populations out of poverty – the world has suddenly become concerned with their energy consumption and consequent emissions. This simply does not fit with the dominant development paradigm, which has been 'grow first, clean up later'.[11]

Not surprisingly, the response from many emerging market governments has been to push back. They make their case on three levels. The first is that the industrialized world is historically responsible for 75 per cent of the existing excess of greenhouse gases above pre-industrial levels. Also, per capita emissions in emerging markets are a fraction of those in the industrialized world. Finally, emerging markets have less money than the industrialized world to pay for the required transformation. In an article entitled 'China says rich countries should take lead on global warming' an official makes it plain that 'as a developing country that's growing rapidly and has a big population, to thoroughly transform the energy structure and use renewable energy would need a lot of money'.[12]

Of course, the reality is that our shared climate will not respond to sensible arguments about historical responsibility, per capita consumption or fairness in terms of the global distribution of wealth. It will respond to aggregate levels of carbon dioxide emissions. And yet, at the same time, emerging markets cannot be asked to rein in their economies, just as the benefits of growth start to trickle down. This proposal would be as unacceptable in Beijing or Delhi as it is in London or Washington, DC. So what is the world to do?

In what was probably a little-read article called 'Climate change: Carry on flying says Blair', the former Prime Minister of Great Britain was clear on the 'danger' of saying to people, 'right, in Britain ... you're not going to have any more cheap air travel, everybody else is going to have it'. So instead he went on to recommend:

> You've got to do this together in a way that doesn't end up putting
> people off the green agenda by saying you must not have a good time any
> more and can't consume. All the evidence is that if you use science and
> technology constructively, your economy can grow, people can have a
> good time, but do so more responsibly.[13]

And therein lies the solution that policymakers, business people, and all of us
as consumers and citizens, consciously or unconsciously, in industrialized
countries or emerging markets, fall back upon when faced with the threat of
climate change: *technology*. As Blair says, none of us – whether in India, China
or Great Britain – want to stop having a good time, and therefore technology
and technological change become, as it were, our last and only hope.[14]

In terms of the technologies that emerging markets can fall back on, technologies for greater energy efficiency will have an enormous role to play in
helping reduce emissions. For instance, Chinese industries are estimated to use
four times more energy in their relative sectors than the global average.[15] But
greater energy efficiency without a dramatic expansion in renewable energy
simply will not be enough:

> In the longer term, any savings achieved by improvements in energy effi-
> ciency will only help to alleviate the problem; they will not in themselves
> solve it. ... [I]f carbon emissions and accumulations are to be reduced
> over the long term, energy conservation measures will need to be
> complemented by measures to develop non-carbon technologies.[16]

For their part, although emerging market governments prefer not to be bound
by emission targets, they are already setting targets for renewable energy. The
Chinese Government has pledged to make renewable energy account for 15
per cent of the country's total energy supply by 2020 and to spend US$200
billion on that effort.[17] Similarly, in 2006 India's former President called for the
country to increase renewable energy's share of power generation from 5 to 25
per cent by 2030.[18]

But such numbers imply an extraordinary technological shift. Consider the
case of India in more detail. By 2030, the population is projected to reach 1.47
billion people, at which point it will become the most populous country in the
world. Increasingly affluent, and desirous of the same standards of living as the
industrialized countries, energy consumption is set to grow dramatically. The
Indian Government's most recent integrated energy report states that:

> To deliver a sustained growth of eight per cent through 2031–2032, and
> to meet the lifeline needs of all citizens, India needs, at the very least, to
> increase its primary energy supply by three to four times and its elec-
> tricity generating capacity/supply by five to six times their 2003–2004

levels. ... By 2031–2032, power generating capacity must increase to nearly 800,000 MW from the current capacity of around 160,000 MW.[19]

If the former President's vision is to be realized, and if India is to increase the contribution of renewables from 5 to 25 per cent of power generation by 2030, it will need to grow the installed base of renewable energy from 8000 MW today to nearly 200,000 MW by 2030. This represents 25-fold growth in just 20 years!

The questions of course remain *how* emerging markets like India will make such a radical transformation so quickly and *who* will make it happen.

&

Most students are caught up in the issues of their day. In my student days, sustainable development was shooting up the policy agenda, and was quickly becoming ensconced in the global lexicon. The only problem was that people still weren't sure what it meant.

As far as I could make out then, renewable energy fitted the 'sustainable development' bill entirely. It would enable emerging markets to continue to 'develop' – in other words consume energy for improved quality of life and economic growth – in a way that was ultimately more 'sustainable', in other words emissions free. Some people propagated definitions of sustainable development as 'a negotiated process', allowing for multiple interpretations and for dialogue. I was personally looking for something more concrete.

Then, as now, it seemed to me that the climate crisis actually created a golden opportunity for emerging markets to build their nascent infrastructures around a new set of renewable energy technologies that will not only help to solve the problem of climate change, but create huge, innovative new industries; enhance their energy independence; produce a cleaner local environment for better public health; and limit large-scale resettlement. In the early 1990s, this concept of emerging markets going where no industrialized countries had gone before took on a fashionable new name, one that was bandied about almost as much as 'sustainable development': 'leapfrogging' became the order of the day.[20]

Because the energy infrastructure was, and still is, far from built in many emerging markets, an opportunity was identified to leapfrog over the conventional fossil fuel technologies used by industrialized countries to a new set of cleaner renewable energy technologies. But, like any new, catchy concept, the reality was that it's a lot easier to say 'leapfrog' than to do it. Leapfrogging told us nothing about how emerging markets could approach this challenge, and what might inhibit or accelerate the process.

In search of greater understanding, and at the outset of my doctoral thesis, I remember talking to a helpful professor and receiving some solid advice: maybe there would be clues in the progress of other innovations.

Following this lead I came across the literature on innovation diffusion. And what I read was compelling. By 'diffusion', the authors simply meant the process by which an innovation spreads to members of a society, and the literature referred to a whole host of innovations about which I knew relatively little: the diffusion of hybrid seeds, the diffusion of VCRs, the diffusion of washing machines, the diffusion of computers and so on. Needless to say, I was not as passionate about the diffusion of VCRs. But it was clear to me that the theories generated by such research could help explain the diffusion of renewable energy technologies in emerging markets.

Having found some theoretical basis for my research, I needed to focus on just one renewable energy technology, renewables as a sector being too broad, with different technologies having different reasons for being, or not being, used more widely. I initially thought that, given the scale of the problem, the scale of the solution needed to be BIG to be worthy of future enquiry. So it was with some surprise that I found myself so intrigued by a much smaller technology: solar photovoltaic (PV) panels applied at the decentralized level – households and small businesses – in rural areas of emerging markets. What caught my attention was simple. Compared to a lot of other renewables at the time, this technology was already being sold in some emerging markets on a *commercial* basis. Its being sold commercially was very compelling, as it portended the possibility of self-sustaining and ever-growing diffusion of solar photovoltaic technology. Moreover, although the application was small, enough for a few lights, TV, radio and so on, it was getting at a really BIG problem: how to get electricity to the then 2 billion people who did not have it, and to do it in a manner that would not further exacerbate emissions.

There are bigger applications of solar that might initially seem more worthy of enquiry, such as building integrated solar systems or large-scale solar power plants. But the case of rural solar always seemed to me more important for the global environment than many initially thought. As the director of sustainable development strategy and operations at the World Bank recently said, 'how the developing world chooses to electrify will determine the fate of the Earth'.[21] Moreover, it struck me that understanding how solar had gained a foothold in rural markets could shed light on the much larger challenge of how emerging markets could accelerate the diffusion of renewable energy.

In the end, my doctorate considered contrasting rates of diffusion of solar systems in India and Indonesia. From this I generated conclusions that would inform my work in the industry, as well as this book. What I found was that rural areas of emerging markets were ready for solar technology. It was no longer a question of waiting for this or that improvement to reduce the cost or improve the functionality. Of course this would help, but what was really needed was for entrepreneurs to bring together financing for solar customers, with a widespread network to deliver, install and service the technology. These were conclusions that bore themselves out once I was engaged in the business of selling solar myself, and they are conclusions that I will return to in this book.

☙

But if *Selling Solar* is largely about explaining the diffusion of solar in emerging markets, my hope is that it will also transcend the case of solar technology, and resonate for the reader in other ways.

First, I will bring to bear a range of theories on innovation diffusion to help us understand and explain the solar phenomenon. The starting point for all of these theories is that an innovation rarely diffuses through a society as quickly as is anticipated, and all of them try to explain this phenomenon. By integrating these theories into one coherent framework, I hope to provide a tool for those interested in the diffusion of other renewable energy and energy-efficient innovations, such as small hydro, solar water heaters, wind turbines, fuel cells, LED lights and electric vehicles. I also hope the framework will be relevant for those interested in green innovation and innovation diffusion more broadly. The book is intended to be of use to those who are studying diffusion from an academic perspective, as well as those who are more proactively trying to expedite the rate at which an innovation spreads.

Second, I want the book to delve deeply into how sustainable technological change is actually achieved. As a student, I remember being somewhat frustrated by the environmental literature, which talked a lot about the 'need' for technological change, but very little about how such change would come about or who would drive it. In the early years of the debates on climate change, many people expressed a sense of urgency that the world must change the way it generates, transports and consumes energy, but there was very little written about exactly how cleaner energy technologies would find their way onto the market. Nobody was really providing analysts, policymakers and business people with the theoretical frameworks to achieve this. What exactly were people meant to do about this problem? Where should they start?

Third, I would like to provide the reader with a greater understanding of the emerging market dimension. Not just in terms of the sound bites that people are now accustomed to, for instance 'large capital inflows' and 'increasing consumption of commodities', but a bit more about the nuts and bolts of actually doing business in emerging markets. And not doing just any business, but renewable energy business, of which thousands will be needed in the days to come. The challenge of diffusing renewable energy in emerging markets lies not just in the scale of the transformation that is required, but also in working through some challenging market conditions. I hope to shed some light on this and help people understand what to expect, and perhaps more importantly what not to expect, when exploring these new markets.

Fourth, history is replete with examples of individuals who combined vision, perseverance and skill to effect profound technological change. When sustainable development was coming of age as a concept, I remember wanting to read more about the people who were trying to effect profound changes in the way we use and consume resources. Specifically, I wanted to hear more about the obstacles they faced, the strategies they deployed for overcoming them and the new problems that emerged as their strategies started to take hold. Unfortunately, such accounts were difficult to find. So looking back, it is not surprising that my own path would focus on entrepreneurs as the 'agents' of sustainable technological change. I resolved that if and when I wrote a book about solar, it would tell the story of the people and organizations that brought about the diffusion of this technology.

Fifth, in the 1980s and 1990s there was a disconnect between the sustainable development movement and the world of business. Business was largely identified as the source of unsustainable development – seen more as the problem than the solution. And in the literature of the day, where business found any promising portrayals, it was usually a story about this or that company adopting an internal paper recycling scheme or some equally 'internal' initiative. There were few, if any, stories of businesses 'delivering' and 'selling' cleaner technologies, the challenges in doing so, and the key factors for success. It seemed to be a big omission. This book belatedly tries to fill that gap – to give the reader examples of where businesses have been trying to bring cleaner energy technology to market, and diffuse it on a large-scale basis in emerging markets, and where policymakers stepped in either to assist this process or hamper it.

Finally, I try to present to the reader a way of integrating entrepreneurship with policy, as it pertains to renewable energy diffusion. I put entrepreneurs at the centre of the analysis, not policymakers. This is because in our largely capitalist global system, it is often the private sector that can bring the most money, management skills and technological resources to the process of innovation diffusion. And it is entrepreneurs in particular who tend to be the most dynamic and innovative in the business community, and historically responsible for bringing innovations to market. That said, it is policymakers who will need to lead entrepreneurs by the nose, as it were, so that emerging markets will have better alternatives to the current fossil-based energy options. As *Selling Solar* will show, governments and international policymaking bodies like the World Bank can have a profound impact by altering the incentives entrepreneurs face in the renewable energy sector. They can literally make or a break a market that entrepreneurs are toiling to establish.

Selling Solar is therefore a hybrid in many senses. It devotes many of its pages to the empirical case of solar, but also tries to bring some theoretical foundation to the case. It delves deep into the details of solar energy diffusion, but also tries to step back and generalize about renewable energy diffusion more broadly. It identifies the transformative powers of entrepreneurs, but also the key role of policymakers in providing the right incentives. It builds on my early experiences in academic research, but also tries to bring a practitioner's eye to the matter. This melding of different objectives and perspectives will I hope make the book interesting to a broad range of people. If this seems an ambitious agenda, so too, at one time, did selling solar in emerging markets.

ᐦ

On our last day of travel in Sri Lanka in that March of 2005, we headed out for Batticaloa on the northeast coast of the island. To get there you first had to go through several military checkpoints, and pass by more than a few bombed-out homes and shelters. There had recently been a flare-up in violence caused by a breakaway faction of the Tamil Tigers, so in addition to the tsunami, the local people were also coping with increased communal tension.

When we arrived at the Batticaloa branch, I was amazed to find that despite the havoc wreaked by the tsunami, the branch and its staff were still selling more than 25 solar systems per month and continuing to carry out after-sales service. Many customers' homes had been washed away, along with the systems they owned, and we were looking at a solution to provide them with replacement systems once they had rebuilt. After reviewing the performance of the branch, the sales manager in charge then offered to take us to the site of his former home, where the tsunami had struck.

En route to his home, we stopped at a Hindu temple located on the beach. As we approached the temple I could see that it had literally been cleaved in two by the enormous power of the tsunami, with one half now leaning at an angle to the still upright half, virtually resting on the sand beneath it. The sea was about 50 metres away, and though largely calm today, it still seemed to gurgle and churn with a ferocity deep below the surface. We were able to walk right through the split in the temple, from one side to the other. It foretold of the awesome power of the waves that had struck the sales manager's home, located just a couple of hundred metres up the beach.

Standing in what was once his living room, I was stunned into silence and reflection. The former two-storey home, about 200 metres from the sea, was now gone. All that was left standing was the front door and some of the supporting wall. Most of the nearby houses had been swept away, revealing only the original foundations. His family had managed to survive by running inland in time, and getting to some height. But the community down the beach had not been as lucky – they had nowhere to run.

As I walked down, I came to a spot called the Dutch Bar, a sand bar named after the early Dutch settlers. This sand bar, on which an entire community had once lived, was stretched out between the sea on one side to the east and a deep wide lagoon on the other side to the west. I imagined it as it was before, shaded under the coconut trees, with each house pressing onto the other, a vibrant community where children would have played in the narrow lanes between houses, and where adults would have lingered in the doorways to chat with passing neighbours.

But now it was all gone. The tsunami took every single home and swept them into the lagoon behind, turning it into a mass burial ground. As I walked through the remains of this community, stepping between biscuit tins, bits of clothing and fractured pieces of furniture, I thought to myself that this is what climate change and its devastating effects will look like. There will be more and more such incidents with sea-level rise and sea surges. Entire communities will be washed away, and those who survive will be destitute migrants.

When you see such devastation, you can understand why people call climate change a weapon of mass destruction. It is a crisis that needs to be faced with the utmost urgency and resolution. Millions of lives are at stake, and only through containing present and future growth in emissions do we have a chance of addressing it. I know that solar systems sold into rural homes in emerging markets will not of themselves solve the climate crisis. But I believe the story of how such a technology came to diffuse in such great numbers serves as testimony to what can be achieved with the technology we have at our disposal today.

The entrepreneurs profiled in this story did not wait for an R&D break-through or a better solar panel to come along. They recognized that, if packaged and sold in the right way, people would buy the solar technology that was already available. In the end, what successful diffusion took was a combi-nation of entrepreneurial vision, persistence and policy innovation to ignite a market for solar that was waiting to happen. It just needed some people to go and do it.

Acknowledgements

The foundations for this book were laid in my early days as a student. Therefore I would first like to acknowledge those who inspired me to pursue my academic interests. Professor Ian Rowlands, then Lecturer in International Relations and Development Studies at the London School of Economics, played a key role in encouraging me to investigate my still unformed interest in energy and climate change. Although he may not have known it, he opened the door that would eventually lead me to write this book, on which he has also provided invaluable input. Ian's early role was later complemented by Dr Gwyn Prins, then head of the Global Security Programme at Cambridge University. Gwyn wrote an elegant editorial on how solar technology could become a 'silver bullet' for emerging markets,[1] and inspired me to focus on this hopeful technology for my doctoral thesis.

My PhD supervisors at the Judge Business School, Cambridge University, subsequently helped give proper shape to my ideas. Dr Chris Hope's legitimate demands for quantitative analysis helped me demonstrate the competitiveness of solar technology in rural markets, and better explain the financials behind selling solar. On the theoretical side, Dr Elizabeth Garnsey's work on entrepreneurship provided me with the key missing links to explain how entrepreneurs affect the diffusion of innovations. Both Chris and Elizabeth were ideal PhD supervisors – I couldn't have asked for better.

Doing a PhD in my chosen field entailed a fairly nomadic life, and I inevitably have quite a few people and institutions to thank. The MacArthur Foundation provided me with the scholarship that made my PhD possible. The Energy Research Institute (TERI) in India, under the guidance of Dr Pachauri, provided me with the perfect institutional setting and support network to do my field work. Dr Griffin Thompson and Judy Siegel, then with the US Export Council for Renewable Energy, provided me with an internship that exposed me to the business of renewables in emerging markets and enabled me to carry out my research at the World Bank. Jerome Weingart generously showed me the world of businesses and policymakers trying to ramp up the deployment of renewables for rural electrification. Michael Northrop and Peter Riggs of the Rockefeller Brother's Foundation not only provided key insights from their early funding of solar markets, but produced a highly influential report entitled 'Selling solar'.[2]

In terms of educational establishments, I would like to thank Trinity College, Cambridge, whose hallowed halls invited me in and strongly supported my work; and the Judge Business School, which provided a tremendously supportive, dynamic environment for a PhD student, as well as a forum that encouraged a cross-fertilization of thinking and research between departments.

In the last 15 years, I have met a few tremendous entrepreneurs setting out to revolutionize rural solar markets. I owe a debt of gratitude to these individuals for sharing with me the frustrations and challenges of selling solar as a start-up entity. They showed me first-hand the way in which an individual's vision, perseverance and unique capacities can be brought to bear to instigate profound technological change. They are referred to anonymously in the book, but they will know who they are, and I thank them for their generosity.

In the industry, I would like to thank Shell as an institution for being interested and willing enough to try selling solar in emerging markets. A big oil and gas company is not necessarily the place you might first think about doing this, but Shell did its best to accommodate and support this effort. I thank Herre Hoekstra and Philippe de Renzy Martin for teaching me a lot about how to get things done; Leigh Vial, who provided key strategic guidance on the business and very helpful edits of this book; and particularly Naledath Palat Ramesh for his steady hand on all matters technical and commercial, and with whom it remains a pleasure to work in Orb.

Catering to a student scrounging for information is not the most attractive of propositions when you are faced with a busy day at the office. So I would like to thank all those individuals at the World Bank who kindly shared their thoughts and time with me. In particular, I'd like to thank Charles Feinstein, Arun Sanghvi and especially Anil Cabraal. Anil has advised more solar projects than anyone I know at the World Bank, and has done more individually to identify the right policies to propel this market than anyone I know.

To stop moving, sit down and write this book took some considerable institutional intervention along the way. The Rockefeller Foundation's Bellagio retreat in Italy provided the most beautiful room any resident scholar could ask for, and was an ideal spot to write a first draft of the book. Later such support would be continued at a lesser-known spot in Bangalore, where Nalini Ramachandran and family took good care of me with warm company, home-cooked meals and thoughtful cups of tea.

My mother, Pauline Juckes, was an early advocate of environmental protection, and strongly supported my interest in solar and renewables. I thank her deeply for the opportunities and insights she has always provided me with. I would also like to thank Genevieve Connors, who I first met while giving a talk on solar in Cambridge and who has always stood out from the crowd. I thank

Genevieve for her encouragement and support in writing this book, for her companionship, her love and understanding through it all. And finally, to my grandparents – both beacons of light in their own way – to whom I dedicate this book.

It goes without saying that the contents of this book are my views and mine alone. They do not represent the views of Orb Energy Private Limited as a company. They are views that I have developed over more than a decade of being exposed to solar in emerging markets, first in academia, then in industry. I hope the reader will find them a potent mixture of strong opinion, sound research and first-hand experience.

To Colonel William Geoffrey Juckes
and Mrs Molly Juckes
of Hatchway Cottage

Part I

Solar and Diffusion Theory

1

Solar in Emerging Markets

Vast swathes of humanity live without any electricity at all. This demands that they seek out far less convenient and more expensive substitutes, with harmful impacts on their health and well-being, and often go without the appliances, services and other benefits that many of us take for granted. And yet the vast majority of this population lives in the 'sunbelt', 30 degrees north or south of the equator, where sunlight is the strongest on the planet and where the sun generates more watts of power per square metre than anywhere else. So why is there any electricity shortage whatsoever?

The technology to tap into the sun's energy and generate electric power – solar photovoltaic technology – has existed in its present form for more than half a century. Of late, this technology has faced a surge in demand. But the irony is that this growth is not coming from the sun-soaked emerging markets, but from the relatively more cloudy industrialized countries.

Solar photovoltaic technology was proactively introduced into many emerging markets in the early 1980s. This was done with much fanfare, hope and promise for the dawning of a new solar era, replete with independent, reliable, renewable energy from the sun. The reality, however, was that its uptake was disappointingly slow. By the turn of the century, just 1 million households in emerging markets were estimated to be using a solar system for electricity – accounting for no more than 0.25 per cent of unelectrified households globally.

But just at the point when many were tempted to give up on solar, some emerging markets turned the corner. So much so that by the end of 2007, more than 7 per cent of the unelectrified households in a country like Sri Lanka were using a solar system. And Sri Lanka was not alone: parts of India, Bangladesh and China also saw a rapid acceleration in the diffusion of solar during the same period. Why was this? Why had such a promising technology been so slow to diffuse throughout the 1980s and 1990s? And why, just at the time when people were starting to lose faith, did it reach a tipping point and rapidly diffuse to thousands of users in select emerging markets? These are the questions that *Selling Solar* sets out to answer.

No Electricity: An Entry Point for Solar

As hard as it may be to imagine, not long ago the entire world lived without electricity. Without power, the most essential need in the home was light – to be able to see between sunset and sunrise. In order to meet this challenge, the pre-electrified world tried several different methods – candles, followed by whale oil, followed by kerosene.[1] But none of these could compete with the ease and convenience of electric light at the flip of a switch. And so when grid electricity arrived in rural America, communities were said to hold a mock funeral for their kerosene lanterns, during which lanterns were buried while the local boy scouts played taps. Indeed, an American farmer from the 1920s probably best captured the taste for electricity when he said at a Sunday gathering:

> Brothers and sisters, I want to tell you this. The greatest thing on Earth
> is to have the love of God in your heart, and the next greatest thing is to
> have electricity in your house.[2]

Today almost all inhabitants of industrialized countries have the convenience of grid electricity. But for the inhabitants of many emerging markets, it is a very different experience. The number of people without electricity is estimated at 1.64 billion – more than five times the population of the US, or 27 per cent of the world's population – and of this, four out of five households are in rural areas.[3] The problem remains particularly acute in South and Southeast Asia, where the number is more than 1 billion, and in sub-Saharan Africa, where it is roughly 500 million people. And this does not include the many, many more people who have a connection to the national electricity grid but who suffer chronic, unscheduled blackouts. Indeed, when the author asked a farmer in South India how often he experienced power cuts, the farmer quickly shot back, 'Better you ask me how often I have any power at all.'

It is not that governments in emerging markets have not had bold ambitions. The Sri Lankan Government would not have been alone in using slogans like 'Electricity for All by 2000';[4] nor would it have been alone in missing the target. But the fact of the matter is that extending the national grid to remote and dispersed rural households, which initially have very low electricity demand, is a costly affair. In areas such as western China, the Amazon or the Himalayan foothills, the cost of a rural connection can be seven times that in the cities.[5] On this basis some have even concluded that complete grid electrification in many emerging markets is, and always will be, too expensive.[6]

When faced with these high costs, governments have tried more decentralized approaches, such as setting up village-scale electricity grids powered by diesel generators. This is where a local distribution grid connects all the

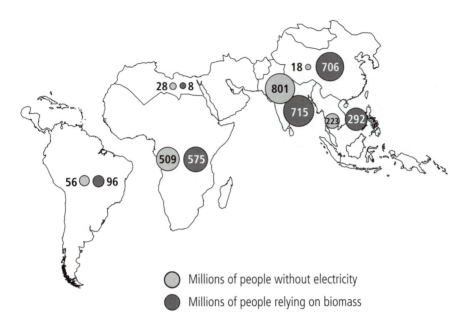

Figure 1.1 Millions without electricity and relying on biomass for cooking

Source: IEA (2002), p12

homes and small enterprises in the village, and diesel fuel is brought in the usually long distances to power a generator at fixed times each day. Not surprisingly, due to the remote location of these systems, the electricity provided tends to be both unreliable and expensive, and thus it has not provided an ultimate solution for emerging market governments in their campaigns to bring electric power to their citizenry.[7]

Of course, in the absence of a solution from their government, people don't just give up and sit around in the darkness without any entertainment or other comforts:

> The world outside the electricity grid is far from one of passive energy deprivation. There is rather a complex and dynamic evolution of energy demands with time, economic development, fashion and rising aspirations. These demands are met by local entrepreneurs and traders, responding often with considerable ingenuity and initiative to the changes taking place in the energy market.[8]

In almost every unelectrified village you can find a local trade in kerosene and kerosene lanterns for lighting, car batteries and battery-charging stations for black and white TV, dry cell batteries for radios, and, for the few who can afford it, diesel fuel and diesel generator sets for powering most modern

Figure 1.2 Carrying home kerosene fuel

Figure 1.3 Transporting a battery to nearest grid point for charging

Figure 1.4 Typical battery-charging station in village

appliances. Travelling around these areas you will often see someone carrying home a bottle of kerosene from the local shop, or a battery strapped to the back of a bicycle, being rolled to the nearest charging station several kilometres away. People want the benefits that electricity can bring and will go out of their way, and spend relatively large amounts of their income, to get it.

While we can admire the resilience and resourcefulness of local populations in the face of no electricity, the fact is the products they are forced to use remain far from ideal. Kerosene, for example, brings with it a severe fire risk. It is so easy for a kerosene lantern to be knocked over and burn down the entire house of an already poor family. It also produces a dim light, making it hard to do schoolwork or housework at night, and, of course, it produces noxious fumes. Combine this with the inconvenience of having to go to buy the fuel, store the fuel and light the fuel, and you have a pretty unpopular product.

Figure 1.5 Different types of kerosene lantern: (a) wick lantern, (b) hurricane lantern, (c) Petromax lantern

Figure 1.6 The process of lighting a Petromax lantern

Equally, there is no great love for diesel generators. In the absence of a reliable electricity grid, generators are being bought in ever-increasing numbers in emerging markets.[9] But generators create noise and air pollution, and also entail certain fire risks. Not to mention the hassle of procuring the fuel, storing the fuel, pouring the fuel and maintaining the generator set, which, because it has many moving parts, needs regular upkeep. And this says nothing about the lifetime costs of running one, since diesel fuel always costs more in rural areas than in the cities, and generally goes up in price, not down.

Figure 1.7 A typical diesel generator

Without an electricity grid and with a choice of pretty unpopular options, it is not surprising that solar technology has entered the rural energy mix.[10] Solar technology makes use of a resource – sunlight – that is truly everywhere, so it can produce electricity without transporting fuels, such as kerosene or diesel, to site. Moreover, it offers electricity, and light, at the flip of a switch, entails relatively little maintenance, has no harmful emissions and, once paid for, does not have much in the way of recurring costs. We can easily see why people had high hopes for this technology when it was first introduced into emerging markets.

Rural Solar Applications

At first, aid agencies tried to put solar to work for unelectrifed populations. In some projects, these agencies tried an approach that would have seemed intuitive at the time – they centralized the solar panels in the middle of a village, or on its outskirts, strung distribution wires to each home, and then transported the solar power to the local families or enterprises. This has since come to be known as a solar 'mini-grid', and its track record in terms of sustainability and cost-effectiveness is not a good one.

Figure 1.8 A solar mini-grid

Pakistan was one of the first countries to experiment with solar mini-grids, setting them up in eight villages in the late 1980s. However, the project failed on two counts. First, it failed in terms of maintenance: if the system is owned and used by a village, who precisely is responsible for its upkeep and for ensuring that everyone uses only their appropriate share of the power? Second, it failed in terms of cost-effectiveness: if the poles and wires to transport electricity and connect the households is the most costly part of rural electrification, then why use them with solar if you don't have to? Faced with these difficult question, the Pakistan post-evaluation study by the World Bank and UNDP concluded categorically that:

> a decentralized approach for household PV systems in which individual households or buildings are powered by individual PV systems is less costly than a centralized approach in which a village is serviced by a single PV array and mini-distribution grid.[11]

A more decentralized approach to using solar technology has come to be known as the 'solar home system'. This approach puts the ownership of the system and the responsibility for its maintenance with the household or enterprise which buys it. The systems are bought by individual consumers (rather than at the communal level as in the case of solar mini-grids), just like generators, motorbikes or washing machines.

Figure 1.9 A solar PV module coming off the manufacturing line

Figure 1.10 Installed solar PV modules (from above and below)

Figure 1.11 A solar home in emerging markets

Perhaps a note on terminology will be helpful at this point. Because solar systems are bought by both households and commercial establishments, the title of 'solar *home* system' seems too restrictive for our purposes, and I instead use the term 'solar system' to apply to the decentralized applications of solar technology. And as a further point of clarification, by 'solar' I mean a solar *electric* system. This is different to a solar thermal system: the technology is different and the use of the sun's energy is different. In the case of a solar electric system, the technology is solar photovoltaic (PV) technology, which uses photons of light from the sun to generate electricity. In the case of a solar thermal system, the technology captures the heat of the sun, often to heat water.[12]

Figure 1.12 Example of a solar thermal system for heating water

How then a does a solar system work? First solar PV panels (what I will call 'solar modules') are mounted on a roof, or nearby pole, and are pointed in the direction of the equator – south if you are in the northern latitudes and north if you are in the southern. The closer you are to the equator, the more horizontal the solar module will be, as the sun spends more time directly overhead. These modules generate electricity from sunlight – photons of light that, upon hitting a solar module, displace electrons to create an electrical charge. This charge is then channelled and conducted from the solar modules through wires either direct to the 'load' (the technical term for the use of the electricity) or to a storage device – a battery – for use at a later time. Often between the solar modules and the battery is a 'charge controller', electronics that regulate the flow of electricity to protect the lifetime of the battery. Finally, because a solar panel produces direct current (DC) at 12 volts, as opposed to alternating current (AC) at 110 or 220 volts, some solar systems also have an 'inverter' to turn DC into AC electricity.[13]

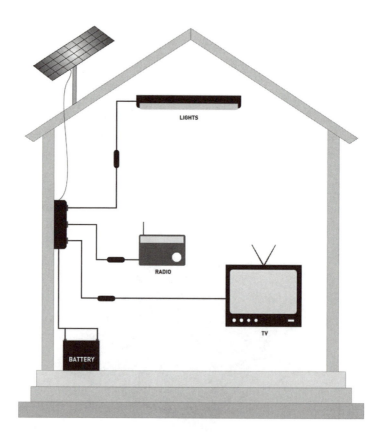

Figure 1.13 Diagram of a typical solar system

Solar systems are ideal for producing electric light at the flip of a switch. When combined with energy-efficient compact fluorescent lights (CFLs), a 'typical' 50-watt solar system will provide a household or small business with four or five lights.[14] Compared to the dim, hot light from a kerosene lantern, a cool, white light at the flip of a switch has its advantages. Moreover, the same system will normally have enough residual power for a small radio or a black and white TV that runs on 12 volt DC electricity.

Figure 1.14 Electric light at the flip of a switch

Figure 1.15 A typical solar light

Figure 1.16 Solar light in a kitchen

Figure 1.17 Radio and TV powered by solar

Figure 1.18 Comparison of (a) kerosene vs. (b) solar light
in village stores

Where customers want to use a colour television, ceiling fan, blender or other appliance, they will need to use a bigger system with an AC inverter. A typical solar system that provides AC power would be about three times larger than a DC solar system – roughly 150 watts. But these are just averages. One of the virtues of solar is that it can be tailored to the precise needs and budget of the family or enterprise in question.

Figure 1.19 Larger solar system for appliances running on alternating current (AC)

Figure 1.20 Solar-powered colour TV and entertainment system

The Solar Promise

By the mid 1990s, enough entrepreneurs and aid agencies had experimented with solar that even the former sceptics were starting to take notice. *The Economist*, not known for its early support of renewables, for example, now described solar for electricity as an 'enticing technology', since 'extending electricity grids from fossil fuel plants to new consumers can be hugely expensive', while 'PV modules can be simply stuck on homes'.[15] Similarly, *The New York Times* reported:

> From India and Indonesia to Mexico and Brazil, solar panels ... are sprouting on thousands of rooftops, lighting up jungles, deserts and other hard-to-wire areas of the developing world that have never been connected to conventional power grids – and are unlikely to be connected anytime soon.[16]

And far away from the mainstream media, rural energy experts were coming around. In 1993, a long-standing expert on rural energy found that 'photovoltaic technology has failed to live up to the expectations of its proponents' and has 'relied upon highly subsidized equipment' and that 'the degree of spontaneous take-up of the technology within the target groups has generally been negligible'.[17] But two years later, the same rural energy expert concluded:

> The self-sustaining commercial diffusion of PV systems, in full competition with the alternatives, is the clearest indication that PV technology has attained a valid and significant role in rural areas of the developing world. The rural areas of many developing countries could see a diffusion of PVs like that of radio cassettes, TVs, video recorders and other high-consumer goods.[18]

The important word here is 'commercial'. The point is that, by the mid 1990s, people started to realize that solar was moving from being a 'handout' to poor 'beneficiaries' by aid agencies to being a 'product' which 'customers' wanted to buy and which firms were trying to sell. Why this created such excitement was simply because those who watched this scene unfold knew that if people could make money selling this technology, then more of it would be offered, more of it bought, and a sustainable chain reaction of events could be set in motion to ensure its rapid and widespread adoption through the emerging markets.

But in relation to this potential, the overall results were still disappointing. Take the case of Sri Lanka. In 1997 it was estimated there were 1.4 million rural households without access to grid electricity. Of these, a large market for solar was thought to exist among roughly 300,000 households regularly using battery-recharging facilities for television and radio services and kerosene for lighting. But between 1982 and 1998, only 5000 solar systems were sold and installed throughout the country – on average just 300 solar systems per annum.[19]

Moreover, even when the World Bank launched a project at the end of 1997 to try to accelerate solar diffusion in Sri Lanka, the initial results were disappointing. The project aimed to add 30,000 solar systems by the end of

2002, which would have represented a significant ramp up in diffusion. However, by the end of 1999, the project had only managed to add about 1000 systems – an average of just 500 solar systems per annum. Solar diffusion in Sri Lanka was not accelerating as expected.

So why was this? Why was it that between 1982 and 1999 only an estimated 6000 solar systems were installed in Sri Lanka out of 1.4 million unelectrified households, and a high-potential market of 300,000 households? This represents only 0.4 per cent penetration of the unelectrified household base over close to two decades. Why was diffusion of this high-potential technology taking so long in Sri Lanka?

Of course, Sri Lanka was not alone. Even if we look at Kenya, which was deemed a solar success story in the early 1990s,[20] the results were not exceptional. Estimates in Kenya of solar systems sold between the mid 1980s and 1994 vary between 20,000 and 40,000 systems.[21] This represented at best only 0.4 to 0.8 per cent of the 4.8 million unelectrified households throughout the country.

The fact is that these numbers reflected the broader picture across almost all emerging markets at the turn of the century. The Global Environment Facility (GEF) and World Bank estimated that by 2000, only 500,000 households were using solar systems across all emerging markets, and if one included solar lanterns (where a mobile electric light is powered by a small module) 1.1 million solar systems were in use.[22] This did not compare well against the 1.64 billion people without electricity,[23] or roughly 400 million homes, representing a penetration of only about 0.25 per cent.

For the proponents of solar, these dismal results represented something of a paradox:

> Over the past decade or so, solar photovoltaics for basic rural electrification has matured and has become a technically proven means of providing basic to intermediate levels of household electricity. Solar can provide comparable services to other means of rural domestic power development, often at a lower cost, and has environmental, social and political advantages. The obvious question then is why is solar PV not a mainstream method of rural electrification?[24]

Indeed why was this? If solar was so ideally suited to the needs of unelectrified customers in emerging markets, why was it diffusing so slowly? This is the first question *Selling Solar* seeks to address.

But it is not the paradox alone that is striking. Just at the point where many were tempted to give up on the technology, there was a sudden surge in diffusion. Take the case of Sri Lanka again. In 1999, just over 500 solar systems were sold across the country, but roughly 18,500 solar systems were sold in 2003 alone, and, by the end of 2006, more than 100,000 systems had been sold on a cumulative basis. Stop for a moment to consider this acceleration in diffusion: between 1982 and 1999, just 6000 solar systems were sold in Sri Lanka; then between 2000 and the end of 2006 a further 100,000 solar systems were added.[25] What happened? What changed?

Here again, Sri Lanka was not alone. A similar surge can be tracked in parts of India, Bangladesh and China. So why was this? Why, after so many years of progressing so slowly, did solar diffusion dramatically accelerate in certain emerging markets at the turn of the century?

Explaining this second question is as important as the first, if not more so. By explaining, first, why solar was slower to diffuse than expected, we can identify the barriers that held this technology back. It is important to isolate these barriers, as overcoming them is the key to diffusion. But by explaining, second, why solar diffusion dramatically accelerated in certain emerging markets, we can examine who lifted the barriers to diffusion, and how they did it. Answering these two questions together gives us a better understanding of what drives solar diffusion, and provides a strong platform from which to recommend policies for successful replication.

Overview of Subsequent Chapters

To help us navigate and explain the progress of solar in emerging markets, it is helpful to have a guide. In our case the guide will be years of research by those interested in explaining the diffusion of innovations as varied as hybrid seeds, cooking stoves and water filtration devices. Although the word 'diffusion' sounds more suited to explaining chemical reactions, in this case it refers to 'the process by which innovations spread to members of a social system'.[26] And, it would seem, we would not be the first to turn to such research for guidance on the question of solar:

> The voluminous literature on innovation and diffusion offers considerable theoretical insight for understanding the process that must occur if solar energy is to be a substantial alternate energy source in the future.[27]

In Chapter 2 we delve deep into diffusion research. What we find is that solar is by no means alone in being slower to spread than anticipated:

> Many technologists believe that advantageous innovations will sell themselves, that the obvious benefits of the new idea will be widely realized by potential adopters, and that the innovation will therefore diffuse rapidly. Seldom is this the case. Most innovations diffuse at a disappointingly slow rate.[28]

But diffusion research turns out to be more helpful in some ways than others. It is very good at identifying the barriers to diffusion, and thus ultimately helps us answer our first question of what held solar back. But it is less good at addressing the second question of why solar diffusion accelerated markedly. To answer this question it is not satisfactory to say that 'the barriers were lifted'. We need to know more about the actors involved, and *how* they did it. Therefore to the existing body of diffusion research, we add an element of what sociologists call 'agency'.

The sociologist Anthony Giddens has defined an agent as an individual or entity with transformative capacity, such that 'whatever happened would not have happened had that individual not intervened'. In this way, agency does not refer so much to intentions, as to capabilities:

> Action depends upon the capability of the individual to 'make a difference to a pre-existing state of affairs' or course of events. An agent ceases to be such if he or she loses the capability to 'make a difference', that is, to exercise some sort of power.[29]

The history of technology diffusion demonstrates the 'power' of entrepreneurs to profoundly influence the diffusion process. But to adequately account for the impact of entrepreneurs, we need to turn to management literature on entrepreneurship and integrate it with existing diffusion research. From this melding of different perspectives we distil an analytical framework that can more adequately address the question at hand.

In Chapter 3 we apply this framework. Doing so helps us conclude that the main barriers to solar diffusion were *not* that potential customers did not perceive its benefits or that solar could not compete with the alternatives. Rather the main barriers were:

1   the absence of consumer finance to make solar more affordable; and
2   the absence of a market infrastructure to make solar more available.

As these conclusions may surprise readers, this chapter goes into considerable detail to substantiate them.

That brings us to the close of Part I of the book, wherein we have developed an analytical framework and used it to isolate the key barriers to solar diffusion. In line with our emphasis on agency, Part II then looks more closely at the actors who were either successful or unsuccessful in overcoming these barriers, and *how* they did it.

Chapter 4 looks at what the early propagators of solar brought to the diffusion process in the late 1980s and early 1990s. We review the role and effectiveness of electric utilities, aid agencies and emerging market governments, and we show why most of these entities were not able to initiate a sustainable and effective process of solar diffusion. Largely in response to these failed initiatives, we consider how, by the mid 1990s, a consensus had formed that solar must 'go commercial'. We then profile the early not-for-profit pioneers who, as if on cue, struck out to set up solar businesses, as well as existing non-governmental organizations (NGOs) which stepped into solar to run it like a business. We also introduce early entrepreneurs from three emerging markets – India, Indonesia and Sri Lanka. In line with the theories considered in Chapter 2, these early pioneers of commercial solar sales were not large corporations or institutions from a related industry, but independent individuals driven by a compelling vision.

Chapter 5 then looks more deeply at three cases of solar entrepreneurship. We see how solar entrepreneurs in India, Indonesia and Sri Lanka faced a similar struggle to mobilize two essential kinds of capital:

1   capital to invest in a market infrastructure (salespeople, technicians, branches, inventory); and
2   capital for consumer finance to make solar affordable to their customer base.

Moreover, they had to learn how to put the limited capital they had to work in a profitable and sustainable manner. This took time, and did not work out for all entrepreneurs concerned. But the lessons they learned, and the demonstration they provided, would ultimately attract new market entrants as well as policy-makers, eager to see how they could help 'scale up' these nascent markets. This combination of new policies and new entrants, all ploughing new resources into selling solar, is shown to underpin the acceleration in diffusion that followed.

Chapter 6 builds on Chapter 5, with a case study of policy formation. We look at how a key lending and policymaking institution – the World Bank – was influenced by the entrepreneurs profiled in Chapter 5, and became active in all three countries where the entrepreneurs were toiling to create a solar market. We see that the World Bank had no ready-made formula to apply to solar; this technology was, after all, very different from the standard set of energy generating, transmission and distribution technologies it was used to supporting. But we trace how the World Bank learned to 'see' the solar markets like an entrepreneur, and in doing so came to establish a highly effective template for supporting solar diffusion. This template was derived from lessons learned first in India, then developed in Indonesia, applied in Sri Lanka, and subsequently replicated in Bangladesh and China. Some divisions of the World Bank were not as effective as others. But overall, the case of solar clearly shows the impact the World Bank can have on successfully accelerating the diffusion of renewables in emerging markets.

Having seen in Part II the power of policy to complement or thwart the objectives of solar entrepreneurs, Part III then becomes overtly prescriptive.

In Chapter 7 we look more carefully at the policies that have worked, and not worked, to accelerate solar diffusion in emerging markets. From our earlier review, we are able to prescribe that only where policymakers can 'see' a solar market like an entrepreneur will they be able to devise successful policies for solar diffusion. In keeping with this theme, we provide eight specific recommendations for policymakers trying to accelerate the diffusion of solar. In doing so, we contrast the policies that have worked in markets like Sri Lanka and Bangladesh with policies that have not worked as well, such as those in South Africa, the Philippines and parts of India. The aim is not, of course, to cast blame, but to record best practice to date, so that policy interventions in the future can become that much more effective.

In Chapter 8 we turn our attention to the future for solar, and consider the huge remaining unserved need in emerging markets. In line with earlier calls from the G8 and others, we set a challenge of reaching 100 million solar homes by 2025, and then consider which of four broad international forces might take us there. We see that, while effective, the World Bank is not replicating its earlier success with the focused intensity required to reach such numbers. We also see that neither bilateral aid, nor expected cost reductions in solar modules, nor new carbon markets, will make up the difference. Instead, we conclude that the only way to reach 100 million solar homes by 2025 is with the establishment of a challenge fund that explicitly adopts these targets, establishes a dedicated and well-resourced team, and works closely with governments of emerging markets to put in place the funds and policies that will drive solar diffusion. We further recommend that this fund be housed within the World Bank itself. This is not how the World Bank typically works, but it is an interesting test case of how its shareholders may need it to work in the future if the challenge of accelerating the diffusion of renewables in emerging markets is to be met.

The final chapter, Chapter 9, presents the findings and lessons of *Selling Solar* in three distinct parts. The first part is specific to solar. Here we answer the questions posed at the outset of the book and summarize the policy recommendations for solar diffusion. The second part then steps back from the case of solar to consider how the analytical framework developed in Chapter 2 can be applied to a range of renewable energy and energy-efficient innovations. The third and final part considers the five 'bigger picture' lessons of *Selling Solar* for accelerating renewable energy diffusion in emerging markets.

It goes without saying that solar, when applied in rural areas of emerging markets, is a relatively small and subtle technology. It is decentralized, often installed by one individual, affects people's lives on a family-by-family basis and has very minor impacts on the external environment. It stands in stark contrast to large coal-fired power plants or large dams, connected to homes and cities by large-scale transmission and distribution projects. Some readers will feel that 'small is beautiful', others will not. But whichever way you lean, the fact is this relatively small technology has the potential to impact people's lives in a very big way, and the lessons it has to offer for renewable energy diffusion are bigger still.

2

Diffusion Theory
and Entrepreneurship

It can be hard to know where to begin when explaining the diffusion of an innovation. There are so many variables that it is easy to be paralysed by the different possible explanations. For this reason, we use this chapter to introduce some theories from the weighty literature on innovation diffusion.

But as we shall see, these theories are better at identifying the factors affecting diffusion than they are at explaining what enabled key actors – such as entrepreneurs – to influence them. Here instead we turn to management literature on entrepreneurship, which helps us better address the questions of 'Who influences diffusion?' and 'How did they do it?'. My aim is to provide the reader with a more complete analytical framework, which can be applied to a range of innovations, and then apply it to the case of solar.

Perspectives on Innovation Diffusion

When we try to explain the rate of diffusion of an innovation, we are basically concerned with the *time* that it takes for more people in a society to start using it. Obviously, when it comes to our concern with renewable energy, we would ideally like societies to start using a lot more renewable energy technologies a lot more quickly, and that is why literature on innovation diffusion is relevant to the challenge.

But of course, it is not just people interested in renewable energy that can benefit from understanding innovation diffusion. For example, companies that manufacture photographic film may want to know how fast digital cameras will diffuse and displace their products; public health officials trying to introduce mosquito nets will want to know how to encourage more people to use more nets more quickly; extension agents propagating the use of new seeds for enhanced crop yields will want to know how to encourage more farmers to sign on in the shortest possible period of time. Indeed, wherever somebody is in a race against time to either understand or accelerate the diffusion of an innovation, the theories we are about to cover will be of some relevance.

What is immediately striking when you start to dig into such literature is that there are an awful lot of different views. Luckily for the reader, somewhere during the digging process I stumbled across the work of a geographer by the name of Lawrence Brown, who very helpfully categorized diffusion research into four broad perspectives:

1   the communication perspective;
2   the economic history perspective;
3   the development perspective; and
4   the market infrastructure perspective.[1]

Each of these perspectives has a slightly different take on the same question of what affects the speed with which an innovation diffuses through society.

What we find as we go on to review the perspectives is that each has something relevant to say about the phenomenon of innovation diffusion, but that none really pulls all the pieces of the puzzle together.[2] Instead, each perspective comes from a different discipline and takes a fundamentally different approach to the question of diffusion.

The Communication Perspective

Those who subscribe to a communication perspective are primarily concerned with the communication that must take place within a society for enough people to be convinced to adopt an innovation.[3] Quite simply, the communication perspective rests its analysis on three key assumptions. First, that upon being presented with an innovation, it will destabilize us and generate a sense of uncertainty deep within that prompts questions and a search for further information prior to adoption. For example, think back to when you first saw a personal computer – did you rush out and buy it immediately? Probably not. Instead you most likely asked yourself or those you knew, 'What's that? What does it do?'.

Second, that save for a select group of innovators, the majority of us in society are risk-averse and will not rush into buying an innovation. So to return to the personal computer, when in answer to your question someone said, 'It's designed for use in your home and office and could really help you save time by allowing you to type and store all your files electronically in one place', you probably responded, or if not, at least thought to yourself, 'Why on Earth would I want to trade in my electric typewriter for that? I'm fine as it is.'

And third, that it is only through a process of communication that we slowly become convinced of the need and irresistible urge to adopt an innovation. So in the case of the personal computer, it was probably through seeing one in your neighbour's or relative's home, or seeing one used by your boss in your office, or seeing it advertised by enough attractive models or happy families, that you finally decided, 'That's a really good idea – I'm going to buy one of those personal computers.' And it is precisely for these reasons that the communication perspective maintains that 'diffusion is fundamentally a social process'.[4]

One type of communication stands out among all others when it comes to convincing people to take the plunge and adopt an innovation. The communication perspective calls the process 'referencing'. We all feel the need for referencing, for finding out more about how others have experienced an innovation prior to jumping in ourselves and taking the plunge. We all want to avoid the risk of wasting our money on something that doesn't work, of being laughed at by our peers or of further complicating our lives. Most often we will talk to those who have already bought and say, 'Excuse me, do you really find that having one of those personal computers makes your life easier? Isn't it all too complicated and difficult to understand and manage?'. And then when someone tells you, 'I can't imagine living without it', you feel a sudden urge to have one too.

This is referencing in action, and it is key to potential adopters developing greater trust in an innovation. Its importance for diffusion was first identified by Ryan and Gross (1943), who set out to explain exactly why it was that over a period of five years only 10 per cent of Iowa's farmers had adopted the new hybrid corn seeds, whereas over the next three years adoption increased to 40 per cent. Their explanation was that in the early stages only the more innovative farmers were willing to try the new seeds, but that once their success became plain for others to see and there was sufficient time for peer referencing on the matter, the more risk-averse then decided they could sufficiently trust the seeds and so started to use them. As such, Ryan and Gross concluded:

> There is no doubt but that the behaviour of one individual in an interacting population affects the behaviour of his fellows. Thus, the demonstrated success of hybrid seed on a few farms offers a changed situation to those who have not been so experimental. The very fact of acceptance by one or more farmers offers new stimulus to the remaining ones.[5]

It was from these initial findings that proponents of the communication perspective developed their categories of adopters – innovators, early adopters, late adopters and laggards – and the S-curve shape of diffusion that has become synonymous with the diffusion of innovations.[6]

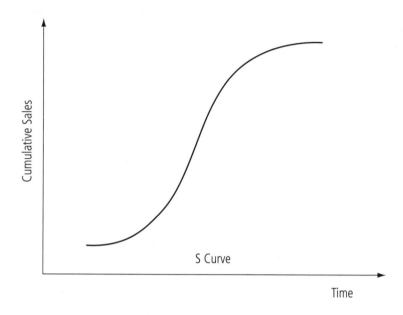

Figure 2.1 Diffusion of an innovation over time

A simplified explanation is as follows: in the early stages of an innovation's life cycle, just a few highly adventurous and more inquisitive innovators are found to adopt. Once enough of these have set an example to others and the word has spread, the innovation takes off as the early adopters, of which there are many more in society, come forward to buy. They are then followed by the slightly more cautious, but just as plentiful, late adopters, and ultimately, bringing up the rear, are the most cautious, fewer in number 'laggards'.

However, Rogers (1983) also recognized that to try to explain everything by the relative 'innovativeness' of adopters and communication between them risked too much of an individual-blame approach for non-adoption and that it was important to be conscious of other processes. He cautioned that we must be careful to include 'system-level' explanations, such as social norms and conventions, particularly in many traditional societies.[7]

We must also be aware that certain people in a society have more influence than others. These are opinion leaders and they play a critical role in either approving or disapproving of an innovation, leading some analysts to describe their disproportionate influence as 'the law of the few'.[8]

We must also consider how the attributes of the innovation itself can also affect its progress.[9] For example, Ryan and Gross felt that because farmers could simply try a little bit of hybrid corn without risking too much – what they called 'trialability' – this aided its diffusion.[10] By contrast, Rogers found 'the perceived complexity' of computers was 'a negative force in their rate of adoption in the early 1980s'.[11]

And lastly, for 'high cost' or 'highly profitable innovations', the 'economic aspects of relative advantage may be the most important single predictor for the rate of adoption'. Although Rogers also states rather categorically that 'to expect that economic factors are the sole predictors of the rate of adoption is unlikely', since studies have shown non-economic factors to be equally relevant.[12] And furthermore:

> What really determines the rate of adoption of an innovation is the adopter's perception of profitability and not objective profitability. There is a vast tradition of social psychology research which indicates the importance of group interaction in determining the selectivity of perception, including perceptions of profitability.[13]

Relevant to the themes of this book, the communication perspective also recognizes the concept of agency. It identifies the role of the 'change agent', defining such a person as a professional who influences innovation decisions in a direction deemed desirable by a change agency.[14] So, for example, change agents might be government agricultural extension officers or public health officers or door-to-door salespeople, and their influence is clearly recognized by the communication perspective: 'most change is not a haphazard phenomenon, but the results of the planned premeditated actions by change agents'.[15]

But the communication perspective ultimately fails to consider the role of individuals and organizations behind the agricultural extension officer or the door-to-door salesperson, and how these individuals or organizations ultimately determine, for instance, how many such agents are available to affect change, how well equipped they are to convince people to change, what exactly they have to offer to entice change or how well incentivized they are to affect change. As an analyst of innovation diffusion notes, 'major barriers to change … lie in the structure and dynamics of innovating organizations', but 'unfortunately, methodologically and conceptually [this] has largely been taken for granted'. Needless to say, the same analyst finds this to be 'a major shortcoming'.[16]

The Economic History Perspective

Whereas the communication perspective explains diffusion by the adopters' perceptions of the risks and benefits of an innovation, the economic history perspective treats all adopters the same – as rational economic agents – and instead explains diffusion by the improvements made to the innovation itself over time:

A better understanding of the timing of diffusion is possible by probing more deeply at the technological level itself, where it may be possible to identify factors accounting for both the general slowness as well as the wide variations in the rate of diffusion.[17]

Taking up the earlier study of the diffusion of hybrid seeds, an analyst of diffusion by the name of Griliches came to a very different set of conclusions to those of Ryan and Gross. Instead of looking at the relative innovativeness of adopters and their communication among themselves, Griliches proposed that the diffusion of hybrid corn could instead be explained by 'differences in the profitability of the changeover from open pollinated to hybrid seed'.[18] This hypothesis was itself based on earlier findings by agricultural extension agencies that 'the greater the efficiency of the new technology in producing returns … the greater its rate of acceptance'.[19]

Griliches's findings had considerable implications for the communication perspective, since it was now said to be 'possible to account for a large share of the spatial and chronological differences in the use of hybrid corn with the help of "economic" variables'. Indeed, he went on to conclude that the 'sociological variables … tend to cancel themselves out, leaving the economic variables as the major determinant of the patterns of technological change'.[20] Others, such as Mansfield,[21] subsequently lent further support to Griliches's economic explanations of diffusion, leading future economic historians to conclude that 'Griliches and Mansfield have clearly demonstrated the power and scope of purely economic explanations in diffusion of individual inventions'.[22]

When a new technology is invented, it is often crude and inefficient, offering few advantages over existing technologies. Think for example about the size of the first mobile phones. But, through a 'continuum of inventive activity', the newer technology is found to become increasingly competitive, with consequent impacts on its diffusion:

If it is true that inventions in their early forms are often highly imperfect and constitute only slight improvements over earlier techniques, it also follows that the pace at which subsequent improvements are made will be a major determinant of the rate of diffusion.[23]

In this way, economic historians have tended to link the diffusion of an innovation to the 'persistent, sweaty, sometimes grim, comparatively monotonous experience' that 'is often called development' of the innovation.[24] Or, as another author concludes, 'the diffusion of technology is inextricably interwoven with its development'.[25]

Historical examples include Diesel's engine, which required more than 20 years of development to find an 'economic role', and only then began to take over 'surprisingly fast: ships in the 1920s, trucks in the 1930s and locomotives in the 1950s'.[26] Similarly, improvements to the incandescent light-bulb by Edison's team of engineers were central to the diffusion of grid electrification itself.[27] The diffusion of the steam engine is explained by Watt's improvements to the Newcomen engine, which opened 'the way to continuing advances in efficiencies that eventually brought the steam-engine within the reach of all branches of the economy and made of it a universal prime mover'.[28] And improvements to high-yielding varieties (HYVs) of seeds and their adaptation to local conditions are said for instance to explain 'the dramatic speed with which new HYVs were diffused among peasants in South and Southeast Asia', and that such examples clearly 'demonstrate the power of the "economic" model of diffusion'.[29]

When we measure the rate of diffusion, we are basically asking how much *time* it takes for an innovation to be adopted by people. For the communication perspective, the amount of time it takes is dependent on the time it takes for people to become convinced through communication. But for the economic history perspective, the amount of time it takes is dependent on the time it takes for the propagators of an innovation to *learn* how to design, develop and manufacture a better product. The idea is that a propagator simply needs experience with an innovation, and as this experience accumulates, so too the product improves in terms of price and performance:

> Falling costs and prices are the rule of technological innovations, a result of learning and accumulating experience in the methods of producing a new product. Empirical evidence concerning the well-known 'experience curve' indicates that the inverse relationship between unit cost and accumulated output (experience) generalizes across a wide range of innovations.[30]

The good thing about this perspective is that it all feels rather like common sense. After all, how many of us have at one time or another taken a conscious decision not to invest in a new innovation because we assume that the price will only come down over time and that the performance will only improve. Noting the price of the VCR, which fell from US$1200 to $300 in the space of a few years, even Rogers, an advocate of the communication perspective, concludes that 'when the price of a new product decreases during its diffusion, a rapid rate of adoption is encouraged'.[31]

The other good thing about this perspective is that it clearly recognizes the impact of entrepreneurs and their firms on the rate of diffusion. In addition to Edison, Watt and Diesel, mentioned above, you can think of Ford and the automobile, Remington and the typewriter, Wozniak and Jobs and the personal computer, and so on. But unfortunately, although the economic history perspective addresses the role of the entrepreneur, it tends to concentrate primarily on the entrepreneur's 'problem-solving' abilities,[32] meaning *technical* problem-solving.

By mainly limiting the analysis to entrepreneurs' successes in overcoming technical problems and producing a better product at better prices, the economic history perspective tends to ignore all the problem-solving that surrounds the profitable *selling* of an innovation in large numbers – problems related to raising capital, distribution, promotions, pricing, taxes, supply chain management and even government policies. For instance, as one analyst reminds us, explanations of diffusion must account for even such seemingly banal things as 'management capacity decisions related to product availability'.[33]

Hughes's 1979 analysis of the diffusion of grid electricity in the US makes the useful distinction between an 'inventor-entrepreneur' and a 'manager-entrepreneur'. In the case of grid electrification, Edison was more of an inventor-entrepreneur, who together with his team of talented engineers developed a high-resistance filament in the light that allowed it to operate at higher voltages. This invention then paved the way for centralized electricity generation and transportation to point of use, as the operator could now use high-voltage transmission to transport the electricity, reducing the losses in the system and so making it financially viable. Based on this initial success, Edison went on to establish electric utilities in other American cities.

However, the expansion of the electricity grid to the millions of homes outside of the main cities was left to Samuel Insull, who was more of a manager-entrepreneur. Although Edison was 'deeply aware of the seamless fabric of economics and technology, he was relatively naïve about the long-term economic and social factors making up the environment within which his systems functioned'.[34] By contrast, Samuel Insull brought both a technical and a managerial capacity to the task. He had been trained 'in the Edison school and absorbed its creative, problem-solving, inclusive, systematic, innovating and expansionist approach', but his problem-solving skills ultimately extended to a wider range of areas:

> His conceptual syntheses involved social and market needs, financial trends, political (especially regulatory) policies, economic principles, technological innovations, engineering design, and managerial techniques.[35]

Thus it was under Insull that Edison's solely urban-based invention was turned into a regional system – bringing electricity to the small town and rural areas – such that by the mid 1920s, Insull presided over a utility with subsidiaries in 19 different states, supplying 8 per cent of America's electricity.

So it seems clear that the economic history perspective could benefit from a broader consideration of the problems entrepreneurs must solve in bringing innovations to market and what ultimately enables them to do so. Certainly, as we shall see, explanations of solar diffusion will mandate that we do so.

The Development Perspective

The development perspective starts from the assumption that potential adopters in a society have unequal access to the resources for adoption. Of central importance among such resources are money, and/or access to credit.[36] Quite intuitive again for the reader is the question asked by one diffusion analyst:

> Where the potential adopter does not have the cash for an innovation which needs financial expenditure, then how can he or she be enabled to acquire the innovation?[37]

The above question refers to diffusion in emerging markets, where it is perhaps most applicable given the wider disparities and irregular flows of disposable income. However, the theoretical point is broadly applicable: it instructs us to take account of the purchasing power of the potential adopter in relation to the costs of the innovation, as well as the facilities that are made available to overcome such purchasing constraints.

Because of its concern with affordability, the so-called 'divisibility' of a technology is important to the development perspective.[38] By divisibility is meant the extent to which an innovation can be divided into small functional and affordable units. For example, many multinationals decided to introduce shampoos and detergents into rural areas of emerging markets by offering smaller, pocket-sized packets that were more affordable than a full box or bottle. But where it is not possible for a product to be broken down into more divisible units, customer credit becomes key to diffusion, especially in places where purchasing power is relatively low. For this reason, some say that in emerging markets 'the most important factor which facilitates access of poor people to new technology is the availability of credit.'[39]

However, this does not only apply to emerging markets. We might consider, for instance, how rapidly the automobile would have diffused throughout industrialized countries without the ability to acquire a loan or a lease on the vehicle. Certainly, it is the loan and the lease that will facilitate the uptake of innovations such as the hybrid electric vehicle, which has relatively high up-front costs but much lower running costs due to its lower consumption of fuel.

Indeed, this brings us to an interesting generalization made in a small article in the *Financial Times* back in 1996.[40] The title of the article was 'The high price of a green machine', and it put forward the idea that the very essence of green innovations is that they tend to cost more up-front. Solar is a good example of this, as is the hybrid electric vehicle or electric wind turbine. The point is that when buying such resource-conserving innovations, the vast majority of the costs are paid at the point of purchase, with comparatively less during operation. This makes the availability of customer credit that much more important for green innovations, and doubly so when they are sold in areas of relatively low purchasing power, such as emerging markets.

The development perspective may seem similar to the other perspectives, but actually it has a significant contribution to make. In relation to the communication perspective, it cautions against grouping adopters as 'innovators' and 'laggards', and recommends instead grouping them as 'high-' and 'low-access' with respect to money and other resources.[41] Rogers has responded to this by recognizing that it is of course much easier for someone to be innovative and try out new things if they have cash to burn.[42] But in the end the communication perspective does not go far enough in examining how broad macro-economic factors, such as the cost of capital, and more micro-level factors, such as adopters' collateral and access to credit, can influence the diffusion process.

In relation to the economic history perspective, the development perspective instructs us to remember that even the most cost-competitive and effective technological innovation can diffuse slowly where the target customers do not have sufficient capital or credit to pay for it. For instance, analysts found that although the adoption of green revolution technologies was potentially profitable, diffusion was restricted in many emerging markets by farmers' limited access to customer credit.[43] The flip-side of this finding is that the diffusion of similar agricultural innovations did not tend to pose the same problem for American farmers, who are 'a relatively prosperous and commercially oriented sample'.[44]

However, the development perspective tends to suffer from an overly static analysis, in which the propagator of an innovation is perceived to be uninterested in reacting to the purchasing power limitations through either radical redesign of the innovation or arranging for customer credit. Certainly this can be the case, for instance where a business decides that a given market simply is not rich enough to justify the effort. But there are also examples of NGOs and businesses responding in just this manner, as with the pocket-size amounts of detergent and shampoo, the $40 wind-up radio, or the $4 filter invented by a Bangladeshi professor to try to remove deadly arsenic from the water.[45]

The development perspective is right to focus on the adopters' access to money as a major constraint to diffusion even once potential adopters trust and/or value an innovation, and even after an innovation has improved in terms of both cost and performance. But in the end, it is overly static. It also needs to be able to take account of the role of entrepreneurs and other propagating organizations in emerging markets that effectively surmount purchasing power obstacles and explain what enables them to do so or not.

The Market Infrastructure Perspective

Of all the four perspectives, the market infrastructure perspective comes the closest in integrating the impact of entrepreneurs on the diffusion process. The perspective itself is most closely associated with the discipline of geography, and its essence is summed up best by Brown when he writes:

> Unless some government, entrepreneurial or non-profit organization makes the innovation available at or near the location of the potential adopter … that person or household will not have the option to adopt in the first place.[46]

The need to pay greater attention to the availability of an innovation was also recognized by Griliches,[47] who noted that 'it does not make sense to blame the Southern farmers for being slow in acceptance, unless one takes into account the fact that no satisfactory hybrids [seeds] were available to them before the middle nineteen forties'. More recently, analysts of diffusion from a more marketing-orientated background have also recognized that 'an empirically observed diffusion pattern may however be governed by bottlenecks on the supply side (production capacity, distribution and so on), so that the natural demand process is decelerated or retarded'.[48]

The research corollary of identifying availability as a key constraint on adoption is to direct attention to the supply side:

> Focus is upon the process by which innovations and the conditions for adoption are made available to individuals or households, that is, the supply aspect of diffusion.[49]

In particular, Brown is interested in the activities of what he calls 'diffusion agencies', defined as 'public or private entities through which an innovation is distributed or made available to society at large'.[50] Diffusion agencies can be 'commercial' entities, such as shops run by dealers and distributors of an innovation, or 'government' entities, such as local agricultural extension offices, or 'non-profit' entities, such as local family planning units.

Examination of diffusion agencies and their activities is particularly relevant to what Brown calls 'infrastructure-constrained innovations'. Where an innovation is infrastructure-constrained, the implication is that 'diffusion will in general occur only where there is the required infrastructure and not elsewhere'.[51] Obvious examples include cable television, high-yielding varieties of seeds which are dependent on irrigation technology, or the internet and telephony in rural areas – for example in India a new approach is being piloted of bringing the internet and telephones to towns and villages through the under-employed communication cables that connect the country's 8000 railway stations.[52] Less obvious but equally infrastructure-constrained innovations are those that must be serviced regularly, or where access to maintenance and repair services is critical, such as photocopying equipment or, as we shall see, solar technology.

Brown then looks behind the local diffusion agency to the propagators, defined as 'profit or non-profit motivated organizations or government agencies acting to induce the rapid and complete diffusion of the innovation'.[53] Diffusion is explained by the propagators' establishment of diffusion agencies and the strategies adopted to promote diffusion, including pricing, promotional communications, market segmentation and channel development. Of the relevant propagators, it is found that diffusion 'may in large part be explained by entrepreneurial actions rather than social interactions',[54] and ultimately that:

> the traditional social science models of diffusion, which focus on adoption behaviour, are found wanting in not considering the role of the entrepreneur in propagating innovations.[55]

This perspective now starts to touch upon the interests and subject matter of this book. Brown has gone further than most in recognizing the variety of ways in which entrepreneurs can affect the diffusion process. As one commentator writes, Brown's analysis represents a shift 'away from the adopter of a new technology to the individuals or organizations working hard to push innovation into the marketplace', and as such it offers 'a way to look at diffusion as a result of entrepreneurial activity, a point of view that is particularly important in assessing the spread of high-technology'.[56]

But Brown does not go one step further to consider what it is that makes the entrepreneurial firm more or less effective in its efforts.[57] Brown does recognize that a propagator's access to capital can affect the rate of diffusion,[58] but this is almost in passing, and he does not develop a specific proposition about the impact of this variable. By contrast, other analysts of diffusion have concluded that diffusion research needs to give greater attention to the 'resource commitments' of propagating firms, since 'the greater the allocation of marketing resources, the more rapid the diffusion process and the higher the diffusion level'. These same analysts lament that 'diffusion research almost totally ignores these intentions and resource allocations of the firms marketing innovation'.[59]

The Missing Element of Agency

To simplify the essence of each perspective, it is perhaps best to remember four core questions that each perspective would have a diffusion analyst ask. The first question, as asked by the communication perspective, is 'Is it attractive?'. For the communication analysts, this is always a work in progress, as the more positive or negative referencing that occurs, the more adopters will either come to value the innovation – in other words perceive it to be attractive enough to adopt – or reject it. The second question, as asked by the economic history perspective is 'Is it competitive?'. For the economic historians, this will also be a moving target, based on the technological improvements that an innovation may or may not be undergoing. The third question, as posed by those of the development perspective, is 'Is it affordable?'. This perspective concentrates on the purchasing power of adopters and their access to credit, and notes that even competitive innovations can remain unaffordable to the majority in emerging markets. And the fourth and final question, as posed by the market infrastructure perspective, is 'Is it available?'. This perspective emphasizes the role of propagating organizations in making the new product or service widely available in the first place.

To summarize, the four core questions to be asked at the outset of any analysis of diffusion are:

1   Is it attractive?
2   Is it competitive?
3   Is it affordable?
4   Is it available?

Answering these questions is the first step in explaining the diffusion of an innovation. The next step is to then link them to the role of the entrepreneur, and explain how such individuals and their organizations are able to influence each of the above four factors. To put it more clearly, *who* will make the innovation more attractive, competitive, affordable and available to the masses, and *how* will they do it? This is the element of agency, and, as we saw in our review, it is not fully developed in the existing theories of diffusion.

If we were to integrate the impact of entrepreneurs with the four factors above, as identified by diffusion research, a schematic diagram might look as simple as Figure 2.2.

But why do we single out entrepreneurs as the key agents of technology diffusion? And what makes them more or less effective in this role? To address these outstanding questions, we will now turn to management literature, which not only substantiates the focus on entrepreneurs, but helps us explain how they impact the diffusion process.

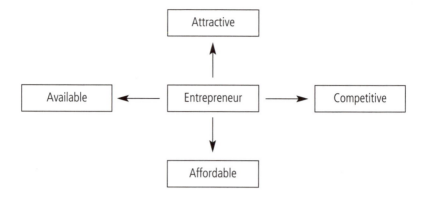

Figure 2.2 Integrating the impact of entrepreneurs on innovation diffusion

The Historical Role of Entrepreneurs in Innovation Diffusion

Historically, it is recognized that commercial firms are 'but one agent for the diffusion of technology'. In many countries, governments and non-profit organizations have been, and continue to be, equally active in promoting innovations – for example rural extension agencies in the US promoting new seed varieties. That said, the historical impact of commercial firms on technology diffusion is widely recognized to be an *important* one.[60]

A firm built on an innovative technology serves as an incubator and carrier of that innovation, and the fate of the firm and of its innovation can often be linked.[61] If the firm goes under, then the impetus behind the innovation's diffusion can die with it. But if the firm continues to grow, then we can expect other firms to enter the market, creating competitive pressures for enhanced marketing, cost and quality improvements, and further development of the infrastructure for widespread availability. For this reason, we need to look closely at the role of entrepreneurs in driving the growth of firms built on or around innovations.

First we should take a moment to define the term 'entrepreneur'. In more traditional economic studies, 'firms are the key actors', while 'individuals are viewed as interchangeable and their actions determined by the firms they are in'.[62] This view sees individuals as largely dispensable. However, there is another perspective in economics which links the growth of new markets directly to the individuals involved. One of the few economists to recognize the broader economic impact of these individuals was Schumpeter, who proclaimed that to be an entrepreneur was to be an agent of change:

> The entrepreneur and his function are not difficult to conceptualize: the
> defining characteristic is simply the doing of new things or the doing of
> things that are already being done in a new way (innovation).[63]

To be clear, the entrepreneur was not to be confused with the inventor, for
while 'the inventor produces ideas, the entrepreneur gets things done'.[64]

Insofar as mainstream economics has attended to entrepreneurs, it has
been to assign them the role of risk-takers.[65] However, studies have found that
many entrepreneurs actively avoid risk.[66] Hewlett-Packard, for example, were
overtly risk-averse.[67] Even for Schumpeter, who stressed the dangers that entrepreneurs encounter, it was not the willingness to take risks, but rather the
capacity to bring about change that was the key attribute of entrepreneurs.[68]

In line with Schumpeter, other prominent analysts have defined entrepreneurs as individuals that create a 'new market' with a 'new customer'.[69] The
implication of this definition is that to be in charge of a new small business
does not make one an entrepreneur. Rather:

> To be entrepreneurial, an enterprise has to have special characteristics
> over and above being new and small. Indeed entrepreneurs are a minor-
> ity among businesses. They create something new, something different:
> they change and transmute values.[70]

According to this definition, it is entirely possible for individuals within large
corporations to be entrepreneurs. There is no doubt that larger corporations
have the research and development (R&D) facilities, the brands, the marketing, the capital and the human resources that entrepreneurs within their ranks
can harness for innovation and diffusion of innovations.[71] For this reason,
where a corporation allows or encourages entrepreneurship, it can sometimes
have a larger impact on diffusion than the struggling start-up company.

However, history has also shown time and again that established corporations often consciously or unconsciously avoid doing what they need to do to
whole-heartedly propagate innovations for fear of destabilizing existing
markets.[72] For example, neither General Electric nor Westinghouse sought to
push new energy-efficient light-bulbs into the marketplace 'for fear of alienat-
ing power utilities that purchased their lamps, generators and other electrical
equipment'.[73] Indeed, every wave in the innovation and diffusion of lighting
technologies, from gas lighting, to incandescent to fluorescent lighting, was
'originated and carried forward by industry outsiders'.[74]

On the other hand, it may not be fear, but simply a lack of vision that
hobbles the large corporation. As Porter writes, 'It is hard for firms steeped in
an old technological paradigm to perceive the significance of a new one. It is
even harder for them to respond to it.' An example given in this regard is the

failure of the established US vacuum tube competitors to enter the semi-conductor market.[75]

Thus by 'entrepreneur' we do not necessarily mean an individual who is working on their own, or has set up their own company, although more often than not, these industry outsiders prove to be the pioneers of innovation. Instead, we mean more broadly *an individual who has the capacity to match resources to opportunities for innovation.*[76]

The relevance of such individuals to the process of innovation diffusion should by now be clear. Using Schumpeter's phrase, entrepreneurs can set off a process of 'creative destruction' in the marketplace, whereby an innovation gradually starts to replace and thus destroy the market for existing alternatives. Initially entrepreneurs may toil and struggle to bring an innovation to market, but if they are successful, they set a precedent which others follow, and on the basis of which rapid diffusion can occur:

> As soon as the success is before everybody's eyes, everything is made much easier by this very fact. It can now, with much diminished difficulty, be copied, even improved upon, and a whole crowd invariably does copy it.[77]

The early efforts of entrepreneurs set off a series of competitive pressures, leading to greater allocation of resources, to improved design, marketing and aggressive pricing, all of which have been found to encourage more rapid diffusion.[78] For example, the successful introduction of the typewriter by Remington encouraged the entrance of competitors with better designs, lower-cost products, and increased sales and promotion activities. The cumulative impact of Remington's early commercial initiative was that the typewriter eventually became 'a ubiquitous fixture of the workplace', and so, as his brochure promised, it became 'a machine to supersede the pen' (until, of course, it was itself superseded by the personal computer).[79]

The role of entrepreneurs in bringing technological innovations to market and stimulating the growth of entirely new industries around these innovations suggests that diffusion research must do a better job of explaining the way in which entrepreneurs are able to have this impact. To do so, I borrow the core concepts of 'capacities' and 'resources' from management literature on entrepreneurship, and integrate them with the four factors earlier identified from theories on innovation diffusion.

Entrepreneurial Capacities

As discussed above, entrepreneurs are those who have the capacity to match resources to opportunities for innovation. There are those in the business

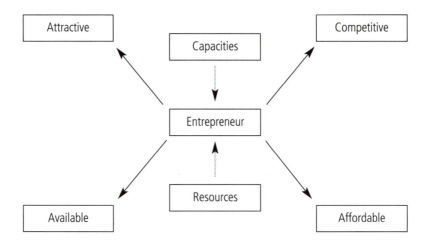

Figure 2.3 What enables entrepreneurs to influence innovation diffusion

world who think of opportunities as quite structurally determined. For example, the arrival of the internet created a massive opportunity for the delivery of new goods and services more directly to the customer. The management theorist, Michael Porter, is often deemed to fall into this more deterministic camp, for example in using the five forces model to explain why it is that some firms are able to grow.[80] However, there are others, such as Edith Penrose, who, before Porter, took a more voluntaristic approach. By this I mean that she did not see opportunities as unmovable, immutable truths, but rather in much the same way as sociologists see the rules and norms in a society – 'all structural properties of social systems are enabling as well as constraining'.[81]

Before business schools were doing it, Penrose set out in 1959 to explain why some firms grew more quickly and more successfully than others. In doing so she concentrated on the capacities developed by the members of a firm over time and through experience. Not surprisingly, she left a lot of room for the agency of entrepreneurs when it came to translating opportunities into growth:

> The set of opportunities for investment and growth that its entrepreneurs and managers perceive is different for every firm, and depends on its specific collection of human and other resources. Moreover, the environment is not something 'out there', fixed and immutable, but can itself be manipulated by the firm to serve its own purposes.[82]

In short, one entrepreneur may be able to find opportunity where others do not.[83] Or put another way, 'different entrepreneurs in the same circumstances might well achieve different results'.[84]

To be fair, even Porter has recognized that 'outsiders', such as entrepreneurs, may be better placed to exploit emergent opportunities since they 'may possess the different expertise and resources required to compete in a new way'.[85] Statements such as this are entirely in line with the thinking of Schumpeter, who proclaimed that:

> In most cases only one man or a few men can see the new possibility and are able to cope with the resistances and difficulties which action always meets with outside the ruts of human practice.[86]

In discussing the capacities of entrepreneurs, and what gives them their powers of creative destruction, Schumpeter placed particular emphasis on entrepreneurial vision, energy and tenacity, rather than on managerial skills.[87] Successful innovation, he felt 'is a feat not of intellect, but of will', ultimately reliant on 'supernormal energy and courage'.[88] There is indeed some truth to this statement. When you review the early experiences of entrepreneurs who are later successful, they have often had to endure tremendous hardship before seeing their innovations take hold.

Yet in explanations of entrepreneurial performance today, analysts tend to give greater emphasis to managerial capacity rather than pure will. For instance, the relatively high rate of failure for entrepreneurial start-ups is to be explained by the fact that entrepreneurs:

> lack the methodology. They violate elementary and well-known rules. This is particularly true of high-tech entrepreneurs. ... But even high-tech entrepreneurship need not be high-risk. ... It does need, however, to be systematic. It needs to be managed.[89]

Recall, for instance, Hughes's 1979 work that found that although Edison made the technological breakthrough, it was Samuel Insull's greater managerial ability that turned Edison's primarily urban-based grid electricity system into a region-wide system. The question, then, is how to account for these managerial capacities.

Analysts of entrepreneurial performance find that 'know-how may be the most critical in influencing the ultimate success or the failure of an enterprise'.[90] Such analysts agree that this quality derives strongly from *prior experience* and *learning by doing*.[91] Entrepreneurs particularly benefit from prior involvement in well-managed companies.[92] Similarly, it has been found that 'repetition', and thus 'an intimate detailed knowledge of the business', greatly improves the chances of success.[93] Thus an entrepreneur who spins out of an existing company often has a distinct advantage over an inexperienced entrepreneur in the same sector.[94]

But entrepreneurs with all the strength of will and managerial capacities in the world will not be able to make a dent in the marketplace if they are not able to harness and mobilize considerable resources.

Resources

By 'resources' here we mean financial resources – capital. There are other resources that business analysts point to, such as human, technological, reputation (brand) and organizational resources.[95] But, in line with Schumpeter, our concern is with capital. Schumpeter emphasized that the commercialization of an innovation 'requires large expenditure previous to the emergence of any revenue' and as such 'credit becomes an essential element of the process'.[96]

By credit, Schumpeter did not mean customer credit, but capital, which has been found to be particularly relevant in the high-tech sector, where product development, manufacturing, sales and marketing, channel development, and so on are expensive and can be prohibitive for the small company.[97] Thus studies of high-tech entrepreneurship have concluded that while 'entrepreneurial people provide the initiative, the energy and the vision to launch a new company ... money provides "the grease", the wherewithal to make it happen'.[98] Similarly, others conclude that:

> Every dynamic process needs to be fuelled. The fuel for the entrepreneurial process is capital. Capital is the catalyst for the entrepreneurial chain reaction. It is the lifeblood of the emerging and expanding enterprises. Capital provides the financial resources through which the ideas of the entrepreneur can be developed, tested and commercialized.[99]

But if capital is key, then it is certainly the case that entrepreneurs often lack 'power on the money market', which is not the case for the larger firm.[100] Recognition of this difficulty for entrepreneurs outside of large corporations has led to a whole host of studies on how entrepreneurs catch the financier's eye.[101]

To a certain extent, different entrepreneurs will have different capacities to affect the flow of finances to their venture – some will create more confidence among investors than others. For example, Edison relied on another individual, a 'finance-entrepreneur', with more 'knowledge of the world of legal, business and financial affairs', to raise the requisite capital for his incandescent lighting projects.[102]

That said, uncertainty always surrounds a new venture and a new technology. Regardless of the objective merits of the proposal, the subjective perceptions of the financier matter. In this regard, 'investor fit', defined as whether 'the investor is interested in, or knows something about, the industry and market', is important.[103] For example, banks were initially ill-suited to fund early entrepreneurs in Silicon Valley, since they 'were unprepared to evaluate the potential of start-up electronic companies that made products that were difficult to understand'.[104] Similarly, the growth of the biotechnology industry was initially dependent on more knowledgeable venture capitalists and business angels coming forward.[105]

Because the mobilization of capital and its investment are so central to whether an entrepreneur can realize his or her vision, it is safe to conclude that potential investors effectively play a key selection role in the diffusion process. In this regard, it is important to note that entrepreneurs in emerging markets often cite a lack of capital as the most serious handicap in the growth of their firms.[106] Analysts must be wary of accepting this interpretation at face value, since 'it is well known that complaints about the unavailability of credit can reflect a wide range of inadequacies in the management of the enterprise'.[107] Nonetheless, there is a general consensus that the financial sector in many emerging markets has historically held back the entrepreneur.[108] And as we shall see in the case of selling solar, this absence of capital can have profound effects on the rate of technology diffusion.

What Role for Policy?

Entrepreneurs do not operate in a vacuum. Policies that are put in place by government can strongly influence their businesses. Of the different perspectives on innovation diffusion, the economic history perspective gives the most detailed attention to the relationship between technology diffusion and policy changes, which are subsumed under the broader heading of 'institutional changes'.[109] In particular, this perspective looks at how policies change to improve the relative economic attractiveness of a particular innovation.

Brown, while an advocate of the market infrastructure perspective, also recognizes that '*institutional* factors influence the diffusion process by affecting the context within which the technological factors operate'.[110] Brown cites a good example of this: the improvement in productivity of ocean-going shipping from 1600 to 1850.[111] The Dutch produced a superior ship for large-volume shipping, as it was lightly built and used simplified rigging that did not require as many sailors per ship. But the problem was that the ship was not conducive to carrying armaments. Thus, although it was superior technology, it was only after levels of piracy had been forced down that it could be adopted for widespread use in large-volume shipping.

Other historical examples include the higher electricity rates charged in Europe at the turn of the 20th century, which led to the earlier introduction and diffusion of metal filament lamps. Although more costly initially, the lamps were more energy-efficient and thus found a market.[112] More recently, the diffusion of solar water heaters in the US was adversely affected by the removal of 'residential solar tax credits' under President Reagan's administration.[113]

Because it will apply to later discussions on solar, it is also worth noting the finding of economic historians that there is a symbiotic relationship between institutional change and technological innovation and diffusion.[114] In other words it is not all one way: that policy changes facilitate or hamper diffusion. Instead, entrepreneurs' efforts to bring an innovation to market can themselves influence policy. In the case of Dutch shipping, for instance, Brown speculates that the arrival of a lighter, cheaper means of shipping actually provided an incentive to force the decline of piracy. As Brown concludes:

> A change in institutional conditions may be necessary for realizing the benefits of technological change, but at the same time the technological change, providing an opportunity to increase profits, may be the impetus to innovate a new institutional arrangement.[115]

There is thus little doubt that governments and their policies can have an impact on the diffusion of innovations and vice versa. But it is best to think of policies as part of the overall structural environment in which an entrepreneur operates. New policies can create opportunities for more or less of these transactions, but it is still up to the entrepreneur to *see* the opportunity for innovation, have the capacity to set up and start selling the innovation profitably, and mobilize the resources required to be effective and sustain the operations. In other words, you can have all the policy change you want, but if entrepreneurs don't see it, cannot translate it, cannot sustain it, then diffusion of an innovation will not happen.

Moreover, as we will see clearly in the case of solar diffusion, it is the early efforts of entrepreneurs, and the nascent markets that they demonstrate, that can influence policymakers to act. Without the examples set by entrepreneurs, policymakers will often not have the inspiration nor the incentive to make policy changes. And that is why this study retains the entrepreneur as the focal point of its analysis, even while recognizing that the actions of government and international organizations can have a tremendous impact on the rate of diffusion.

Figure 2.4 schematically adds this policy component to our analytical framework for diffusion.

Policy effectively 'surrounds' the entrepreneur and the diffusion process. It affects the extent to which entrepreneurs can surmount the barriers to diffusion, and it affects the flow of capacities and resources that enable them to do so. Moreover, as we have considered, there is a two-way flow between the entrepreneur and policy, with each influencing the direction of the other. We

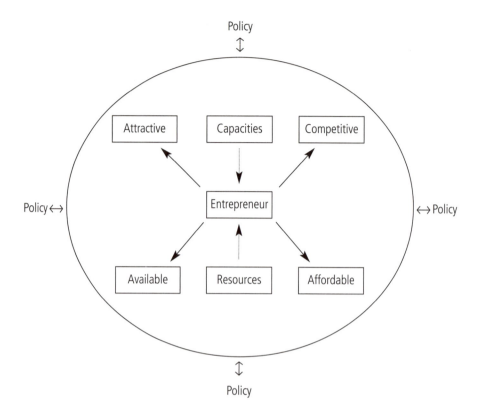

Figure 2.4 An integrated analytical framework for explaining innovation diffusion

will see this process in action in Part II, when we review our case studies of solar entrepreneurship and policy formation.

Summing Up

We have seen that diffusion research can help us identify key barriers in the diffusion process. Specifically, it asks us to consider four core questions relating to the diffusion of an innovation: Is it attractive? Is it competitive? Is it affordable? Is it available? Answering these questions will go a long way towards establishing the barriers to the diffusion of an innovation. However, we have also seen that doing so will not give us a full explanation. For this we need to add an element of agency, particularly the impact of entrepreneurs.

Historically, the entrepreneur has been a key agent in the diffusion of innovations. In terms of what empowers an entrepreneur to fulfil this role, it is clear that it is a mix of essential capacities and resources to affect change. Beyond the sheer will of the entrepreneur, we need to look closely at an entrepreneur's prior experience and learning-on-the-job, and we need to look closely at an entrepreneur's connection with investors in raising sufficient capital. We also need to consider an entrepreneur's structural environment – specifically the impact of policy on entrepreneurs and the impact of entrepreneurs on policy. With this, we now have a full analytical framework with which to approach our case of solar diffusion in emerging markets.

Theory Applied to Solar

Having developed an analytical framework in the previous chapter for explaining diffusion, we now apply it to the case of solar in emerging markets. Specifically, we apply it to the first of our two questions posed at the outset: 'Why was solar slower to diffuse than expected throughout the 1990s?'.

The excitement surrounding solar's introduction into emerging markets in the late 1980s and early 1990s meant that much was written on it. These 'reports from the field' are a rich source of information, and when viewed through the lens of our analytical framework on diffusion, they help us arrive at the key factors that were holding solar back. Furthermore, by isolating these barriers, we set the stage for later discussions on what enabled entrepreneurs to overcome them and thereby accelerate the diffusion process.

Communication Perspective: Is it Attractive?

The communication perspective demands that we enquire more deeply into how customers *perceive* the risks and benefits of buying a solar system, and ask whether overall they find it an attractive proposition.

There is no doubt that households in emerging markets value electricity. However, a demand for electricity does not necessarily translate into a demand for solar. From the household's perspective, electricity from a reliable grid is often preferable in terms of service.[1] Take the example of the Government anti-poverty programme in Mexico, where rural households initially rejected solar systems on the grounds that they were being subjected to yet another experiment by bureaucrats in the cities.[2] Similar reactions were recorded in Sri Lanka, where 'overcoming perceptions of both the government and the public that PV is inferior to the grid has been a barrier', especially given the Government's high profile campaign which 'had the public believing that everybody would be linked to the grid by the year 2000'.[3]

The perception that the grid is just around the corner can indeed be a negative perception that weighs on customer adoption of solar. Whether due to wishful thinking or genuine belief, households will be wary of making the investment in solar when they feel that the grid is coming soon, or even when they feel it is coming within the next year or two. In Indonesia, before the economic crisis of the late 1990s, sales of solar were strong. But they would nonetheless dry up in areas where PLN (the electricity utility), with the blessings of the Government, dropped poles by the side of the road prior to elections to raise expectations of the grid's imminent arrival. On the other hand, in other countries some analysts also found that rural households were starting to wise up. In Sri Lanka, for instance, households were said to have come to the realization, after years of failed promises, 'that the grid will not reach them in the short term and PV will meet their immediate needs'.[4]

Although the grid is by and large preferred by all, we also need to remember that not all grids function as well as they do in the industrialized countries. In Kenya, for instance, where rural households regularly suffer blackouts, a survey found that 50 per cent of adopters saw 'reliability' as an advantage of solar compared to the grid.[5] India provides the classic case of the grid being perceived to be highly unreliable and solar to be an increasingly reliable backup, as we will discuss in more detail later in the book.

In the absence of the grid, or a reliable grid, rural households have the option of using a petrol, kerosene or diesel genset. A small petrol genset supplies 13–22 times the rated wattage of an average 50-watt solar system; it is thus considered by some to be more appealing to the rural households, offering 'considerably more flexibility'. And since it is cheaper on a dollar per kWh basis, it frees up resources for 'greater increases in the standard of living'.[6] But as prescribed by the communication perspective described in Chapter 2, this is a classic case of why it is important to understand the customers' *perceptions* of the economics and not just the economics themselves.

First of all, because many rural households have limited electricity requirements, they do not focus on the extra 'flexibility' of a genset, which will by and large remain unused. Rather they focus on the recurring cost of having excess capacity in the generator, and the fact that fuel prices in rural areas generally go up and not down. In the Dominican Republic, for example, the same critics of solar quoted earlier also found that because agricultural income is seasonal, farmers were even selling their generator sets in order to buy solar, where the fuel costs are all paid up-front. Furthermore, they concluded that where there is insecurity about future price rises in fuel 'the $/kWh economic advantage [of the genset] is less important'.[7]

In Kenya, rural customers were found to 'relish the idea' that, once the panel was bought, electricity costs were minimal: two-thirds of all respondents in a questionnaire cited 'free electricity' as an advantage of solar.[8] Furthermore, in Kenya the same authors found that customers perceived not only that solar was less costly, but that it was more convenient to turn on and off, was less vulnerable to fuel price fluctuations, saved journeys, and was far less hazardous.

Compared to other alternatives, such as kerosene for lighting and battery charging for radio and television, we find that the perceptions in favour of solar are stronger still. The primary use of electricity by formerly unelectrified homes is lighting and entertainment (see, for example, the findings from Indonesia in Table 3.1).

Table 3.1 Appliance use in households with electricity: The case of Indonesia

Activity	Low income (%)	Middle income (%)	High income (%)
Lighting	100	100	100
Television	31	63	83
Ironing	21	51	77
Refrigeration	1	6	9
Water pumping	1	4	26

Source: World Bank (1996a), p42

In Kenya the findings were that 'first and foremost the Kenyans surveyed use their photovoltaic systems for lighting needs' and that 'the prospect of improved lighting is often a main factor in the decision to buy a solar panel. Over two-thirds of those questioned in Kenya identified 'quality of light' as a significant advantage of solar.[9] Solar is also perceived as being much more convenient as it provides light at the flip of a switch. Those surveyed were 'grateful for the journeys saved by their PV system' – journeys otherwise made to procure kerosene fuel – and over two-thirds cited the overall convenience and safety of solar as an advantage.[10]

In addition, solar meets households' entertainment needs in a more convenient fashion than taking a battery to the local charging station, which requires two trips on back-to-back days – one to drop it off, and one to pick it up once it is charged. A four-country case study in Kenya, Zimbabwe, the Dominican Republic and Sri Lanka found that rural households generally perceive an advantage in using solar to power a black and white television, because it removes the burden of transporting a battery for regular recharging.[11]

We might also note that social norms (identified by the communication perspective as a factor to consider) tend to be conducive to solar. A solar system can attribute status to the household or enterprise that uses it. In the Dominican Republic, for example, '[electric] lights at night are very visible, and electricity allows a family to effectively become the "local cinema", to invite the neighbours around, to watch soap-operas, and so on'.[12] Similarly in Kenya:

> Ownership of a PV system can earn the household a local reputation, because neighbours can see the lights at night-time and friends and relatives are often invited over to watch the television. In fact, one household reported that the advantage of owning a solar energy system is that solar is 'a highly visible status symbol'.[13]

So clearly the perceptions of solar compared with the most commonly used alternatives – kerosene lighting, battery charging and generator sets – are very positive, and give solar a relative advantage in the eyes of potential customers. But for that to be acted upon, a customer must also develop trust that the system will work. Could it be that diffusion was held back by a lack of trust in the technology?

Sales of solar often occur in clusters, where potential customers have first waited to see how the system worked, and only then bought their own solar system based on the positive referencing of their neighbours. This is confirmed by the four-country case study in Kenya, Zimbabwe, the Dominican Republic and Sri Lanka, where it was found that:

> Villagers spend much time visiting each other. As with all new technologies, the first home that installs a system gets scrutinized by the rest of the village. If the first system is successful, other community members soon follow suit and buy systems.[14]

This is the referencing process in action, as discussed by the communication perspective. Likewise, other studies concluded 'that word of mouth plays a central role in educating the Kenyan public about PV technology'.[15] In Zimbabwe it is reported that 'PV systems are typically found in clusters – one innovator in a community buys a system and convinces other community members to follow'.[16] And again in Mexico, where a large commercial propagator of solar technology states:

> We found that the demonstration effect was absolutely vital to sales. ... Many do not believe it will work at first, but seeing the lights at night for one month has a positive impact on perceptions.[17]

The vital importance of referencing in the case of solar relates to its up-front costs. For the typical rural unelectrified customer in emerging markets, a solar system can represent anywhere from 20 to 30 per cent of their annual income. It is therefore quite natural that before making this kind of investment, potential customers would first want to find out from their neighbours, friends or peers how well it has worked. When the author asked one propagator of solar whether being an NGO engendered more trust in the customer, he replied their NGO status had not:

been absolutely essential for developing trust among households. Anyone will be distrustful of someone selling a $500–$800 system. Instead trust is developed when they can see their neighbours' system working, and neighbours getting enthusiastic about it.[18]

This of course means that the quality of the solar system and after-sales service becomes critical to diffusion. The after-sales service required is not complex: it entails topping up the battery (in the case of flooded lead acid batteries that are not maintenance free), or replacing components in the light fixtures and electronics. But very often in the 1980s and 1990s, solar systems were parachuted into rural areas and installed without any back-up after-sales service, which meant that in the end the systems failed. This in turn gave solar a bad name, and though it is difficult to quantify, we might speculate that it has been a barrier to diffusion:

In the absence of a support infrastructure, many solar electric systems have failed, and these failures have led people to say that solar technology is not viable. However, solar system failure is almost always due to the lack of proper design, installation, management or maintenance, and not solar power systems.[19]

It is ultimately the propagator of solar that must decide on the design of the system, monitor effective installation and provide after-sales service. Without this, it is clear that households will come to distrust solar as an alternative, and its diffusion can suffer as a result. In Fiji, for instance, under-sizing of solar systems and poor maintenance by the implementing government agency meant that all 300 systems installed between 1983 and 1985 had failed by 1989. Not surprisingly the rural populace in those parts of Fiji became disaffected with solar and came to see it as a technology of last resort.[20]

Thus the communication perspective has helped us identify a couple of potential barriers to solar diffusion: wishful thinking about the arrival of the grid and the negative referencing from poorly maintained or designed solar systems. These are significant potential barriers, but, as we shall explore in Part II, they can be overcome by entrepreneurs with the right approach. More significantly, we can conclude that provided a solar system is designed and installed well, potential customers perceive solar to be an attractive proposition compared to alternatives such as kerosene, battery charging and generator sets. Could it be, then, that what was actually holding back solar in the 1990s was that it could not compete economically with these alternatives?

Economic History Perspective: Is It Competitive?

In talking about the cost competitiveness of solar, it makes sense to focus on the solar photovoltaic module. Of all the components in the solar system, solar modules have been and continue to be the highest-cost component and have shown the greatest potential for dramatic cost reductions.[21]

A typical solar module is made up of what are called PV cells – these individual cells are connected together in series and laminated and encased in a solar module. The earliest PV cells were made in the 1870s with selenium and were able to convert light to electricity at 1–2 per cent efficiency.[22] But by 1954, Bell laboratories had built the first silicon-based PV cell, which converted 4 per cent of the sun's rays into electricity and which was adopted by the US space programme for generating power in space.

The impetus from the space programme subsequently reduced the cost of PV cells by 90 per cent. But it was only with the oil crises in the 1970s and a push from governments to displace oil that PV prices really started to drop and early terrestrial applications for such things as telecommunication repeater stations and remote research facilities started to emerge. In the early 1970s the cost of PV power was $600 per watt, meaning that the average 50-watt module cost US$30,000! But by 1980 the cost had fallen to around $20–25 per watt, and it continued to fall to $6 per watt by 1990 and approximately $4.5 per watt by the mid 1990s. It is no wonder that around this time, energy analysts proclaimed that the 'development of photovoltaics has been nothing short of remarkable'.[23]

Some still felt that the time was not right for solar in emerging markets – they felt that more time should be given for the costs of the solar module to fall further: 'The economics of PV applications are unlikely to allow for an unsubsidized widespread adoption of this technology in the near future.'[24] But others came to a very different conclusion. The World Bank, for example, concluded as early as 1994 that PV technology was competitive for rural electrification:

> For many purposes they are already the least-cost option. Costs and performance compare well with diesel generation, for example, and sometimes with grid supplied electricity in rural areas, depending on the community's distance from the grid.[25]

A further World Bank study confirmed in 1996 that for areas of low population density, low initial electricity demand and long distances from the grid, PV was already competitive with the grid from a purely economic point of view.[26]

Of course, customers in emerging markets, particularly in rural areas, have not tended to pay the full cost of electricity from the grid (see Table 3.2):

Table 3.2 Costs and rural retail tariffs for grid electricity in selected emerging markets (US cents per kWh)

Country	Fuel	Generation and transmission	Distribution	Total	Average rural tariff
Bangladesh	4.6	9.2	10.6	24.4	16.0
India	2.1	5.8	8.7	16.4	0.5
Indonesia	3.8	4.1	9.8	17.6	5.8
Malaysia	2.3	8.8	4.4	15.5	7.2
Philippines	5.0	2.8	7.5	15.3	9.2
Thailand	5.0	3.8	8.3	17.1	7.0

Source: World Bank (1996a), p44

Under circumstances of heavily subsidized grid electricity, solar PV plainly cannot compete. The cost of electricity from a solar system in the Dominican Republic in the mid 1990s was estimated at almost US$1.9 per kWh,[27] and $2.5 per kWh in Zimbabwe and Kenya,[28] whereas the highest tariff in Table 3.2 is $0.16 per kWh and the lowest is $0.005 per kWh.

But we must remember that solar in rural areas of emerging markets is not competing with the grid. Given the choice, most rural customers would prefer a connection to the national electricity grid, especially if the electricity is reliable and subsidized. But the reality is that the electricity grid is simply not available to 1.64 billion people in the emerging markets. So instead of comparing the cost of solar with grid electricity prices, we need to compare it to the alternatives people are actually using in the absence of the grid.

After comparing it to a 650-watt gasoline generator set, the earlier critics of solar concluded that on a cost-per-kilowatt-hour basis it was still too expensive, and thus concluded that 'PVs are clearly not competitive with fossil fuel power' for rural electricity supply.

Table 3.3 Cost per kWh of solar and petrol genset in the Dominican Republic

	Up-front Cost	Cost per kWh
Solar	$870.83	$1.926
Genset	$609	$0.462

Source: Erickson and Chapman (1995), p1132[29]

Moreover, these analysts felt that even under favourable conditions of higher fuel taxes, zero per cent interest rates and 30 year system lifetimes, 'PV systems are still non-competitive with gasoline-powered electric generators'.[30]

Certainly on a per-kilowatt-hour basis, the petrol or diesel genset can be a more cost-effective option than solar. Furthermore, it generates AC power for standard 220-volt appliances, such as colour TV, and provides greater flexibility to increase the power output and duration when required – for example to run a few extra appliances or to run later into the night. By contrast, an average 50-watt solar system (without a DC to AC inverter) generates only DC electricity at 12 volts, suitable for black and white TVs and radios, and once the power in the battery is used up, there is no more until the sun comes up the next day.

But these relative advantages of a generator obscure the fact that, for many rural homes in emerging markets, using a 650W generator would be 'overkill', because their electricity requirements generally do not extend beyond lighting, radio and television.[31] To meet these basic needs by running a genset would mean paying for tremendous excess capacity. Looking at the case of India, where customers were buying solar mainly for back-up lighting purposes, we see that the smallest diesel genset then readily available on the market was three times more expensive to run on a monthly amortized cost basis:

Table 3.4 Monthly amortized costs of solar and diesel genset in India

Product option	Cost to customer
37W solar system, later upgraded to 74W	US$10.1
500W diesel genset	US$30.4

Source: Miller and Hope (2000), p89[32]

Furthermore, as we considered earlier, unelectrified households may also prefer solar to a genset due to the regular expense of purchasing fuel, the burden of transporting the fuel, and the risk of non-availability or future price escalations of fuel.[33]

Instead, of using a genset, the vast majority of rural households tend to secure basic lighting and entertainment services with kerosene lanterns and battery charging.[34] Taking kerosene first, households use one of three different lanterns: either a plain wick lamp, which works like a candle with, a wick sitting in kerosene; or what is called a hurricane lantern, which is an old-style lantern encased in glass that again uses a wick, but where you can turn a knob to increase or decrease the flame; or a Petromax lantern, which uses pressure to generate a much brighter light from kerosene. With regard to battery charging, households purchase a car battery, and then every 1–2 weeks, depending on the extent of use, take it to be recharged at the nearest grid charging point for a fee.

When you compare solar to such competing products, you find, first of all, that solar gives a better quality light than kerosene (see Table 3.5).

Table 3.5 Comparison of kerosene lanterns and electric light

Light source	Lumens
Wick lantern	40
Petromax lantern	300
Compact fluorescent bulb (11W)	550

Source: Miller (1998)

Second, as the World Bank concluded in the mid 1990s, solar is actually more cost-effective than the combination of kerosene and battery charging:

> Solar home systems provide energy services at a lower economic cost than the kerosene or battery option. ... Moreover, PV systems have the added benefit of being able to provide more and better light, and more conveniently, than batteries or kerosene.[35]

These assertions were backed up the World Bank's findings in the field (see Table 3.6).

Table 3.6 Monthly amortized costs of solar and kerosene/battery charging

Solar home system		Kerosene and batteries	
Equipment	Monthly cost ($)	Equipment	Monthly cost ($)
50 watt SHS: 8 hrs of area lighting 6 hrs of task lighting 60Wh for radio/TV	8.25	2 wick lanterns 1 mantle lantern 1 battery	9.25
100 watt SHS: 12 hrs of area lighting 14 hrs of task lighting 150Wh for other loads	13.75	3 wick lanterns 2 mantle lanterns 2 batteries	19.25

Source: Cabraal et al (1996), p18

A similar World Bank study also analysed the competitiveness of solar, but this time by various socio-economic groups (see Table 3.7) and concluded that 'PV systems are generally financially competitive in providing the services demanded in each socioeconomic group'.[36]

Table 3.7 Comparison by socio-economic group between expenditure on conventional alternatives to electricity grid and monthly amortized cost of solar

Socio-economic group	Appliances	Existing monthly expenditure ($)	Solar systems	Solar monthly amortization ($)
Low-income	Kerosene lamp Candles	2.30	Lantern	1.49
Lower-middle-income	Kerosene lamps Torches	3.95	20 watt	4.42
Middle-income	Kerosene Lamps Radio cassette Torch	8.00	50 watt	10.81
Upper-income	Kerosene Lamps Radio cassette Torch TV Car battery	17.60	100 watt	18.98

Source: Foley (1995), p45

The same study quite rightly cautioned that analysis of the competitiveness of solar systems needs to be done on a country-by-country basis, as installed prices vary from country to country due to the selection of components, taxes and import duties, and so on. But if we look at three countries which were analysed in depth in the mid 1990s – India, Sri Lanka and Indonesia – we find that solar was indeed competitive with kerosene and battery charging by this time (Table 3.8).

It is often assumed, and often still stated, that the 'high' cost of solar PV modules is the reason for its slow diffusion in emerging markets. But from this analysis, we can see that even by the 1990s, solar was already cost-competitive with the alternatives used by customers in the absence of a reliable electricity grid. As this may come as a surprise to the reader, it is worth repeating: *solar was already cost-competitive in rural unelectrified markets.* But if cost was not the issue, what then was holding solar back?

Development Perspective: Is it Affordable?

When rural customers get enthusiastic about their solar system, they will tell you 'the beauty of solar is that you get free electricity'. This is, of course, not entirely true, since a solar system costs money. What customers mean, however, is that once paid for, they have very little running costs. With kerosene or a diesel generator, the running costs are high. But with solar, the fuel customers would have otherwise bought is provided by the sun, which rises every day free

Table 3.8 Monthly amortized cost of solar system compared to kerosene and battery charging in India, Indonesia and Sri Lanka

	Product	10-Year amortized cost (US$)	15-Year amortized cost (US$)	20-Year amortized cost (US$)
India	2 basic lanterns and battery charging	6.10	6.20	6.20
India	2 Petromax lanterns and battery charging	12.50	12.70	12.70
India	**2 light 37 watt SHS**	**8.60**	**7.70**	**7.60**
Indonesia	2 basic lanterns and battery charging	8.20	8.40	8.40
Indonesia	2 Petromax lanterns and battery charging	15.00	15.10	15.20
Indonesia	**2 light 37 watt SHS**	**6.70**	**5.90**	**5.70**
Sri Lanka	2 basic lanterns and battery charging	5.90	6.00	6.00
Sri Lanka	2 Petromax lanterns and battery charging	11.00	12.30	12.30
Sri Lanka	**2 light 37 watt SHS**	**7.40**	**6.50**	**6.20**

Source: Miller and Hope (2000), p90

of charge. The only ongoing costs of running a solar system are battery changes every 3–5 years and possibly new electronic components (for example the charge controller or inverter) every 5–10 years. The bottom line, however, is that compared to a diesel generator or kerosene lantern, where the up-front costs are low and the running costs relatively high, in the case of solar 75 per cent of the lifetime costs are paid at the time of purchase.[37]

This cost structure of solar would not be such an issue if unelectrified households in emerging markets had the same purchasing power as households in Organisation for Economic Co-operation and Development (OECD) countries. If your average income is US$40,000, for instance, then affording a $600 solar system with four or five lights is not an issue. But at the risk of stating the obvious, the average customer in rural areas of emerging markets does not have this kind of purchasing power. For the typical farmer in Sri Lanka, for instance, who has 2–4 acres of land and who manages to harvest two crops per year, buying a $600 solar system typically entails 20–30 per cent of his or her annual income. The system will pay for itself in just four years compared to kerosene and battery charging,[38] but these up-front costs are nevertheless high relative to annual incomes.

Thus, it is not surprising that solar systems first found rapid uptake in pockets of relative affluence. Take Kenya, for example, where the average income of a solar customer was estimated in the mid 1990s to be US$2800 – three times the mean household income in Kenya at the time.[39] And a similar pattern has been reported in other emerging markets, such as the Dominican Republic.[40]

Such affluence is often clustered in geographic pockets of fertile land and cash crops. In Kenya, for example, it was found that 'the rapid growth in sales has occurred because of the relatively prosperous and sophisticated rural middle class in the densely populated and fertile highlands of the country'.[41] Similarly, professionals such as doctors, nurses, professors and teachers were found to be early adopters of solar in emerging markets because they had enough disposable income to purchase a solar system outright on a cash basis.[42]

But how many people in rural areas could afford to pay outright? The most generous estimate was that 15 per cent of the rural unelectrified households in the world were able to pay on cash terms.[43] The more conservative figure was that only 5 per cent had this kind of purchasing power.[44] On this basis, analysts tended to conclude that the 'lack of relatively large cash sums required for the purchase of PV installations is the most significant obstacle to their wider use by rural families'.[45]

If we think back to the development perspective described in Chapter 2, we recall that a technology that is more 'divisible' will tend to diffuse more easily, because its costs can be broken down into more affordable (bite-size) amounts. But a technology like solar cannot easily be broken up and sold in smaller bits (without compromising the functioning of the system).[46] In such situations, consumer finance becomes essential for rural households to manage the up-front costs:

> Institutional arrangements have helped to introduce new technologies (even those that are perceived as expensive as solar photovoltaic power) into rural settings. The key feature is an arrangement that allows the high initial cost of the technology to be converted to an operating cost, thereby enabling modest payments from households.[47]

Most people assume that the cost of solar technology has been the key barrier to its diffusion, however, analysts in the 1990s were coming to very a different conclusion – that while the cost of solar technology was typically:

> deplored by all as the main impediment to acceptance, no lowering of prices ever yielded a corresponding increase in physical turnover. ... [T]he minimization of costs therefore is (currently) not a proven instrument of dissemination.[48]

This view was supported at the same time by analysts at the World Bank, who concluded that:

> Even with ... cost reductions, unless adequate financing arrangements, geared to low- and middle-income households, are in place, solar home systems cannot play a significant role in rural electrification.[49]

To test this conclusion, we can take an absurd example. Imagine for a moment that instead of $4.5 per watt, the cost of a solar module had fallen so steeply that by the mid 1990s, a 50-watt panel cost only 1 US cent – effectively nothing. What would have been the effect on diffusion? The answer is not that much. Because the solar module then represented only 35–40 per cent of the average retail price of a system, the price of a 50-watt system with four or five lights would still have been US$400. And at US$400, this would still have been more than 50 per cent of the mean income in Kenya, for example. Thus to make the product more affordable to the majority of customers would still have required consumer finance.[50]

Of course, many emerging markets *have* a rural banking infrastructure. It's just that very few, if any, finance institutions came forward in the 1990s to lend for solar. The product was still new, the firms selling it were small and new, and the banks were reluctant to lend for a product that was not seen to provide an income stream (like a tractor or a water pump).[51] So there was little, if any, consumer finance for solar.

To illustrate the impact on diffusion, analysts offered the following comparison to the automobile:

> In the case of the car purchase, a well-established financial infrastructure links customers to manufacturers to capital markets, and a wide array of financing choices is available from banks, leasing companies and dealers. ... Imagine the negative effects on the automobile industry if every customer had to pay the full cash price. And imagine the positive effects on the SHS industry if the same financing options available to car purchasers were available to solar home system buyers.[52]

Returning to our perspectives on innovation diffusion, we can see why the development perspective emphasized the role of finance. Even though solar as an innovation was already cost-competitive with the alternatives in unelectrified markets, its diffusion in the 1990s was hampered by the absence of consumer finance. That said, it was not the lack of finance alone that held back solar diffusion. The market infrastructure was also missing.

Market Infrastructure Perspective: Is it Available?

The market infrastructure perspective instructs us to consider the presence of local diffusion agencies that are actively propagating an innovation, as well as providing installation and after-sales service. In the case of solar in rural areas of emerging markets, we can imagine why such an infrastructure would be important. Unelectrified households tend to live in more remote locations, where existing support infrastructure of all kinds is weak. Many would not even be aware of solar as a solution, and even if they were, they would be wary because of the up-front costs. Even if they were convinced to buy, they would struggle to find a sales point, and would struggle even more to find a trained technician to help them install the system and to turn to in the event that it broke down.

In the early to mid 1990s people started to realize that the lack of this infrastructure was holding solar back.[53] Some proclaimed the 'need for a solar infrastructure'.[54] Others found that after consumer finance, 'a second crucial element is the building and strengthening of a local market infrastructure'.[55] In Sri Lanka, for instance, it was found that in addition to the lack of credit, the main obstacle to wider diffusion was an 'underdeveloped sales and distribution infrastructure'.[56] Indeed, the importance of such an infrastructure can be inferred from the statement of a solar executive in Asia: 'If I had the retail outlets that Honda has for diesel generators, we'd be a massive business.'[57]

In terms of a sales infrastructure, the early experience in solar diffusion suggested that it was not enough to set up sales points and wait for the customers to come in. It was necessary to go out to the customer, effectively selling door-to-door, to raise awareness and convince customers to part with a large chunk of their annual income for a new technology.

In the Dominican Republic, trained technicians were said to 'constitute the "front line" in PV promotion in terms of influencing public perceptions of the product ... because they are the ones who work most closely with the clients'.[58] Here each technician was treated as a small-business owner responsible for sales, installation and maintenance of systems. And giving some hint as to their importance, it was found that solar diffusion largely kept up with the number of such technicians, which grew from:

> zero in 1992 to more than 20 [in 1995] actively installing systems in each of the country's 18 departments. ... The number of systems installed during each year has grown exponentially with the number of small businesses, jumping from 60 installed during 1993 to 300 during 1994 and to 550 during the first half of 1995, and by the end of 1995 it was estimated that over 1000 systems had been sold.[59]

In Mexico, a major electronics company trained over 60 dedicated sales agents, called *promotores*, and asked them to demonstrate and sell the product, provide upgrades, and carry out limited servicing. Their conclusion was that these agents were 'the most valuable asset in the diffusion of solar home kits'.[60] In Kenya, it was concluded that the driving force behind the relatively more rapid diffusion of solar in the late 1980s and early 1990s was the combination of hundreds of trained sales agents plus rural technicians.[61]

Returning to the terminology of the market infrastructure perspective, it is important to also consider the extent to which solar is an 'infrastructure-constrained innovation'. It may not be constrained in the same way that a telephone requires a connection to a national telecommunication infrastructure to work. But it is constrained in the same way that the early diffusion of the photocopier may have been constrained – that is, if it is not installed well and serviced regularly, it can break down, and if there are any technical difficulties, it helps to have a technician to troubleshoot.

It is not enough, then, to put up sales points and put sales people into the market. It is just as important to have an installation and after-sales service capacity:

> Of course, it is easy to open a store and sell systems; it requires much more to develop a service capability. But if solar systems are to become an integral part of rural electricity development, service must be provided.[62]

Installing a solar system is not easy, and most of us would get something wrong in doing it ourselves. The solar module has to be positioned correctly towards the sun: both its tilt angle and the direction it is facing. It also has to be secured well, to ensure that it does not disappear with the next typhoon or monsoon rains. And if a household has installed a system that powers four or five lights, then the lights will also need to be installed properly, the entire house wired and the lights connected to wall-mounted switches. Furthermore, additional sockets need to be arranged for other appliances, and the charge controller needs to be mounted and connected to the battery. In addition to this, there would then be a need for customer education on how best to use the system and manage household energy requirements, as well as an understanding of what to do to maintain the batteries, and who to turn to for support if the system fails.

This need for a strong installation and service support is something that comes up time and again in the early reports on solar diffusion. For example, experience in the South Pacific found that the success of solar electrification programmes was highly correlated with training and equipping of technicians.[63] Moreover, to do their job effectively, these technicians needed to have access to a ready supply of spare parts for servicing.[64] Customers could not be expected to install, maintain and service the systems themselves – they fundamentally needed assistance:

> While the simple design and dependability of the solar home system allows a single technician to service a large number of customers, the need for local technical support remains. Users can perform simple maintenance functions. However, field experience shows that very few households can service their system themselves over long periods of time.[65]

The absence of this essential technical infrastructure in many emerging markets meant that by the turn of the century it was estimated that 10–20 per cent of household solar systems around the world were no longer operational.[66] Returning to the communication perspective, we can in turn conclude that this would have damaged customer perception of solar, and further served to limit its early diffusion.

In the end, when we talk about a market infrastructure for solar, we are talking about sales points, delivery channels, trained sales people, trained and equipped technicians, and access to spare parts. This kind of infrastructure is often taken for granted when it comes to buying a more established product, for instance a new stove:

> A European wants a new cooker. They will choose from the cookers available to them, undertake to pay the capital and running costs, often by monthly payments, make space in their kitchen, arrange for gas or electricity … organize delivery, installation and maintenance. … These actions are easily done in a consumer society, because the industrial, commercial and financial infrastructure already exists to facilitate such transactions. In other circumstances and in other societies, this infrastructure may be incomplete and the receipt of technology may be impossible unless these problems are identified and addressed.[67]

In the 1990s, a market infrastructure for solar had only begun to be built, and that too in only a handful of emerging markets. Overall, this critical infrastructure was simply missing. Neither the product nor the trained technical support that customers required to purchase a solar system was easily available, and consequently diffusion suffered.

Summing Up

Our aim in this chapter was to use the analytical framework we developed in the previous one to help us identify the key barriers to solar diffusion in the

1990s. In doing so, we found that solar was not by and large held back by unfavourable customer perceptions, or its inability to compete on a cost basis with the alternatives. On the contrary, customers perceived significant advantages to buying and using solar (provided it was properly installed and maintained), and solar was already cost-competitive with the alternatives people used in the absence of a viable electricity grid. The larger obstacles to solar's diffusion proved to be:

- the lack of consumer finance; and
- the lack of a market infrastructure.

Having identified these key barriers, we now turn, in Part II of the book, to explore the role of entrepreneurs in trying to overcome them. In those countries where diffusion subsequently picked up at the turn of the century, it was largely because entrepreneurs either directly or indirectly addressed the main barriers we identified in this chapter. What followed when they did was unprecedented levels of solar diffusion.

Part II

Case Studies in Entrepreneurship and Policy Formation

4

Solar Goes Commercial

When solar was introduced into emerging markets in the 1980s, it seemed everyone wanted to get into the business – in addition to the earliest entrepreneurs, there were aid agencies, utilities, government departments, NGOs and socially conscious individuals. Though a bit chaotic, this was not totally unexpected. Solar, after all, was seen as having a big potential for poverty alleviation. This attracted many different types of individuals and organizations into directly distributing the innovation. Moreover, nobody really knew for sure at this stage who would be better or worse at doing it.

This chapter reviews some of the early players in the solar market and their experiences.[1] In line with our discussions on agency in Chapter 2, we are interested to see what kind of 'transformative' impact such entities were able to have in the solar market. In short, who proved to be the most effective in selling solar, and why?

What we see is that, in general, the public sector actors such as utilities, aid agencies and government departments were not well suited to the task. The more this developed into a pattern, the more that commentators started to call for solar in emerging markets to be commercialized just like any other technological innovation. And in line with this call, some early not-for-profit pioneers decided to set up commercial businesses. Some NGOs got into the business, and decided to run it like a business – concerning themselves with revenues and cost recovery, in addition to their social objectives. Entrepreneurs who had either been in the business for a while or were just entering it started to develop larger-scale plans. And by the end of the 1990s, even big business started to enter the market.

Over roughly a decade, solar went from being a technology of interest mainly to government, aid agencies and NGOs for public welfare objectives to being an innovation around which entrepreneurs and other businesses built big plans with the intention of earning commercial returns. This sea-change in perceptions, and in the types of actors backing solar, set the scene for accelerated diffusion to follow.

Public Sector Diffusion

Different public sector entities became involved with solar. Utilities at first, because it seemed it might fit well with their existing operations – though ultimately it didn't. Aid agencies, because it was deemed to be complementary to their missions. Government departments, because it was part of a broader social welfare objective. We will review each of these in turn, and then consider in depth the case of the Indian Government's approach, and its drawbacks.

Given their existing infrastructure of trained technicians, distribution channels and rural offices, national electricity utilities seemed in theory to be the ideal propagators of solar. For example, a US laboratory for renewable energy set up a collaborative venture with electricity utilities in Brazil in the early 1990s for the diffusion of solar. When asked why they chose utilities as their partner for solar, they were clear: utilities knew exactly where the unelectrified customers were located and had strong networks of technicians strategically placed throughout the state.[2]

However, in line with the discussion in Chapter 2 about existing industries not wanting to destabilize their own business and not being able to see new opportunities, it soon became clear during the 1990s that utilities found this new emerging solar market quite unappealing. When it came to rural electrification, their knowledge base primarily pertained to grid extension, around which they had established standard, comfortable practices.[3] Moreover, at the time, most electric utilities in emerging markets were struggling to make ends meet as it was, without introducing a new business into their mix. They simply did not have the appetite for something as new as selling decentralized solar systems:

> PV electrification is ... not an activity that plays to the natural strengths of an electricity utility. If it is to be undertaken by the utility, it requires the development of an additional range of skills and capabilities. In the poorer developing countries, where utilities are under-funded, have too few resources, and are incapable of carrying out the basic tasks of repair and maintenance on the existing systems, asking them to take on PV electrification is pointless.[4]

There were plenty of one-off demonstration programmes by utilities, such as in Sri Lanka as early as 1981,[5] or in Brazil, as mentioned above, in 1993.[6] There was also the case of Eskom, the South African utility, entering the solar market in 1998 (as we shall see in Chapter 7, this remained at the scale of a demonstration programme as well). But there were very few instances, if any, of utilities adopting the role of long-term, effective propagator of solar in emerging markets.

Even earlier than the utilities, the international aid agencies were engaged in similar one-off demonstration programmes. However, in the early days these projects tended to be managed from afar, with not nearly enough retained capacity or retained learning on the ground:

> Turn-key systems were packed into shipping cases, air-freighted and trucked to project 'target groups' in remote areas of the Third World, while Western experts were flown in to complete the installations. So from the late 70s to 80s, many projects 'engineered' to perform mainte-nance free ... failed because of lack of local involvement. When fuses blew or when rodents chewed through wires, local farmers hundreds of miles from the nearest town wondered where in the world they could find someone who knew enough about this miraculous technology to fix it.[7]

Such projects demonstrated that without local trained technical support as part of the ongoing market infrastructure for solar, solar diffusion would fail. This was confirmed by another rural energy analyst at the time, who found that while the PV panels in such projects continued to function, without sufficient local technical support, the ancillary equipment frequently failed under the harsh operating conditions.[8]

Beyond utilities and aid agencies, there were various national-level govern-ment departments selling solar directly. But these entities would come to show that government departments generally do not have the capacity nor the incen-tive to provide the customer with a well-designed, high-quality system, delivered upon order and serviced over the long term. Furthermore, the systems tended to be sold at highly subsidized rates, in line with their public service objectives and the expectations of the citizens. This meant that customers got used to the low subsidized price, and other private-sector play-ers could not compete with the government-subsidized channel. And because these programmes did not run like a business and cover all their costs with some modicum of profit, there was no capacity for growth in diffusion, other than through additional government spending – solar diffusion essentially remained capped at whatever the following year's government budget for solar would be.

A World Bank report on the experiences with solar in various South Pacific islands found that 'in no case have the PV systems performed consis-tently as intended by the governments or expected by the users'[9] and that the programmes were fundamentally dependent on further cash injections from the outside to add new installations (in other words to grow).[10] Similarly, in the Philippines (where the potential for solar is enormous, with 7000 islands and a population of 85 million people), the Government decided to do it directly. Using either local cooperatives or local government agencies as vehicles for diffusing highly subsidized solar systems for homes, or centralized solar systems with battery charging (where a home brings their battery for charging to a centralized solar system), the Government managed to diffuse only 133 kilowatts of installed capacity of solar in various applications by 1999.[11] Or to put it into perspective, less than 3000 solar systems (of 50 watts) over more than one decade among an unelectrified population of more than 3 million – penetration of a mere 0.1 per cent.[12]

Because government agencies often took the lead in trying to diffuse solar in the 1980s and early 1990s, it is worth reviewing in a bit more detail why they did not emerge as more effective agents for solar diffusion. To do so, it is illuminating to consider the case of India.

Government-Led Diffusion: The Case of India

In India, the Government's solar programme was initiated in 1976, with a focus on R&D and solar manufacturing,[13] and in 1980 the Government launched the National Solar Photovoltaic Energy Demonstration Programme.[14] Like other emerging markets, the Government deemed electricity to be an entitlement rather than a commodity, and a prime objective of the solar programme was to meet the needs of unelectrified rural households.[15] As illustration of this sentiment, we can refer to the head of the solar programme in Uttar Pradesh – the most populous state in India – who found it 'deplorable' that complete electrification had not yet been achieved, and supported the Government's solar programme on the grounds that 'people have a right to electricity. Why should we deny them?'[16]

The Government's solar programme was run by the Ministry for Non-Conventional Energy Sources (MNES, now called the Ministry of New and Renewable Energy, MNRE). India was then, and possibly still remains, the only country with a full-fledged ministry for renewable energy. As a civil servant within MNES at the time recounts, the programme received support from the highest levels:

> Indira Ghandi was a strong proponent of renewable energy technology, and Rajiv was stronger still. This support has been unique in the world, with an entire administrative network set up down the line – from the ministry to the nodal agency to the district.[17]

Nodal agencies were set up as state-level implementing bodies of MNES, with district offices under them. The process for selling solar was as follows: the district office collected orders for three months; these were then aggregated by the nodal agency, which put out a tender to the manufacturers that met

Government specifications; the district office would then supply the systems at a subsidized rate to the households. In Uttar Pradesh, for instance, which had 68 district offices, 50 per cent of the cost was paid by MNES, 30 per cent by the customer and roughly 20 per cent by the state.[18]

But the system of government procurement and tendering did not create the right incentives for high-quality products. As a manufacturer and participant in the tenders recounted, 'Manufacturers have an incentive to secure tenders through reduction in capacity and quality components. Tenders are secured on the basis of lowest cost.'[19] Similarly, a former adviser to MNES recalled:

> Because it is target-oriented, the Government has made all kinds of compromises. System integration has been a real problem. For example, the sizing of the batteries – say you require four hours, but this doesn't fit the budget, the system will be redesigned to use less amp-hours, which the user doesn't know about, creating a mismatch in user expectations and system capacity. This has at some point affected every PV application.[20]

In addition to creating incentives for low-quality products, the programme had neither the resources not the incentives to carry out effective after-sales service. As a consultant to the Government PV programmes lamented, 'For 10 years I have been doing performance reviews and seeing the nation's money wasted due to a lack of servicing.'[21] Because the situation he describes is so revealing, it is useful to quote the consultant at some length:

> Let me give you the example of Kerala. During the first round of the operational review in March 1995, we found only eight solar PV water pumps in working order out of a total of 30. We found that many of the non-working systems only needed minor repairs – for example the carbon brushes. With small adjustments, we – as we brought technicians – were able to raise the number of operational pumps from 27.6 per cent to 58.1 per cent. In each case, not a single technician had ever gone back after the sale of the system. We also found that yet more systems could have been made operational with slightly more repairs – adding a further 25.8 per cent to the total of operational systems. So with adequate servicing that means that 80 per cent of the pumps in Kerala could be functioning today. Servicing is just so critical!

Overall, in terms of system performance, the results were not good. India's Comptroller and Auditor General found that 'most of the [PV] systems were not working, mainly due to lack of proper maintenance, poor performance of the systems and apathy of the users'.[22] Specifically, the report found a failure rate of 33–100 per cent for solar street lighting and 25–94 per cent for solar home systems.

In addition, the rate of diffusion had not been strong by the mid 1990s. The Government had managed to distribute only 36,000 solar home systems (the subject of this book) and 37,000 lanterns (a lesser substitute for a solar home system) by 1996 (see Table 4.1). In nominal terms, this is more units diffused than most emerging markets at the time. But if we consider that the programme had been running for more than 15 years and the country had roughly 100 million homes without electricity, it is a very low rate of penetration – roughly 0.08 per cent of the unelectrified population.[23]

Table 4.1 Number of PV systems installed under MNES schemes in India by 1996

PV application	Installations
Street lights	30,917
Lanterns	37,465
Centralized power plants	141
Solar home systems	36,519

Source: Prabhakara (1996)[24]

Despite these results, there was no move within MNES towards a more private-sector approach:

> If I depend only on private channels, the companies will not go to the backward areas, which doesn't meet the development policies of the Government of India. Take the example of motorcycles, which are privately disseminated: there are a very small number of dealers – we do not want the same for thing for solar lights.[25]

Of course, a decade later, the number of motorbike dealers in rural India would tend to call into question such conclusions. But still other MNES officials agreed: 'It is all very nice to talk about rural entrepreneurship, but you need a lot of people in one area for an entrepreneur to make money.'[26]

Instead, officials made the case for 'parallel markets' in solar: in the same way as the Government distributes rice and bread to those who cannot afford it, so too it should distribute solar. Yet the adviser to MNES's solar programme was aware of the internal contradictions in the concept of parallel markets:

> In states where there is a strong state network, it will be difficult for [a solar business] to initiate its schemes.[27]

A Gathering Consensus: Go Commercial

It seems that by the mid 1990s, enough commentators and analysts of the solar markets had seen enough public-sector solar projects and programmes not perform to their potential for them to decide to call for an alternative. For example, after many years of funding government-led diffusion of solar, the German aid agency GTZ came to the conclusion that commercial enterprise was the most 'effective transmission belt for the dissemination of SHS technology'. And they went on to prescribe that:

> The dissemination, or better the commercialization, of Solar Home Systems as a product should rely on private enterprises as the main executing organs and on their self-interest as the driving force, for it is precisely that self-interest which guarantees a certain degree of sustainability. ... The promotion of private-sector activities is the means most likely to yield sustainable achievement of this goal.[28]

Similarly, after a review of PV programmes around the world, analysts within the World Bank came to the conclusion that:

> PV programmes must be operated as businesses [which] generate revenues sufficient to recover capital investment, service debt, pay for administrative and support services, cover payment defaults, and, in the case of for-profit operations, provide satisfactory returns for investors.[29]

It was not that the private sector had necessarily installed more systems than the public sector. But private-sector approaches in Kenya, Sri Lanka and the Dominican Republic, for instance, were already showing the capacity for individuals and businesses to sell solar in a more commercial fashion, outside of government channels. Kenya in particular had a big impact on the perception of how rural solar markets would and should evolve.

According to reports by a close observer of and participant in the Kenyan solar market, this market was initially sparked by a highly committed American development worker and renewable energy enthusiast. With the help of US aid money, this individual set up solar demonstration projects to create a local demand and, once these were established, launched training programmes to train technicians in solar installation and maintenance. Between 1985 and 1988, his organization only sold 150 systems, but through its training programmes, it established a network of local technicians who, even before his departure, established their own businesses and began to compete.[30] This network of businesses then caught the eye of other businesses, spawning an entire local industry and further propelling solar sales, such that by the mid 1990s:

over 12 firms supply photovoltaic equipment to households. Hundreds of agents, service personnel and technicians form the infrastructure of Kenya's photovoltaic economy. ... Kenya's private sector, from large multinational firms to local cottage industries, is a driving force in the expansion of photovoltaics in the country.[31]

Of course, the private-sector approach was not perfect. For instance, people could point to under-sized systems and poor service in Kenya, just as we saw in India. But it was the potential for self-sustaining, ever-growing sales of solar, without continual infusions from the next annual government budget or aid agency handouts that excited people. In short, by the mid 1990s a very clear consensus had emerged around the idea that solar would and should be driven by the private sector.[32] And as if on cue, we start to see an interesting trend in the solar markets: the early not-for-profit pioneers spinning out to set up solar businesses.

Not-for-Profit Pioneers Go Commercial

As we briefly reviewed in the case of Kenya, one of the more interesting, and ultimately effective, actors in solar diffusion would prove to be individual entrepreneurs initially motivated more by the 'promise' of solar energy – to deliver renewable energy solutions to the world's poor – than just the money to be made from selling solar. Although these individuals were not entrepreneurs in the sense of making money, they nonetheless fit Schumpeter's definition, discussed in Chapter 2, in the sense that they set out to effect profound technological change. The following paragraphs take some time to profile two of these individuals in particular, as they would provide inspiration to future entrepreneurs and policymakers and lay the seeds for diffusion in several markets we will go on to consider in detail.

An entrepreneur from the US started his work in solar as the director of a high-profile solar NGO. He first got the idea that there might be a big market for solar in the emerging markets while consulting for an American PV manufacturer. As he concluded at the time, 'The global market for solar [was] the off-grid stand-alone small system, and [the PV manufacturer] had no clue about that.'[33] Without strong interest from the PV manufacturer in developing this market, he decided to try to do it himself:

> I saw that this should be a business; I should go to the solar companies and say I will develop projects in x countries and you pay me – that will be my business. Or I will sell 100,000 systems to the Government of Zimbabwe and tell them how to put them in. ... This was the idea until I realized that it was a little harder to do. You don't just waltz into Zimbabwe and sell 100,000 systems.[34]

Instead of establishing a company, the entrepreneur reasoned that 'the other way to do this was to set up a non-profit which could raise money as a development issue'.

Having studied the market, he knew that consumer finance was a key barrier to selling solar, and so his NGO became specifically dedicated to setting up 'credit funds' in different emerging markets, with the objective of demonstrating that people were willing to 'pay' commercial prices for their solar systems, provided that someone was willing to make a loan, the product and technical support available to them.[35]

Largely with the help of foundation grants, he was able to set up funds in five different emerging markets by the early 1990s – India, Nepal, Sri Lanka, South Africa and Zimbabwe.[36] From these early projects his initial views were borne out – people without electricity were willing to pay for solar on a cash or credit basis as an alternative to the grid if someone supplied it: 'We knew from experience that the demand for electricity was there, rural people could afford it, and they would pay for it in large numbers if credit financing was available.' And he had also seen that people were willing to pay cash, too: 'If quality and reliable local service are available, many farmers will gladly pay cash for a solar home system.'[37]

But the entrepreneur was also aware that he was not developing the market in the way he knew it needed to be developed:

> What we learned was that the only way solar rural electrification was going to happen on a mass scale in the developing world was if private companies undertook to do it.[38]

In line with the growing chorus that solar in emerging markets should become a larger, commercial activity, a prominent US foundation held a seminar in 1995 to explore how this might happen. It was at this seminar that the entrepreneur in question decided it was time to set up a commercial business, doing what he was already doing as an NGO. Because he could not convert the NGO, he had to step down, and start a new company, with the same mission, from scratch. The company was officially incorporated in 1997, and we will return to consider the further impact this entrepreneur had on solar diffusion when we consider the case of India.

Interestingly, a similar story unfolded in Central America at roughly the same time. In the Dominican Republic, a US entrepreneur with a background in business and an interest in development launched a training programme in solar engineering and technology in 1986, using grant money from the US Department of Energy, the Peace Corps and various foundations. To organize this activity, he established an NGO that would go on to train a network of solar technicians and six different solar component or equipment manufacturers. It was on the back of this network, loosely affiliated with the NGO, that by the late 1980s and early 1990s solar started to be sold on a commercial basis – cash and credit – to rural customers. By 1995, estimates were that this NGO had spurred the sale of roughly 5000 systems in the Dominican Republic.[39]

Having seen that there was a market, and having also heard the calls for the commercialization of solar, the entrepreneur went on to establish a company in both the Dominican Republic and Honduras that would attempt to sell systems on a cash, credit or what is called fee-for-service basis, which is essentially 'rental' of solar systems. The aim, for instance, in Honduras was to quickly scale up to 50,000 households out of an unelectrified population of 500,000.

In an earlier-cited article critical of solar, there is an implicit criticism made of the role of 'Northern' entrepreneurs in trying to bring a solution not yet ready to market to the South[40] – it is viewed as a sort of missionary-style, neo-imperialist phenomenon. That, of course, is one view. The other view is that these individuals were highly motivated by the prospect of a simple, elegant technology to transform the well-being of rural households without electricity. To begin with they could not figure out how to make it a viable business. But having secured an initial understanding from their not-for-profit work, they then transformed themselves into more commercial entrepreneurs. A similar trend can also be seen with existing NGOs starting to get into the business of selling solar, but doing it according to business principles.

NGOs Go Commercial

Like utilities, NGOs in theory seem ideal propagators of solar. They tend to have a strong base of existing rural customers and engender a good deal of trust. Moreover, they often have a well-developed network of field officers who could in theory support sales, installation and service. But, like utilities, many NGOs have expertise in different areas than solar – for example micro-finance, social work and development projects. Thus they will not necessarily be geared up for the things that solar requires – for example, designing a portfolio of solar products, controlling quality of installation and service, and establishing and controlling multiple stock points. Moreover, like government depart-ments, NGOs will tend to sell to customers without taking account of the full costs of doing so, and so are then reliant on future handouts.

For instance, an NGO in India made a name for itself by taking technicians from remote rural areas and, despite their lack of education, training them in solar installation and servicing. They were called 'barefoot technicians'. In this way, the NGO developed good village-level projects, but it did not establish a commercially viable way to take their operations to scale. This stands in contrast to other NGOs who entered the industry a little later but ran their operations on a much more commercial basis.

At the same time that early individual pioneers of solar were deciding to get out of NGOs and get into the business of selling solar, one of the largest NGOs in Bangladesh – Grameen Bank – was planning to establish a new solar operation. It would not be a business in the sense of being an independent company, maximizing profit. It would still retain the ideals and approach of the Grameen Bank – to maximize the well-being of its customer base. But Grameen would run it like a commercial business. It was established in 1996 and called Grameen Shakti (*shakti* meaning power).

Grameen could bring an existing base of 2 million beneficiaries to its new solar business, most of whom did not have electricity. Grameen also had hundreds of centres or distribution points for a variety of goods and services – medical, schooling, micro-finance and so on – where they had existing procedures, sometimes even computerized, to enable them to track movements of cash and stock. Moreover, they could couple finance with the solar product, thereby overcoming the two main obstacles to wider diffusion under one roof.

In the end, as we shall see in Chapter 6, Grameen Shakti has become one of the most successful solar energy businesses in emerging markets. But this was only possible because, despite being an NGO, they decided to approach it like a business. They raised external start-up capital on semi-commercial terms, and they took a decision to sell their systems for commercial prices (though roughly 10 per cent lower than neighbouring markets, probably to reflect their social priorities). With this, they moved beyond demonstration projects to setting up a basis for self-replicating and growing sales of solar. This was entirely in line with what the pundits were calling for in the mid 1990s, when they extolled the virtues of commercializing solar technology.

Of course, in addition to commercially minded NGOs and the not-for-profit pioneers who became commercial entrepreneurs, there were those who approached solar as a business from the moment they got involved. The following section introduces three different sets of entrepreneurs who will be profiled in more detail in subsequent chapters.

Introduction to the Entrepreneurs

The first case study comes from India. By the early 1990s, India had developed a strong manufacturing and distribution base: installed production capacity of 18 megawatts per annum, 5 cell manufacturers, 8 module manufactures, and 50 system integrators who designed, installed and sold total systems.[41] But none of these players were particularly interested in selling directly into the rural markets. The reason for this was that they preferred selling into the Government programmes:

> Government orders are easy as there is a chunk to be allotted, with few decision-makers who can be influenced. But in the rural markets, there are millions of decision-makers to try and influence, and to do this requires more effort, meaning that your costs go up and, at least in the short term, your profits go down.[42]

Similarly, the general manager of a major Indian PV manufacturer noted that:

> The consolidated market is easier to serve … as the rural markets are dispersed. Here, the problem is 'How do I reach them?'. The reach is where the costs come in for us. You need many of these little, little, little centres, and then one needs to manage these centres, and they will grow and how to orchestrate them?[43]

Thus, as a World Bank review of the market revealed at the time, although 'there were projects that would lead to PV being placed in rural areas, such as lighting for tea plantations', there were 'none that led to building rural-sector delivery mechanisms'.[44]

In most states in India, the Government programmes for solar were too strong, crowding out any direct commercial sales of solar. But in Karnataka, the Government solar programme was largely non-existent at this time – intentionally so, as it would turn out. This created a space for the American entrepreneur profiled earlier to enter in 1993 and forge a working relationship with an Indian entrepreneur that would soon transform into a commercial partnership.

In 1995, the two entrepreneurs established a company that initially sold 40 solar systems on credit to rural customers in Karnataka. It was seeded with as little as US$30,000 in capital. It would have to operate on a shoestring for several years, until the entrepreneurs were able to mobilize sufficient resources to grow. During this time, invaluable lessons would be learned, and the company would serve as an example to policymakers and other businesses that it was indeed possible to set up commercial operations serving the rural solar markets in India.

Our second case study comes from Indonesia. In 1987, R&S – a Dutch manufacturer of solar modules partly owned by Shell – established a sales office in Indonesia, in which Philips also took a stake in 1991. It is estimated that both invested roughly US$3 million in the business. The sales office was successful in selling 20,000 systems to the Government over a six-year period, prior to Shell and Philips deciding to exit the business in 1993. Although the business did not directly develop the rural solar markets in Indonesia, the managing director's experience in running the Indonesia operation informed him that there was a big potential in doing so.

Rather than leave with the business, the managing director (heretofore 'the entrepreneur in Indonesia') decided to stay and pursue his vision. In 1994 he established a company, and started selling solar directly to the unelectrified parts of Indonesia. Initially the company served West Java and to a lesser extent Central Java. But by mid 1995, it had also expanded into the province of Lampung in Southern Sumatra. By mid 1996, there were 46 rural sales points cum service centres, serving between 50 and 60 sub-districts in three provinces in Indonesia. There were a total of 180 employees: 40 in head office engaged in administration and system assembly, and in each service centre a local manager, a secretary, and one or two assistant technicians.

Sales grew very quickly, because the entrepreneur combined a strong market infrastructure with four-year credit terms for his customers. Between 1994 and July 1996, the company sold over 8000 solar systems – an unprecedented figure in the diffusion of solar at this time. But it was never easy, and the company was always short of cash. Eventually disaster struck, but before it did, the entrepreneur in Indonesia had set an example that would go on to radically influence the diffusion of solar in other countries.

Our final case study comes from Sri Lanka. Two entrepreneurs, then living in Canada, returned to Sri Lanka as part of a post-university trip around the world. It was mid 1985. They didn't know it when they set out on their journey, but once in Sri Lanka they would be gripped by a vision of selling solar and stay.

Their initial interest was in solar water pumping – to develop a mobile solar pump, with only a secondary use for lighting. In pursuit of this market, they set up a company and worked on sourcing machinery to manufacture solar modules in Sri Lanka. In 1988, they teamed up with a third entrepreneur and together secured vital start-up capital from local banks. With investment capital in hand, they were able to procure the machinery they needed, and in the same year they produced their first solar modules.

But while they initially thought the market would be for water pumping, they quickly found that the 'real' market was selling solar to households that were reliant on battery charging for TVs and kerosene for lighting. They would learn many other lessons like this, often the hard way. They still had to figure out how to reach the market, how to make solar more affordable and how to keep the costs of the operation low. And they would have to do all this amidst the social and political turmoil sweeping Sri Lanka.

Ultimately, the two founding entrepreneurs dropped out to reduce the cost burden on the business, remaining only as shareholders. The third entrepreneur, who joined in 1988, decided to stay on and take the business forward. He had a marketing background and had now developed considerable know-how in what customers wanted, how to deliver it to them and how to operate in the rural markets. But the business was strapped for cash, and faltering. In line with Schumpeter's emphasis on 'will', he managed to keep the company alive on a shoestring, until, several years later, his business was acquired, and he finally had the resources required to grow. As we will see in Chapter 5, he would go on to have a transformative impact on solar diffusion in Sri Lanka.

Big Business

It wasn't just in India that the PV manufacturers decided to stay out of selling solar directly in rural areas. It was a global phenomenon throughout the 1990s. There are a few exceptions to this, such as a small-scale manufacturer in Mexico, where an influential director acquired 'a love for PV', and, on his behest, the firm developed a solar home system kit and sold it through a network of rural *promotores*.[45] Yet, by and large, the PV manufacturers preferred to leave the selling of solar in rural markets to local dealers and distributors.

Other big businesses also decided to stay out for much of the 1990s. In 1995 there was a flurry of excitement when Bechtel announced that it was setting up a subsidiary called EnergyWorks, that would sell renewable energy systems and services in unelectrified areas of the developing world, but unfortunately nothing came of this, and EnergyWorks never made a significant impact.[46]

Thus, in line with our discussions in Chapter 2 and the theories surrounding technological innovation, it is interesting to note that the entrepreneurs under consideration were all from *outside* the solar PV manufacturing industry. They were the consummate industry outsiders – individual entrepreneurs with a vision for a big business in areas of the world largely deemed 'too difficult' by the PV manufacturers that would, in theory, have had the most interest in the market.[47]

It was not until the end of the century, once entrepreneurs had started to demonstrate the commercial potential in the rural solar markets, that some bigger businesses also decided to enter. For instance, Électricité de France and Total entered rural solar projects in Morocco in the late 1990s. And Shell set up a division specifically targeting the rural unelectrified segment; through this division it 'directly' entered the markets in India, Sri Lanka, the Philippines, South Africa, Morocco and Indonesia. As it was unique in doing so, it is worth reviewing the entry of this 'big' business in more detail.

Shell already had a foothold in renewables through its investment in a modules manufacturing company in The Netherlands. But it was not until 1997 that the company decided to commit significant resources, and establish Shell Renewables as a fifth core business, standing alongside its core oil, gas, and chemical divisions. Shell commited US$500 million to renewables over a five-year period, and from 2002 a further $500 million. Although Shell

Renewables initially made some small investments in biomass, it settled on wind and solar as the renewables it would back, and established two companies to develop these sectors: Shell Solar and Shell Wind Energy.

To quickly scale up, Shell Solar acquired Siemens Solar in 2002 and overnight assumed a position as the fourth largest manufacturer of PV modules in the world. But in addition to manufacturing modules, Shell Solar was clear from the start that it would need to sell directly in certain markets in order to fully realize latent business opportunities. In the emerging markets, where it felt that a direct presence could create a long-term business, Shell Solar established a stake in two solar operations in South Africa and Morocco that worked under government concessions; it worked with a local Chinese partner to implement a 78,770 solar home systems project in China; and it established four 100-per-cent-owned subsidiaries in the Philippines, India, Sri Lanka and Indonesia to sell solar into these local markets. In each case the emphasis was on having a local, on-the-ground presence to reach homes or businesses without access to reliable grid electricity.

As discussed earlier, there are virtues to large companies entering a market. They obviously bring a good deal of money, and many can bring a better-known brand to win the trust of customers and key stakeholders such as banks and local governments. In addition, many individuals within large corporations have a good deal of managerial experience and capacity which they can bring to a business.

But at the same time, many employees in large corporations lack specific knowledge required to innovate in a new sector, or specific knowledge about the country in which they are operating. Furthermore, although they bring strong management, many large corporations will bring a strong aversion to risk, which means they will not seize opportunities in front of them in the same way as entrepreneurs. They also often bring a strong set of procedures, which can imply excessive costs, delays and constraints. Lastly, corporate agendas tend to be much more fickle than the single-minded determination of an entrepreneur.

In Chapter 5, it will be shown that companies such as Shell Solar had a big impact in the markets they entered. But this was largely following a lead pioneered by earlier entrepreneurs. Eventually Shell Solar exited the business, while many of the original entrepreneurs remained.

Summing Up

A lot of different players tried their hand at propagating solar throughout the 1980s and 1990s. We saw that the public-sector propagators, such as utilities and aid agencies, did not have the capacity or resources to effectively drive forward solar diffusion. At the same time, some countries and some early pioneers were demonstrating that a private-sector approach might work better. By the mid 1990s a consensus had emerged that solar diffusion should become a more commercial activity.

In line with this consensus, we saw how early not-for-profit pioneers switched over to being more commercial actors. We saw NGOs diversify into this sector, but apply strict commercial criteria to their operations. And we saw how early entrepreneurs had already set up in various local markets, planted a flag and were trying to sell solar systems on a larger-scale commercial basis.

There was little role for big business in the early formation of the rural solar industry. Industry outsiders were at the helm. Big business entered later, after entrepreneurs had demonstrated the potential. In the interim, entrepreneurs would go through lean years of struggle to raise the requisite resources to grow. Some would break through, and some would not. But through the example they set, new actors would enter with more resources, and new policies would be initiated that would significantly propel diffusion. The impact of these entrepreneurs would thus go well beyond their own direct sales of solar in the marketplace.

5

Entrepreneurs as
Agents of Change

An entrepreneur must overcome two critical barriers to sell solar in large numbers in rural markets. As discussed in Chapter 3, these are the lack of finance for solar consumers and the lack of a viable market infrastructure for sales, installation and service.

Addressing these two barriers is not an either/or option. There is a symbiotic relationship between a market infrastructure and consumer finance, and both are equally important. For instance, a bank will not make loans available to a rural customer unless they know that a service infrastructure exists to maintain the solar system for which they lend. Or the other way around, a business cannot afford to put in place a market infrastructure if it does not have consumer finance in place to sell sufficient volume. You can have all the branches, salespeople and technicians you want, but without consumer finance to make the product more affordable, there won't be enough volume to cover costs, and the business will go broke.

To put in place consumer finance and market infrastructure fundamentally takes capital – the 'life-blood' of the entrepreneurial start-up. As we shall see, the early solar entrepreneurs needed to raise two types of capital. The first was capital to help them build their market infrastructure; the second was capital for consumer finance, which they did not need to own, but which they needed to mobilize to make their products more affordable. Once they had raised or mobilized this capital, they needed to have the capacity to put it to work in a profitable and sustainable manner. And here they had to learn, sometimes the hard way, what worked and what did not.

In the end, their activities would stand as a demonstration for others to follow. Policymakers would be encouraged to scale up the solar markets that these pioneering entrepreneurs had created. And new businesses would enter, sometimes with more resources for sales and marketing. Both would lead to radically enhanced diffusion of solar.

This chapter tells the story of how entrepreneurs radically influenced the progress of solar diffusion in their markets. We look closely at three case studies profiled earlier – in India, Indonesia and Sri Lanka. But before doing so, it is useful to consider the hard realities these entrepreneurs faced in entering this market and trying to set up a market infrastructure for solar and finance it.

Hazards of the Job

When the entrepreneurs in question started out – some in the late 1980s, others in the early 1990s – they were facing the challenge of selling solar to customers who basically did not know about, or understand, the innovation. So the first thing the entrepreneurs had to do, in line with the communication perspective described in Chapter 2, was to figure out how to make solar attractive enough to customers that they would to want buy it. This is hard for any innovation, but an innovation that costs on average 20–30 per cent of the annual income of a rural unelectrified customer is, needless to say, not an easy sell.

As we will see, almost all the entrepreneurs landed on the same solution. They needed to have door-to-door salespeople who could go out to explain the innovation. Here we can refer back to the role of change agents, as highlighted by the communication perspective. These salespeople would serve the function of introducing solar, trying to sell its relative advantages compared to kerosene or diesel, for instance, trying to persuade the customer to buy, and, hopefully, closing orders.

But in line with the market infrastructure perspective, to convince people that solar was an attractive option in the first place, a diffusion agency had to make the product and service readily available to them. Not surprisingly, when customers part with a large amount of their annual income, they want to be able to see, feel and touch the system soon after investing in it; and fundamentally, they need to believe that it is going to work. This meant putting in place stock points close to the customers, and setting up an efficient system of distribution to such points.

It also meant identifying and training technicians to install and service solar systems, and ensuring they had some access to spare parts. But the entrepreneurs were also facing a situation in which there were very few salespeople or trained technicians in their local markets who knew the first thing about solar. So they first had to recruit those with an interest and some basic skills, and then train them in solar sales, customer handling, system design, installation and after-sales service.

And once they had their sales and technical teams, their stock points, and their distribution system in place, the entrepreneurs would then need to *manage* it. As the entrepreneur in Indonesia would say of his own business:

> People do not often think about how to manage a commercial system to disseminate solar. It is a question of establishing organizational rules, discipline and oversight.[1]

Most activities within any well-controlled business, whether big or small, require some systems and procedures. But this is especially critical in the case of solar, because much of the activity is happening hundreds of miles away from the view of the entrepreneur. How to be sure that salespeople were saying the right things to close the sale? That the stock was going out when it was meant to? That the technicians were installing and servicing to the right standards? That all the money for every sale was coming back? The business of selling solar in rural markets would prove to be quite complex.

Finally, even if a customer was now convinced by a robust and well-managed market infrastructure, they still needed to be able to afford the product. This is where arranging finance was critical for the entrepreneurs. But financing an unelectrified household in the emerging markets is not necessarily straightforward. Many households in rural areas do not have a bank account, and even if they do, a direct monthly debit may not be possible. There is no centralized database to check credit histories. The customer may be far away, and will struggle to bring the money into an office each month, in which case it must be collected. And though this varies, the legal and policing system may not be strong enough to recover the equipment or seize collateral should the customer default.

When entrepreneurs were getting into the solar business, banks were largely ignorant and distrustful of the innovation. So the entrepreneurs had to figure out ways to either convince the banks or to do financing themselves. Learning how to sell solar is difficult enough, and takes a good deal of managerial capacity. Now add to this the difficulties of doing consumer finance, and you have a very difficult operation to run. Needless to say, deciding how to offer consumer finance would prove to be critical – to the point that it could determine the fate of the business.

The entrepreneurs profiled in this story all brought useful prior experience. But equally, all of them had something to learn. There would be a host of questions and puzzles to resolve. How to finance the customer? Should we do it ourselves or work with banks? If doing it ourselves, should we retain ownership of the asset – in other words rent or lease it – or sell it and provide a loan? How to balance cost and quality in components? And where to find lowest-cost components, with sufficient quality, for improved margins? What do the customers want? What should our product portfolio be? What are the best ways of selling solar? Where should we sell it? What should be our sales pitch? What are the key sales schemes? How high can we price solar to deliver a strong gross margin, while not killing off demand? How to establish effective controls over inventory in remote locations? How to manage receivables from banks, and governments, and ensure all is collected?

Some entrepreneurs had more of the answers in some areas; some were more proficient in others. But it simply was not possible for all the entrepreneurs to have all the answers on day one. Developing the essential capacities took time and learning, often the hard way. For some there would be a second chance; for others not.

Entrepreneurs in India

The American entrepreneur had already launched a successful project in Sri Lanka to demonstrate the viability of solar systems and the capacity and willingness of rural unelectrified customers to pay for them. But when it came to India, he said:

> I had no immediate plans to enter India with a solar power project, because the size of the place intimidated me, and I wasn't sure how or whether to start. India was a bit scary.[2]

It was in January 1993 that the Indian entrepreneur arrived at the offices of the American entrepreneur's NGO. He had been trained as an engineer at one of India's elite universities, but had little business background. As part of his graduate studies in solar energy in the US, he had conducted field work in both the Dominican Republic and Sri Lanka, and had seen how to sell, install and service solar. About this experience he later recounted, 'It was very formative to go and see these models in action.' It gave him the confidence that these models could be replicated in India: 'When you talk of high risk, it means you do not know the market. I perceived the risk as low, because I had seen the market working elsewhere.'

The American entrepreneur was interested, but didn't know where to begin. In the summer of 2003, the Indian entrepreneur travelled across the country and chose the state of Karnataka. Why Karnataka? Mainly because in certain pockets there was good purchasing power, and because electricity supply in rural areas was chronically unreliable. So whereas the Indian entrepreneur originally thought they would serve unelectrified markets, in the end they served markets where people had power, but it was so unreliable that they were willing to turn to solar as an alternative.

It would take roughly a year of visits and pre-feasibility work before the American entrepreneur was ready to launch in India. It was at this point, much in line with the emerging consensus of 'going commercial', that the American entrepreneur decided that 'they could "commercialize" this endeavour right

Figure 5.1 Grid failure in India

from the start in South India by drawing on the local entrepreneurial spirit and talent and simply forming a company'.

This would prove easier to say than to do, however, because India at this time only allowed 51 per cent foreign ownership – it had to be a joint venture. It would take more than six months before the entrepreneurs could launch their new business, in March 1995. Later, when the rules allowed for 100 per cent ownership, the company's structure was changed again. Mired in red tape, it was not until 1998 that the company emerged as what the American entrepreneur said was the first 100 per cent foreign-owned solar company in India.

In late 1994 the American entrepreneur was using his networks to arrange the initial seed capital. The Indian entrepreneur, having finished his postgraduate studies, was on the ground, preparing for the initial project. In the end the American entrepreneur scraped together US$30,000 as seed funding, about which he recalled at the time:

> It was nothing, including my time and [the Indian entrepreneur's] salary. But it got us off the ground. … I don't think I found much more money, so it's been a shoestring operation.

With the funds in hand, the first thing the entrepreneur did was set out to identify technicians who could also act as salespeople (this was the model he had
seen at work in the Dominican Republic). As a trained engineer, proficient in
solar installations, the Indian entrepreneur placed a lot of importance on the
quality of components used and the training of these technicians. In line with
this approach, the Indian entrepreneur was quick to emphasize that 'I conceive
of [our enterprise] as a promoter of solar', and in the early days he even turned
down sales in areas which were too remote to service, because, as he said, if he
made them, 'solar gets a bad name'.

This concern with *promoting* solar could be dismissed as not sufficiently
commercial. However, it should more properly be seen as an integral component of the entrepreneurs' strategy for eliciting demand. In line with the
communication perspective discussed in Chapter 2, the entrepreneurs were
setting out to ensure that solar would become a 'trusted' and 'valued' innovation, perceived as superior to kerosene, candles, diesel generators and so on.

Figure 5.2 Customers
using solar lights for
wedding ceremony
at home

Figure 5.3
Customers
using solar
lights for
family-owned
village shop

Figure 5.4 Entire family watching television powered by solar

Figure 5.5
Customer with
solar-powered
televisions

In line with these values, the Indian entrepreneur personally tested the components they initially procured; he personally trained all his technicians in the early days; and he personally spot-checked as many installations as he could. He was very hands-on. And the results were recognized. As an independent consultant examining the progress of the business reported in 1996: 'The [enterprise's] installations are of the highest quality and conform to high safety standards.'[3]

In addition, the Indian entrepreneur had learned from his earlier observations of the markets in the Dominican Republic and Sri Lanka that the enterprise would have to offer excellent after-sales service. Thus he explicitly positioned the enterprise as not only a sales but a 'service' company. In a discussion with a potential battery supplier in the early days – 1996 to be precise – the Indian entrepreneur explained that their 'philosophy is that solar cannot be done just like any other business – it requires dedication to service'.

Figure 5.6 Typical solar home

Figure 5.7 Less affluent
solar home

Figure 5.8 Larger solar installation in suburban setting

Figure 5.9 Larger solar installation in rural setting

From the outset, the entrepreneurs introduced a one-year guarantee and a policy of free service visits for the first year. Subsequently, the customer was required to pay a nominal fee for each service visit plus the cost of replacement parts. They also arranged for communication points for the customers, for example a local TV dealer in one town. As a result, the same independent consultant's report concluded that 'the customers seem very satisfied with their prompt service … and know how to communicate their problems to [the enterprise] in case of failure'.

Figure 5.10 Technician demonstrating solar module at local agricultural cooperative

Figure 5.11 Technician providing customer with after-sales service

The Indian entrepreneur first established the company's head office, with a small assembly shop, on the southwest coast of Karnataka. The first rural outlet, called a 'service centre', was established about 50 kilometres away in a rural district south of the head office. He would later establish a second service centre in the north of Karnataka in early 1995, and a third service centre by February 1996 in the neighbouring state of Andhra Pradesh.

In parallel with building the market infrastructure, the Indian entrepreneur also set out to solve the thorny issue of consumer finance. The US$30,000 raised by the American entrepreneur was intended not only for identifying and training technicians, but to finance an initial round of customers. It was used to reach 25 rural households, from whom the Indian entrepreneur was then responsible for collecting the money.[4] The loan period was three years, but the latter quickly found this to be a problem. Indeed by

Figure 5.12 Technical and sales personnel operating from first service centre

Figure 5.13 Small assembly
shop for solar lights

early 1996, his team was reporting 'problems with collection' and that 'people are not finishing their payments'. The Indian entrepreneur described this as 'a learning experience' – the central lesson being that he would rather not be in the consumer finance business.

Whereas the entrepreneurs originally had a vision of establishing a subsidiary finance wing to complement sales of solar, the Indian entrepreneur concluded from this experience that:

> to do this, you need a larger structure, and you need a lot of time and effort on this instead of sales. You effectively become a finance house. I do not think we are now in a position to do finance. It is better to let the rural banking network assume this headache.

The Indian entrepreneur was certainly right that India had a large rural network of banks, which, if they could be brought into lending for solar, could have a huge, transformative impact in the market (Table 5.1).

Table 5.1 India's rural credit infrastructure

	Commercial banks	Regional/rural banks
Number of banks	28	196
Number of semi-urban branches	10,900	1079
Number of rural branches	21,952	13,290

Source: Dikshit (1996)

In line with the stereotype of entrepreneurial resourcefulness, the Indian entrepreneur tried to identify an alternative source of consumer finance. In 1994 he approached an acquaintance of the family who he thought could help – a deputy general manager (DGM) in the Syndicate Bank, then on secondment to a rural subsidiary bank in North Karnataka. Recognizing the importance of finance to sales, the entrepreneur was persistent in his pursuit of the DGM. As the DGM recounts:

> I did not have confidence that [the Indian entrepreneur] would come back to me. So many youngsters have lofty ideals, but do not follow through. I was surprised when he contacted me in three months time and said he would come and do this. I said, 'welcome'.[5]

Like the two entrepreneurs, the DGM would come to see solar as providing rural inhabitants with one of 'the basic necessities' of life – light. The DGM lamented that 'in India millions of households do not have any light except the traditional lamps'. And he quickly developed the arguments for why his bank should finance it:

> Light is a necessity for a man's life. TVs and washing machines are not essential, but light is. So if we finance a range of consumer goods such as TVs and washing machines, we should certainly support solar.

The Indian entrepreneur had now identified a well-respected, powerful technology champion within a bank that was itself supportive of innovations for rural development. Having initiated earlier schemes in the bank, the DGM possessed the credibility to drive through the solar finance scheme. As his colleagues confirmed, 'He is a very strong character and highly influential, and he *pushes* an innovation.'[6]

Figure 5.14 Syndicate Bank headquarters in Manipal, Karnataka

The DGM's influence in the Syndicate Bank had been built over a lifetime of service, and a record of having successfully launched loan schemes for rural innovations such as biogas technology and hybrid seed varieties. Moreover, the bank itself had its very origins in rural banking, and so was receptive to the technology's rural application.[7] It was also a pioneer of other new rural technologies. As the chairman of the Syndicate Bank recounted, the bank was the first to engage in agricultural financing, when most banks considered this a 'non-banking sector', the first to lend for hybrid rice seed varieties, the first to lend for biogas technology, and:

> now solar energy. We at Syndicate are fundamentally concerned about the rural economy, and today electricity is not reaching the rural people. Solar electricity is an alternative, and so we should finance it. Ultimately, anything that benefits the rural people we should finance. So once again, this time with solar, we find that Syndicate is first.

Figure 5.15 Syndicate Bank's rural subsidiary from where solar finance was launched

And so, from the bank in North Karnataka, the DGM was able to launch India's first commercial consumer finance scheme for solar. It was initially restricted to North Karnataka only, but by early 1996, the DGM had relocated to Andhra Pradesh, and orchestrated a nationwide programme under the banner 'Solar Electric Lighting Scheme'.[8] The entrepreneurs' company was identified then as the sole vendor – an alliance which no other Indian supplier of solar had so far been able to establish.

The benefits of the Syndicate Bank entering the market were considerable, and would bode well for diffusion going forward. The average solar system sold by the entrepreneurs' firm at the time was a 35-watt, four-light system for 21,600 rupees (Rs), which in dollars terms was then US$635. But the Syndicate

Bank was now offering four- to five-year loans, with just 10 per cent down payment, and 12 per cent interest up to a maximum of Rs 25,000. With this scheme in place, the up-front cost to the customer was reduced to US$60 and the monthly payment to just US$12–15 (Table 5.2).

Table 5.2 35-watt solar system under Syndicate solar loan scheme

	Karnataka		**Andhra Pradesh**	
Down-payment	$62	Rs 2100	$62	Rs 2100
Monthly payment	$12	Rs 420	$15	Rs 498
Bi-annual payment	$59	Rs 1996	$73	Rs 2470

Source: Miller (1998)

Moreover, in line with the discussion on the power of opinion leaders in Chapter 2, the bank's entry gave customers the confidence to 'try' the technology. As one early customer from Andhra Pradesh explained:

> We took it because the bank took on the risk. As it was a new system, we did not know about it and how it would work, but like this we could not afford to take the risk. We took the loan in the end because the bank was involved.

Or as another customer succinctly put it: 'If it fails, I'll just drop it in the bank.'

Figure 5.16 A rural branch of Syndicate Bank offering solar finance

Furthermore, the Syndicate Bank branch managers played a key personal role, promoting the technology in line with their internal mandate to introduce the scheme. As one of the earlier-quoted customers went on to say: 'Any company can give a guarantee. It was the assurance of the branch manager that mattered. Only the branch manager can say whether the assurance that the company gives is good.' He went on to conclude, 'The only reason I bought the system was because of the branch manager.'

The entrepreneurs now planned to rapidly grow sales and installations on the back of the new finance scheme. In 1996 the aim was to sell 1860 systems. However, by the middle of that year, these targets already seemed out of reach. In fact in roughly two years, between October 1994 and August 2006, the company had struggled to sell just 250 systems. The key barrier was no longer the lack of consumer finance, but the lack of capital in the business to develop and support a market infrastructure. This meant the Syndicate Bank and its subsidiary in North Karnataka were eager to lend for solar but could not. As the senior manager of the latter bank explained:

> We can only expand our loans if there is a larger service network. [The enterprise] is now in the infant stage. … We are ready to finance more borrowers, but we need the distribution and sales network.[9]

To emphasize this point he concluded that 'there is only so much the bank can do – it cannot initiate a demonstration and do promotion unless the support of [the enterprise] is there'.

Not only could the entrepreneurs not build out their market infrastructure, but they didn't have the capital to hold sufficient inventory. As the enterprise's local manager in Andhra Pradesh lamented at the time:

> We have found that those who use solar always demonstrate a pride in their system and tell others. … However, we have not had the capital to follow up on this demonstration.

And he went on to say, 'We can get orders for 25 systems now, but *when* will we be able to install them?'. A similar sentiment was expressed by officials of the Syndicate Bank in the same state: '[The bank] has now generated a demand for the systems in the rural areas, but [the enterprise] is not in a position to supply – there is a gap.'[10]

Consequently, the DGM offered a working capital loan to the Indian entrepreneur. The former knew from his prior experience in financing innovations like electric pump sets and biogas digesters at Syndicate Bank that it was not enough to create demand for an innovation, the supply-side needed support too:

I was convinced with the bio-gas technology – I had seen it. The next point is who will do this. If the farmer decides to have a bio-gas system, who will do this? So we encouraged people to manufacture the drum, the burner and do the civil construction works. With bio-gas we financed both the manufacturers to increase supply and the end-users, dealing with both ends. After we did this, other entrepreneurs came into the market.[11]

When the DGM perceived that the entrepreneur was not meeting the demand generated by the bank scheme, he protested 'You must have more technicians!' and later complained that:

> Just from the seminar last week I received several orders, which have been passed on to [the enterprise]. But they are not yet prepared to meet the order. Solar lighting has to be done on a turn-key basis by local technicians – fast and simple.[12]

To fix this problem he advised that:

> They could take a loan of less than 200,000 rupees for 12.5 per cent. I've been telling them this for a long time now. What [the enterprise] needs to do is to build its rural infrastructure, and for this they need capital.[13]

However, the Indian entrepreneur was worried about the interest burden, and presumably defaulting on a loan and letting down a close ally.[14] Even before he settled back down in India, the Indian entrepreneur was approaching others to see if they wanted to fund the operation. But he was not finding an 'investor fit' – a concept we discussed in Chapter 2. For example, he recalled:

> I was communicating with a US-based representative [of an Indian electronics manufacturer] who had taken on the idea of doing solar all over India – this had gone very smoothly as I knew the head of [the electronics manufacturer]. However, they were a safe player and did not want to focus just on solar, they wanted to diversify into purifiers and so on. ... But solar electrification was my objective no matter what. I was focussed on this. Our ideas were not matching. Our objectives were completely different: he wanted to make money through the diversified approach, and I wanted to do solar electrification. If I had wanted to [just] make money, I would not have gone into the solar business.

He also approached several private investors in the Indian community of the northeast US, 'But they were not willing to sponsor the idea from the very beginning, and were expecting high returns on their money – around 25 per cent. They equated this with any other business, not thinking that it was a *solar* business.' Furthermore, they 'had a short-term perspective of two years and wanting their dividend'.

In 1996, at the peak of cash-flow difficulties, the Indian entrepreneur also made enquiries with a venture capital (VC) firm in Bangalore, the capital of Karnataka. The VC firm had an existing investment in the Indian PV sector – a PV manufacturer in South India – and so looked promising. However, the entrepreneur was under no illusions: 'There is a sense in which venture capital is not suited to rural solar electrification. What is venture capital? It is high risk, so it expects high returns.'

The VC firm in question received the majority of its money from institutional investors, and, as a representative of the firm explained, these investors expected 'A return of 5–6 times what they put in. ... The figure to remember in terms of our expected returns is 40 per cent compounded over 10 years.'[15] Moreover, 'If the company is new, then the risk is higher. Thus the expected returns also have to be higher.' The representative nonetheless asked the Indian entrepreneur to submit a business plan, but the latter decided against it, explaining that:

> It was simply a case of us not being able to meet their expected returns. If solar electric lighting could provide 40 per cent returns, compounded over 10 years, then it would be absolutely everywhere by now!

Not finding an 'investor fit' at capital costs they felt they could afford, the entrepreneurs turned to an institution that should have had an interest in lending to them. Partly influenced by the success of the American entrepreneur in other countries, the World Bank had launched the Renewable Energy Resources Development Project in India in 1994. Responsibility for implementing this project in India lay with the Indian Renewable Energy Development Agency (IREDA), which had a US$50 million line of credit for PV at low rates of interest. In theory, this was ideally suited to the entrepreneur's requirements.

However, the line of credit was not for development of a market infrastructure or working capital. It was explicitly designated for consumer finance. IREDA and the World Bank had to 'see' each customer at the end of the transaction. Thus the Indian entrepreneur needed to first secure all the names of all the customers that would be financed under a discrete solar project, and then supply these customers in one shot, while subsequently managing the collection of money from these customers over time.

The Indian entrepreneur had identified an organic agricultural cooperative in his area of operations that was willing to buy roughly 100 systems. The amount sought was about US$50,000, on concessional terms of 4.5 per cent, to finance these 100 customers. Thus, after already taking the names and the down payments from each customer, he put forward an application to IREDA.

At first, IREDA directed the application to a private-sector bank they were using to help disburse the PV line of credit. But the representative at this private bank was not disposed to lending to the rural solar sector:

> If we are talking about the rural market, the key feature is whether the money will come back. This market has been spoiled by politics. There have been constant loan write-offs by the politicians. A rural farmer knows very well that the write-offs will occur with the next elections. Private finance does not want to lend to rural people. ... The rural market is very high risk.

The perception was that rural areas were lawless, rendering private rural finance difficult, if not impossible. After postulating that the entrepreneur would be 'shot' in trying to collect the monthly deposits from rural customers, the representative of the private bank went on to explain that:

> When we, as a private finance organization, try and lend in the remote areas, the people expect the same treatment from us. Maybe the first one or two times, you might collect your repayment, but on the third instalment you will get beaten up. And the villagers have the support of the politician – they are politically very strong since this is his vote bank. You simply cannot do business in such areas.

The Indian entrepreneur then took his application back to IREDA for direct funding. Not surprisingly, it did not sail through smoothly. Instead it was marked as having a 'high institutional risk', because the entrepreneurs could not properly secure the loan, because the company was a start-up and because it was not clear they could manage the collection of the funds from the customers. Moreover, the rural solar markets were simply not IREDA's priority. As the then managing director of IREDA confirmed:

> The rural market is a high potential market, but it is difficult to reach. ... Our strategy is to encourage rural adoption through a step-by-step process. By this I mean go from urban, to semi-urban, to rural and then to remote, such that the PV would reach the remote user over a period of time, at which point the costs will have come down and awareness will have gone up. You cannot go straight to the tail end – to the remote areas. This is an accepted delivery pattern for all services and products in this country. All items, such as TVs, communications and so on, began in the urban end and went to the remote end. Reaching out now is very challenging.[16]

Blocked from securing any loans under the World Bank project, the entrepreneurs could not grow their business until they received new money. But it was not just the lack of capital that was hurting the business. Part of the issue related to internal decision-making and learning, and part to the prevailing set of policies in India at the time.

We can point to several areas where the entrepreneurs were learning by doing, perhaps incurring higher costs than necessary and otherwise damaging a poor cash position. For instance, with very limited funds, the enterprise was 'spread thin' across two neighbouring states. Ideally, it would have saturated Karnataka prior to entering the second state of Andhra Pradesh.

In addition, the Indian entrepreneur was only retaining a 10–12 per cent margin on the price of a solar system. He felt this was sufficient to cover all his costs. Yet the American entrepreneur felt differently: 'He has to go for 20 per cent.' When it was suggested that he think of increasing the margin by raising the price from Rs 21,650 to Rs 25,000, the Indian entrepreneur countered that at this price he would lose the rural market. He sought to keep the price where it was, based on his belief that rural households would not generally pay more than the cost of a colour television set for a solar system. However, this assumption was not proven.

Finally, an independent consultant felt the entrepreneurs could do better on procurement. Instead of aligning with one manufacturer, the entrepreneurs should 'use [their] brand to push for better prices and to play off manufacturers', and:

> constantly be in touch with all manufacturers of panels, batteries and so on and track their latest prices. This marketing intelligence should be used to forecast quarterly demand and to order components in bulk after tough negotiations from a quality supplier. The company can reduce its costs of goods by at least 15 per cent if they are purchased in a professional manner.[17]

In addition, we can point to the way in which existing policies were hurting the company's margins. PV module duties in India at this time were high – high by international standards and higher than they would be in later years (Table 5.3). With the Indian entrepreneur feeling that he could not raise prices further, these duties (a tax on solar) were unduly constraining the margins of the entrepreneurs.

Table 5.3 Declining import duties on PV modules in India

Year	1992	1994	1996	2005
PV module duty in India	110%	45%	30%	0%

Source: NREL (1994)

That said, with just US$30,000 in the bank, until funding was increased every-thing else was just tinkering. It wasn't until the middle of 1996 that more resources started to come on stream. The first investment came from the energy finance wing of a large US foundation – US$50,000 for a minority share in the company. However, receipt of the money was then delayed by government procedures on foreign ownership. This application initially stalled in MNES, who queried why the enterprise should be foreign-owned, and then got stuck in the Government's bureaucratic channels on foreign direct investment.

The American entrepreneur was playing a key role in raising these resources – a role that was set to continue for the next several years. The next investment came hard on the heels of the first – a long-term loan from the United States Agency for International Development (USAID) of US$160,000. This enabled the Indian entrepreneur to shift the head office to Bangalore and build his management team. The business was now starting to take shape. But the key investment came two years later, in 1998, when the parent company, due to the successful fund-raising efforts of the American entrepreneur, was able to start an ongoing process of investing US$1.2 million into the Indian enterprise over the next few years. Finally, although they faced difficulties in securing the funds, this was be followed up in 2003 with a long-term loan of US$1 million from the International Finance Corporation (the private arm of the World Bank), under a programme called the Photovoltaic Market Transformation Initiative (PVMTI).

The entrepreneurs now had the funds to grow. Moreover, by this time, they had learned the hard way what worked (and what did not) in growing the busi-ness. For instance, to focus on selling solar and not financing it; to concentrate just on the state of Karnataka; and to play off key suppliers to bring down their costs of goods. Between 1996 and 2005, the enterprise would go on to sell 42,000 solar systems and establish a profitable company with more than 180 personnel. Moreover, as the American entrepreneur would later be told by a visiting delegate of the United Nations Environment Programme (UNEP): 'You have done more in 12 years than create a great company. You've created an industry.'

This was indeed the case, and in 1999 Shell Solar entered the Indian market directly. The entrepreneurs' early initiatives were now providing an example that later arrivals could follow. The difference was that Shell Solar could bring more resources to the table on day one to effect the diffusion process – more than US$2 million. Moreover, Shell Solar was able to leverage these resources under PVMTI to arrange a low-interest debt facility of an addi-tional US$2 million. With these resources, Shell Solar was able to hold more inventory and establish more branches. In just three years, the company estab-lished 25 branches, largely in Karnataka, with a trained base of more than 200 employees.

Figure 5.17 More retail sites and field staff serving the local solar market

Figure 5.18 More door-to-door salespeople selling solar

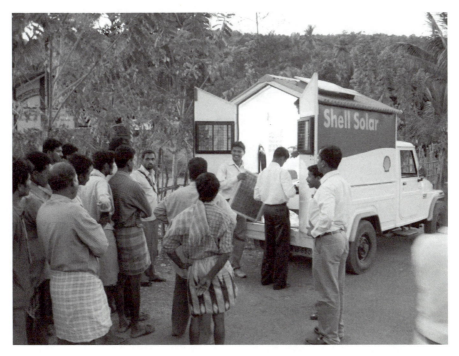

Figure 5.19 More village-level demonstrations of solar

The entrepreneurs and Shell Solar were joined by several other local players, also focused entirely on selling solar in the rural markets of Karnataka. And with more sellers now in the marketplace, more banks became involved. At the last count there were 16 on 17 different banks who had signed agreements with various providers of solar systems in Karnataka.

Then on the back of this nascent rural solar industry, UNEP got involved. Having seen that the supply side had already developed well in Karnataka, UNEP, with the support of the UN Foundation, launched a low-interest loan scheme in 2003 to provide an extra incentive on the demand side. UNEP identified two participating banks with large rural networks to reach the intended customer base – Syndicate Bank and Canara Bank – and offered five-year loans at just 5 per cent interest.

The project got off to a quick start in 2003 (fiscal year 2003/2004), particularly through the Syndicate Bank, who already knew this technology and market well. The existing players in the market were then joined more forcefully by a network of roughly 60 dealers and sub-dealers of TATA BP Solar (a joint venture between the Indian conglomerate TATA and British Petroleum). Not surprisingly, with low-interest consumer finance and a strong market infrastructure now in place, sales of solar systems surged in 2004 (fiscal year 2004/2005).[18]

Figure 5.20
Advertisement for solar loans under UNEP low-interest loan scheme

It only fell off the next year because Syndicate Bank, which at this point was financing 60 per cent of all the systems, hit its overall quota under the programme and had to step out, though of course Syndicate continued to finance solar under its existing programme, at its normal interest rate of 12 per cent (loans at normal rate of interest not included in Figure 5.21). In the end, the UNEP policies resulted in the sale of 18,000 solar systems in just three and a half years. But had there been more funds, it could have had an even bigger impact.[19]

What started as just a trickle of solar sales in the mid 1990s by two entrepreneurs grew into thousands of systems per year being sold by a multitude of players and financed by an even larger number of banks. As of the end of 2007, the best estimates were that over 100,000 solar systems had been installed in Karnataka through private-sector channels since the entrepreneurs launched their commercial enterprise in 1995.[20]

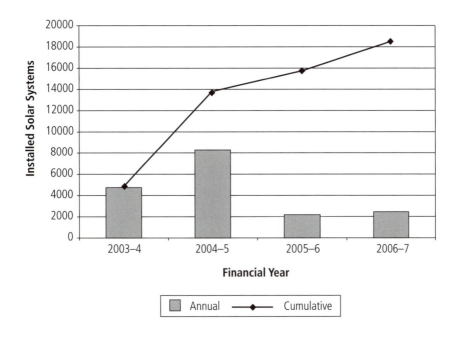

Figure 5.21 Low-interest solar loan scheme propels diffusion in Karnataka, India

Source: Crestar[21]

In line with our discussions in Chapter 2, the key to the increase in the diffusion of solar proved to be entrepreneurial tenacity, combined with raising sufficient resources and developing the capacities to deploy them in a profitable manner. Then, through their demonstration effect, the entrepreneurs attracted the attention of big business and policymakers, who helped to further drive the diffusion process.

As we have seen, a bigger company like Shell Solar could bring considerable resources to the task of diffusing solar, with some significant results. It was estimated to have sold more than 30,000 solar systems between 1999 and mid 2007. But in line with our earlier discussions in Chapter 2, while large corporations can bring more resources to the task of technology diffusion, their agendas do not tend to remain as steadfast as those of entrepreneurs. Shell Solar exited the business at the end of 2007 by selling it to a small Indian company.[22] Meanwhile, the American entrepreneur went on to establish a new solar company back in the US, and the Indian entrepreneur continues to sell solar through the same enterprise he established; still committed to the markets of Karnataka, and now also serving new markets in Kerala and Gujarat.

Entrepreneur in Indonesia

The entrepreneur in Indonesia was setting out to build a big business: 'Solar has to be done as a "mass consumer market". We need to sell solar like Coca-Cola.'[23]

He had a background in business and finance and came from Europe. As the former managing director of a solar business based in Jakarta, his mandate had been to do whatever government solar projects came along: homes, clinics, schools, telecommunications and so on. However, one of these projects convinced him that customers were actually willing to pay market prices for solar and that he could set up a business, independent of government projects, around it:

> After [the government project] I had the conviction that it would be possible to do solar home systems on a commercial basis. ... I saw a huge market and felt there was the possibility to develop a huge company. If you think about the commercial market amongst those who are willing to pay with cash, you arrive at a market of 10 million modules.

He had also seen that there was a degree of rural purchasing power: 'I knew there were 5–10 per cent in rural areas who could afford to pay in cash. I was convinced there was a capacity to pay in rural areas, or rather, I "knew" this to be the case.' And he was convinced of the rural demand for electricity: 'What people really seem to care about, however, is electricity – to watch the last few minutes of a soccer game on TV is what they want.'

With this experience, he was quite clear on what needed to be done.[24] He decided he would build his 'own' sales and distribution network. His mantra was simple: he wanted to control as much as possible in the start-up of his operation. And more to the point, he could not find any other suitable distribution points in rural Indonesia that could handle the requirements of stocking, selling, installing and servicing solar.

From early 1994, he opened one or two branches per month (called 'service centres'), creating a network of 46 service centres in West Java and Lampung by mid 1996.[25] The centres were responsible for holding stock, coordinating sales, installation and service, and collecting money. Although this might appear an expensive way of doing things, the entrepreneur was adamant that the cost of each branch could easily be covered by a minimal volume of sales each month. Moreover, this network of branches was critical to the entrepreneur's ability to supply and service the rural demand that he managed to generate.

In each service centre there was one local manager (who handled a lot of the sales and money collection), one secretary, and one or two assistant technicians. In addition the company possessed a considerable fleet of vehicles: there

Figure 5.22
Installed solar module
on customer's roof
in Indonesia

Figure 5.23 Typical solar home

Figure 5.24 A satisfied solar customer

Figure 5.25
Family next to system,
with enclosed batteries
and electronics

were two motorbikes per centre, used for installation and servicing, and head office had ten vans and one truck for distribution. At head office the company not only organized distribution and managed the network of service centres, but it had an assembly plant for electronics and framing of solar modules. After its launch the company quickly grew to a total of 180 employees by mid 1996, with 40 employees at head office and the rest operating out of the centres.

Figure 5.26 Employee outside typical service centre

Figure 5.27 Employees arriving for work at head office

Figure 5.28
A warm reception
in head office

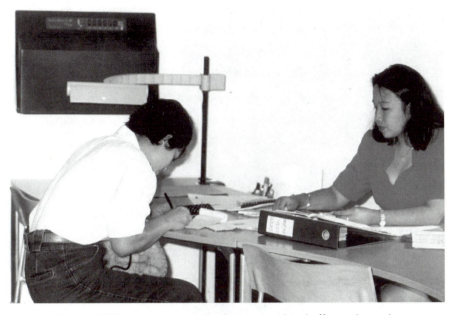

Figure 5.29 Serving customers who come to head office to buy solar

Figure 5.30
Assembly of electronics

Figure 5.31
Framing of solar modules

The entrepreneur had already learned about the relationship between after-sales service and the growth of his business. He saw that under the Government's solar programmes in Indonesia, 'no resources were allocated for servicing'. Witnessing high levels of technical failure, he reasoned from the outset that 'service is absolutely critical'. As he explained to a meeting of UN officials:

> We are in the business of selling a service. The only way for us to survive as a business is to ensure that we provide adequate service. One reason we stopped doing the Government programmes is that under these you have to go to small, remote, out of the way islands, for political reasons, where service then becomes impossible.

The commitment to service was based on an awareness by the entrepreneur of the important role that 'referencing' played in a customer's decision to buy solar. A survey commissioned by the entrepreneur found that:

Figure 5.32
Technician carrying out
after-sales service

in their evaluation whether or not to buy a [solar system], they will
consider the merits of solar energy based on examples set in their village.
… Word of mouth is our most important marketing mechanism – more
important than a brochure.

The survey also found that satisfied customers can become unofficial sales
agents for the company:

People do not believe the salesmen on their word: proof of good quality
is needed. I noticed that people who are satisfied with their system like
to help our salespeople to find new customers.

This is all very much in line with the findings of the communication perspective, discussed in Chapters 2 and 3.

Given that servicing depends on trained technicians, the Indonesian entrepreneur organized regular training programmes. Training 'covers all subjects,
such as company history, strategy, marketing and sales, administrative

procedures, after-sales [service], technology, and logistics'.[26] Training was organized roughly once every three months and entailed the training of typically 20–30 new staff members.

Figure 5.33 Training of new employees near head office

Figure 5.34 Customers in service centre, paying their monthly instalment on solar loan

But the entrepreneur knew this was not enough. He knew that to be able to sell solar in larger volumes, and cover the cost of his market infrastructure, he would have to find a way to finance the customer. He first checked with the banks in Indonesia, but found they were only offering loans up to two years. They were also highly sceptical about lending for solar. Reasoning that a two-year loan would not do enough to make solar affordable for the customer, he set out to establish his own finance scheme.

The entrepreneur sold his solar systems at the prices listed in Table 5.4. But once he introduced his own finance scheme, only 10 per cent of his customers paid the up-front price. The rest opted for finance, which required a 25 per cent down payment but no collateral or additional security of any kind. The solar system was deemed to be sufficient security.

Table 5.4 Solar products and prices of Indonesian enterprise

Solar product	Price (rupiah)	Price (US$)
One panel, 50 watt	1,020,000	441
Two panel, 100 watt	1,730,000	742
Three panel, 150 watt	2,540,000	1090

Source: Miller (1998)[27]

An independent survey of customers in West Java and Lampung confirmed that by making the initial hurdle for the customer only 25 per cent of the system price, the entrepreneur was meeting the needs of his customer base. In a market survey of rural households who expressed an interest in buying a solar system, the vast majority wanted the lowest possible down payment (Table 5.5).

Table 5.5 Preferred means of payment by customers interested in solar in West Java and Lampung

Financial scheme	West Java (%)	Lampung (%)
Cash payment	5	14
Down-payment of Rp 400,000	30	29
Down-payment of Rp 300,000	10	14
Down-payment of Rp 250,000	55	43

Source: World Bank (1995b), p22

The entrepreneur was clear that the interest rate was not the issue. Provided the down payment and the monthly amount fit the customers' needs, he could sell in large volumes. He charged the prevailing rate in rural Indonesia at the time for consumer durables – 30 per cent on a declining balance. But because he offered a longer-term loan of four years (remember the banks were only offering two), he could bring the monthly amount paid down to US$12 for a 50-watt system (Table 5.6).

Table 5.6 Lowest down payment and monthly payment options under Indonesian enterprise's loan scheme

Product	Down payment (Rp)	Down payment (US$)	Monthly payment (Rp)	Monthly payment (US$)
50-Wp SHS	240,000	103	27,000	12
100-Wp SHS	690,000	296	36,000	15
150-Wp SHS	990,000	425	54,000	23

Source: Miller (1998)

Once he arrived at a figure of $100 down-payment and only US$12 per month, the entrepreneur had unlocked a large market. According to a World Bank market survey in Indonesia, this resulted in a total market of 250,000 households in the provinces of West Java and Lampung alone (Table 5.7)

Table 5.7 Assessment of market potential for solar on credit in West Java and Lampung

Steps for identification of prime commercial market	West Java (% of sample)	West Java (number of unelectrified households in non-urban areas)	Lampung (% of sample)	Lampung (number of unelectrified households in non-urban areas)
Total	100	2,061,000	100	736,000
Total with interest in buying SHS	64	1,319,000	67	471,000
Total with energy expenditure greater than Rp 15,000	14	288,600	24	103,000
Total willing to purchase a solar system with credit	7	144,300	21	154,600
Total owning a TV or spending 20,000 Rp/Month on lighting and entertainment	6.3	130,000	16.3	120,000

Source: World Bank (1995b), pp17–21

According to the entrepreneur, the firm managed to retain collection rates of 95 per cent under its consumer finance scheme. But even with a perfect rate of 100 per cent, the entrepreneur was facing a much more fundamental issue – lack of capital.[28]

His profitability was good. He made a margin of 30 per cent on the system price, which he felt was 'not a magic number', rather it was the one that is most 'comfortable in developing the organization'.[29] Plus he earned a 30 per cent margin on the consumer finance:

> We have increased our prices over the last three years. Initially they were low to capture the market. Now presently the profit is nice. … You can build a much stronger organization this way. You simply have to have a reasonable income. If the margin is 30 per cent on the system and 30 per cent on the finance, then that is the perfect profit for us.

As is the case with many small businesses, however, it was not the profitability of the business but the cash in the business that was the problem.

Under his consumer finance scheme, the down payment covered only part of the cost of the system. The entrepreneur had to find the rest until the customer repaid it month by month. As demand increased, he needed more capital to fund the consumer finance scheme. The business was sailing perilously close to the wind. By mid 1996, it could only make payment to its suppliers at the end of each month, once the customers had paid their monthly instalments.

The cash in the company simply was not sufficient both to allow for dramatic growth in his market infrastructure and to finance his customer base:

> We manage a credit system and, in fact, nothing would have been possible without combining sales with credit. However, as the down-payment is only enough to meet 30 per cent of the system cost, and as the money is tied up in the loan for typically four years, from a company point of view, there is a shortage of working capital.

The entrepreneur achieved sales of 400–500 solar systems per month by the end of the 1994. At the time, these figures were unprecedented among solar businesses targeting rural markets. But ironically, they were too high. In order to correct the deteriorating cash position, the entrepreneur actually had to reduce the monthly sales to 200–250 for 1995 and 1996, which allowed the cash-flow situation to stabilize.

In a way, the entrepreneur was too successful. His finance scheme and market infrastructure were creating too much demand:

> The strange thing is that the more sales we have, the less cash we have at our disposal due to the credit programme. It is stupid, but I could stop selling and use the money that keeps coming in to simply strengthen the organization.

The entrepreneur reported that 'we began the company with a personal investment of US$400,000–500,000' and that this was used to establish the first series of service centres and to design the wall-mounted display box.[30] But this wasn't enough – he was seeking a further investment of US$2 million to try to improve his cash-flow position.

The entrepreneur first tried approaching the banks in Indonesia. But found it to be 'extremely difficult'. He didn't have much luck with the banks back in Europe either:

> I would visit a bank and not even be allowed to finish my presentation. I went to a Dutch bank once and only got half way through the presentation when the manager stopped me and asked why I was wasting his time. That is the feeling in most banks about commercializing solar in rural areas, and I understand this. As a banker I would do the same thing. A banker simply likes the money in the way that they are used to. The bank is risk-averse and conservative, while selling solar is new in so many ways.

It was not a question of possessing inadequate security, since he had considerable collateral to offer in land and houses. Rather, his proposal 'was more or less rejected straight away'. The financiers told him that the loan requested was too small, and the proposal was too risky. But in the entrepreneur's opinion it was that it was just too innovative, too different:

> It was a question of being a new company, with a new strategy, entailing a new concept and a new product. PV has always been a government-dominated area. The bank's perception of electricity is large-scale, oligopoly, involving the Government. By contrast I was presenting a proposal for small-scale electrification, which was fully private, for rural, perceived-to-be-poor people, who had never taken a loan before. The banks are used to working with one customer in electricity-generating projects. But here I was asking them to work with thousands if not millions.

And he continued, 'Presenting [our] proposal to the bank entails telling them about five "new" things at one time – it is not just one new thing. In the end you are simply "finished".'

Of particular significance was the entrepreneur's proposal to on-lend the bank's money to rural households. The entrepreneur found that 'the banks do not believe that we can handle a rural credit programme'. Independent confirmation of this assessment came from a World Bank consultant looking at the solar markets in Indonesia: 'From a bank's point of view, not only are the dealers relatively unestablished, but [solar] is a new business, in a not very attractive market segment.'[31]

The perceived risk of lending for rural credit was heightened by the duration of the entrepreneur's most popular credit package – four years. According to the same consultant, the banks in Indonesia have a 'rule of thumb that the longer the period of the contracts, the larger the losses'. Furthermore, both the product and the enterprise were viewed as unestablished: 'the banks do not see the panels as fully commercial (this is a pilot project)' and '[the enterprise] and even more so the other dealers are not seen as having a well-established track record'.

Given that an investment was not forthcoming, the entrepreneur reasoned that he should turn to organizations with more to gain:

> The key is this: you have to go through parties that have an interest in cooperating with you. It is that logical and that simple. If you cannot get your money from a bank, then go to a party that actually has an interest in your work. For us that was the manufacturers. And their support has made the difference.

The entrepreneur perceived that solar PV manufacturers 'have their own "interest" in cooperating with us, as they ultimately have to move modules'. He identified a state-owned Italian manufacturer of solar modules that was willing to provide six-month, interest-free credit. The entrepreneur emphasized time and again that 'supplier credits make financing possible'; 'we would never have made it without the credit offered by [the supplier]'; 'without the supplier credits, it simply would not have been possible to launch this initiative'; and 'if the supplier had not trusted us, we would have been broke by this stage; this cannot be over-emphasized'.[32]

But supplier credits for the entrepreneur were more of a stop-gap. The big potential lay in securing the World Bank's 1997 Indonesia Solar Home System project. The entrepreneur had played a central role in lobbying for this project, and during the preparation process was asked to inform its design.[33] Indeed, the World Bank manager who spearheaded the loan drew inspiration from the success of the entrepreneur.

The project, described in more detail in Chapter 6, targeted the sale of 200,000 solar systems over five years. Its two core components were working capital loans for firms selling solar (which would have improved the entrepreneur's cash flow), and a grant per solar system installed, disbursed directly to the firm responsible for invoicing the customer (which the entrepreneur could have used to further improve margins or reduce prices). Simply put, it would have been ideal for the entrepreneur, and for the firms that would have followed his lead.[34]

But then crisis struck. Just as the World Bank project was signed by the Indonesian Government, the Asian economic crisis sent the country reeling. With the rupiah plummeting, overnight the cost of a solar module in local currency virtually quadrupled. No longer able to afford to procure and sell modules, his sales came to a halt. This was soon followed by customer loans rapidly dropping off, and very quickly the business collapsed.

In a book that has as one its core theses the agency of entrepreneurs, it may seem strange to use a case study of a business failing. But this entrepreneur nonetheless had a profound effect on the future of solar diffusion. Not as it happened in Indonesia, but on an island just across the Indian Ocean – Sri Lanka. The World Bank project in Indonesia was inspired by the entrepreneur's initial success. And although it could not be implemented properly in Indonesia, it would find rebirth in Sri Lanka, where it would lead to unexpectedly high rates of diffusion.

Entrepreneurs in Sri Lanka

Unlike the entrepreneurs profiled earlier in the book, the three entrepreneurs in Sri Lanka had no prior solar experience. But they did bring what one of them described as the 'right combination of knavish energy and enthusiasm'.[35]

One of the entrepreneurs was trained in economics, one in engineering and one in marketing. All three of these disciplines found their use when it came to selling solar in Sri Lanka. But without any direct solar experience, there would be a lot of learning by doing; often the hard way.

When the entrepreneurs launched their business, they initially thought the market was in solar water pumping. Their idea was to come up with a mobile solar-power pump:

> There was a lot of sun, a lot of people didn't have electricity, and this idea had potential and scope. We first thought of mobile solar water pumps for farmers, mainly for irrigation but with secondary use for lighting.

But when it came to making and selling a product, they found that instead the market was among the thousands of households that were using kerosene for lighting and battery charging for entertainment. Interestingly, a market survey they had commissioned had written off this segment – finding that the rural population was too enthralled to the promises of grid extension and low-cost electricity made by the politicians. But in practice, this is where they would find the market; and the market wasn't small – there were an estimated 2.5 million unelectrified households in Sri Lanka in 1986.

To tackle this potential market, the entrepreneurs would need to learn on their feet. They initially felt it necessary to manufacture solar panels to serve the local market, but later the last remaining entrepreneur of the original three would exit the manufacturing business to focus on sales. To reach the market, they initially tried to go through a big distributor of consumer durables, but decided in the end to focus on building their own small, tight-knit network of dealers and sales agents. They initially tried to work with a big bank for solar, and when this didn't work they tried their own consumer finance, and when this didn't work they would settle on cash sales.

Figuring all this out took time and money. The entrepreneurs had initially done well to raise start-up capital from two prominent development banks in the country. (We might observe here that the other entrepreneurs, in India and Indonesia, did not have the same success in encouraging banks to provide start-up capital.) Most of this money was sunk into the machinery to manufacture modules, as well as head-office expenses and managing 23 different teams that were organizing demonstrations and promotions for solar power.

Initially, it looked promising. Through a combination of road-shows (to demonstrate the product) and building a network of dealers, the entrepreneurs increased sales to 150 units per month by August 1998. But then there was an island-wide strike called by the local communist party (JVP), and many businesses, including theirs, ground to a halt. At this point, it would have been easy for the business to be engulfed in the orgy of violence and chaos consuming the country. If their business and staff had been targeted as anti-JVP, it would have spelt the end.

To avoid this fate, the entrepreneurs resourcefully placed an ad in the newspaper asking young people to send in an essay about how solar technology could help their village. The response was more than they expected, and on the back of this they organized multiple three-day training programmes with 20 participants at a time, specifically targeted at the youth. As one of the entrepreneurs recounts: 'we felt among them would have been sympathizers or even JVPers, so we were able to break barriers in the village and continue to do business'. This initiative probably saved the business, and earned them the right to soldier on.

That said, there were many more obstacles to come. The entrepreneurs still had not figured out how to get consumer finance to their customer base. The large banks in the country were not interested or willing to take the credit risk. The entrepreneurs also knew they needed to build their market infrastructure. They did not have a dedicated channel to make stock and service available close to the customer. They had mobile promotional teams, and a few dealers, but not a dedicated and permanent channel. Moreover, the business was quickly running out of money.

So in what seemed like a coup at the time, the entrepreneurs concluded a deal with the largest nationwide retailer of consumer durables – Singer – to stock, sell and finance their systems, all under one roof. Singer had several hundred dealers around the country, not to mention their own dedicated Singer shops and financing facilities. The deal saw them selling 600 systems up-front to Singer, which was significant since they were not even selling 100 units per month at this time.

But the promise in this partnership was ultimately not realized. It seemed perfect: the entrepreneurs were bringing a new product that Singer could add to its portfolio of consumer durables sold in rural areas. But in line with the discussion in Chapter 2, and Schumpeter's contention that only a few people are 'able' to see the opportunity inherent in an innovation, Singer and their dealers just didn't see it.

What they saw instead was the hassle of selling door-to-door, developing installation and servicing procedures, and taking the risk on financing a prod-uct they knew nothing about. They were comfortable with most customers walking into their shops and selling and financing products that everyone knew – TVs, fridges, sofas and so on – and on which they earned a steady, consistent margin. In the end, it would be left to the entrepreneurs – individuals from outside the established consumer-goods industry – to 'see' the opportunity and persevere. Only the entrepreneurs properly understood the product, under-stood the potential and were singular in their focus to drive the market forward.

It was now 1991, and in the absence of a promising partnership with Singer, or a bank to finance customers, the entrepreneurs had established a tight-knit group of dealers that were selling systems on a cash basis. Through this network they could sell 300–500 systems per year. But this was not enough to cover their costs. Instead, to make ends meet they found a big project part-ner in BP, which was implementing a large 1000-system project. BP needed a local firm to take care of sales, installation and service, and the entrepreneurs' firm was selected to do so. And when the project ran into difficulties with money collection from the customers, the entrepreneurs were again called in to sort it out. The project provided them with a lifeline, enough to see them through another year.

But by 1992, the business was in trouble, and radical steps had to be taken. The company was not selling enough to cover costs, so two of the original founding entrepreneurs left the company. As one of the departing entrepre-neurs said: 'We felt it was a drain on resources for all three to remain. [The third entrepreneur] continued to run the business.' But the departing entre-preneurs did not abandon the business. In a critical move, one of them encouraged a Malaysian businessman with whom he was doing another deal to take a 50 per cent stake in the company. The company's debts were all settled, it was renamed and it was effectively given a fresh lease of life.

At this point the third entrepreneur (hereafter 'the Sri Lankan entrepreneur' or just 'the entrepreneur') took control of the company. He knew what needed to be done – build a channel to the rural customer base and organize finance. But he had to run the operation on a shoestring. Although its debts were settled, the business did not have sufficient resources for expansion. The entrepreneur would end up putting his own money into the business to keep it afloat – a testament to his commitment.

In an effort to cut costs and improve focus, the entrepreneur got out of manufacturing solar modules. Instead he started to import modules from one of the larger global solar module manufacturers. Similarly, he consolidated around a network of 8–10 dealers, all of whom were selling solar systems either on a cash basis or through their own credit. And he sought out projects that would enable him to supply in bulk and cover his costs at one shot – for example a telecommunications project he landed in 1998, which helped the company finally turn a profit. But at times, probably out of sheer frustration, he tried bolder moves to see if he couldn't stimulate a bigger rural market, for instance selling to a village on credit terms and trying to collect money from them directly over time. Not surprisingly, he ended up unable to collect the instalments, and wrote off the loss – something he could ill afford at this time.

The entrepreneur needed something else, something that would lead to a more dramatic shift in the marketplace. Thus, as early as 1993, he started lobbying the World Bank to develop a solar project.[36] After four years of market studies and reviews, the World Bank was ready to launch the 1997 Energy Services Delivery Project, which would effectively mimic the Indonesia project: a grant per solar system installed (starting at US$120 for a 50-watt system) and lines of credit for companies and banks to on-lend to solar customers. It was an attractive policy framework, and it caught the eye of Shell Solar.

At the end of 1998, one of the founding entrepreneurs contacted Shell Solar to see if there might be a potential for a partnership in Sri Lanka. Shell Solar was just starting its process of investing in the rural markets, and Sri Lanka was a key target country. After roughly a year of initial meetings, feasibility studies and due diligence, Shell Solar was ready to invest. On top of the amount received for acquisition of the business, Shell Solar invested more than US$2 million over the next two or three years. Moreover, the entrepreneur would be retained by Shell Solar as its managing director in the expansion phase. He now had at his disposal the resources to build the market infrastructure he knew the market needed, but which earlier he could not afford.

It is important at this point to note the beneficial effect of Sri Lanka's policy on foreign direct investment. Unlike India, where the entrepreneurs faced controls and delays on 100 per cent foreign ownership, Sri Lanka had no such barriers. Instead it had a 'fast track' system through the Board of Investments. Because Shell Solar committed to invest a certain amount of equity in the new venture, it was able to fund the company and close all formalities within just a couple of months of completing the acquisition.

While finalizing the negotiations and acquisition with Shell Solar, the Sri Lankan entrepreneur was working on a new consumer finance arrangement. The American entrepreneur (from the India case study), through his earlier promotional activities in Sri Lanka, had encouraged an NGO called Sarvodya to enter the solar market. Now their micro-finance arm, Sarvodya Economic Enterprises Development Services (SEEDS), was in the business of not only lending for solar but selling solar. The Sri Lankan entrepreneur sensed that the managing director of SEEDS was not pleased with their performance as a seller of solar, and he pursued the partnership in earnest.

By mid 1999, after a year of trial and error, the SEEDS managing director was getting the sense that when it came to selling solar, they were in the wrong business. SEEDS had earlier established two of its own sales and distribution points, hired staff to sell, install and service systems, but soon found that they were not able to manage sales, installation and service of solar to the standard they had hoped for. So when the Sri Lankan entrepreneur approached the managing director, himself an innovative leader, and made a compelling case that SEEDS would do better to focus just on financing solar, the managing director took note.

In May 1999 the entrepreneur signed a preliminary letter of intent with SEEDS. And once Shell Solar had actually finalized the acquisition in September 1999, there was that much more credibility. The entrepreneur was able to make a convincing pitch that he was serious about investing in an extensive market infrastructure to sell, install and service solar home systems in large numbers, and that the systems sold would be of good quality, that warranties would be honoured and that a certain number of after-sales visits would be done for free. To prove his point, he could point to pictures of new, Shell Solar centres – branded branches – already established in some market towns of Sri Lanka, staffed with trained technicians and sales people, already selling into the market. Finally, after several months of negotiations, the managing director of SEEDS agreed to step back from selling solar themselves, and formed an alliance with the entrepreneur to finance solar customers in December 1999.[37] This agreement would go on to revolutionize the solar industry in Sri Lanka.

Figure 5.35 Unelectrified household in Sri Lanka, with family outside

Figure 5.36 Typical solar home

Figure 5.37 Less affluent solar home

Figure 5.38 Lifting a solar
module above shadow
caused by trees

Figure 5.39 Solar system powering road-side shop (also serving as home)

It is not surprising that the entrepreneur's success in coaxing SEEDS into the market made the difference. Once in the business of financing solar, SEEDS found that 80–90 per cent of the solar loans they disbursed were for the longest duration possible – this was similar to the experience of the entrepreneur in Indonesia. Until 2003, SEEDS offered a five-year loan at 24 per cent interest with 20 per cent down-payment. At the prevailing prices from 2000 to 2003, customers typically paid – US$100–120 as down-payment and US$10–15 per month over five years for a 50-watt system with five or six lights. With these terms of finance, SEEDS found that roughly 700,000 unelectrified homes could now afford to buy solar.[38] So again it is not surprising that after SEEDS entered the market, the demand for solar dramatically increased.

With Shell Solar's investment, the entrepreneur could capitalize on this demand. He proceeded to develop local branches – Shell Solar Centres – to act as stock and coordinating points for door-to-door salespeople and technicians for installation and service. It was a similar approach to that in Indonesia. The number of these solar centres quickly ramped up to 16 over a two-year period, and with this, so too did the number of trained salespeople and technicians driving sales forward.

Figure 5.40 Solar light in rural kitchen

Figure 5.41 Solar powering a stereo and television

Figure 5.42 Sitting in solar light, watching television

Figure 5.43 Enjoying solar-powered television at end of day

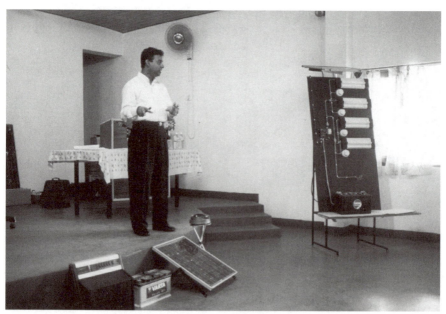

Figure 5.44 Training in sales and service of solar

Figure 5.45 Training technicians in basics of solar module

Figure 5.46 Training technicians in battery-handling

Figure 5.47 Field staff operating out of rural branch

Figure 5.48 Sales personnel and technicians massing for village demonstration

Figure 5.49 Technician installing solar module on rooftop

Figure 5.50 Wiring solar module to electronics and battery

Figure 5.51 Customer education post-installation

With both credit and the market infrastructure now in place, sales surged from what the entrepreneur was used to – for example 20 per month in 1999 – to 200 per month in 2000 and 500 per month in 2001. And they would keep growing until in 2003 the company was selling some 1000 systems per month. Critical to being able to keep up with this demand was the investment by Shell Solar to finance the growing inventory that was required, as well as the growing accounts receivable – payment by the banks often took 60–90 days from installation.

At the end of 2001, the entrepreneur then created a further opportunity for growth. He got news that a particular province in the south of the country, inspired by the development of the solar market, wanted to do its own dedicated grant scheme. The province's initial plan was to orchestrate a mass tender for solar systems, and then dump them in the market at subsidized prices (which would have distorted prices and future solar sales in the area). The Sri Lankan entrepreneur was able to convince this government not to do this, but rather to build on the same policies as the World Bank project – for example make grants available based on sales by the business direct to the customer, and enable the customer to choose from a variety of firms in the marketplace.

Thus, by the end of 2001, firms participating in the Sri Lankan solar market were not only benefiting from a grant per system installed of

Figure 5.52 More retail sites established to serve the local solar market

US$70–120 under the World Bank project, but an additional US$100 from the Uva Provincial Government, albeit that the provincial government grant had to be subtracted from the system price – it was not left up to the company to decide how much to pass on. This had a huge impact, leading to the surge in sales at the end of 2001. Moreover, the provincial government grant would serve as an example to the central government, and it would later be expanded to the other poorer eastern provinces, as well as to the north. Today this additional grant has been retained as a key policy tool by the central government, and extended on a countrywide basis.

While this was happening, the local solar industry was steadily growing. There were already two other players in the market that quickly signed with SEEDS after the entrepreneur. Once the entrepreneur and these competitors demonstrated the potential in the market, a new local entrant – Access – joined, and committed a lot of resources (at least the same amount as, if not more than, Shell Solar). On the back of their own credit scheme, this company was able to grow very quickly. Indeed, in 2001 they grew to owning about 35 per cent of the local market share (although their market share quickly dropped when their credit scheme did not work out). By the start of 2002, there were five solar providers in a growing market, most of whom were using the SEEDS facility to finance their customers. And by the end of 2007, there were a total of 14.

Moreover, once SEEDS set the example, it was possible for the entrepreneur and other solar companies to approach other potential banks and bring them in too. From 2000 to 2003, it is estimated that SEEDS's share of the solar

Figure 5.53 More advertisements for solar: Example of billboard advertising solar

market was as high as 90 per cent, but with the entry of other finance houses such as Lanka Oryx Leasing Company (LOLC) and Alliance Finance, this share subsequently dropped to 50 per cent by 2005.[39]

With multiple firms building a market infrastructure to sell and service solar (albeit to different standards), with multiple banks actively financing solar, and with an additional grant from the Uva Provincial Government, the industry-wide sales of solar simply took off. From only 500 systems per annum in 1999, the market jumped to nearly 15,000 systems per annum in 2001. Then with a follow-on World Bank project orchestrated at the end of 2002, the scene was set for unprecedented diffusion. By the end of 2006, more than 100,000 solar systems had been sold and installed in Sri Lanka, representing more than 7 per cent of formerly unelectrified homes and more than 33 per cent of the estimated market among unelectrified households using kerosene and battery-charging services in place of grid electricity.

Shell Solar sold an estimated 50,000 of those systems before exiting the Sri Lankan solar market as part of its global exit from the solar industry. But while Shell Solar exited, the entrepreneur remained. Having already spun out of Shell Solar and set up a new solar business in 2003, his enterprise now remains one of the largest solar providers in Sri Lanka. It is a testimony to the enduring commitment and tenacity of entrepreneurs, as discussed by Schumpeter, and again stands in stark contrast to the shifting agendas of larger corporations.

When reflecting on the Sri Lankan experience with solar, and why solar sales increased there, GEF and World Bank analysts have pointed to the country's 'long history of rural microfinance' on which financing for solar could build.[40] In another study it was concluded that once the microfinance institutions (MFIs) became interested, solar diffusion under the World Bank's project simply took off:

> Though SHS installations were slow for several years after the project began, once MFIs became involved, installations have begun growing rapidly, from 1000 in June 2000 to over 3200 by the end of March 2001.[41]

But nowhere in these analyses is the question of '*why* it was that MFIs decided to enter this market when they did' considered. They had not entered the market in the past two years of the project's existence, despite the presence of the two or three firms on the ground. Nor had they entered the market during the close to two decades that solar was already being sold in Sri Lanka. So why did they choose to come in now?

It is because such questions are rarely explored and answered by those adopting a more macro-view of diffusion that I specifically developed the concept of agency in Chapter 2. Very often people will explain technology diffusion with statements such as 'the price came down', or 'credit became available', without looking at exactly how this result was brought about, how those involved made it happen and why they were able to do so effectively.

As we saw in the case of Sri Lanka, it was not simply a question of there being a long history of microfinance in the country, or an arbitrary decision of microfinance institutions to become 'involved' in the market. It was a question of an entrepreneur 'convincing' the country's largest microfinance player to scale up their solar finance activities, and then having the right capacities and right resources to build a market infrastructure that could support this increase in finance with strong solar sales, installation and service. Once our profiled entrepreneur had done this, he was quickly joined by other players in the market, who in turn encouraged other finance partners to enter. With the twin pillars of a strong market infrastructure and consumer finance now emerging in Sri Lanka, solar diffusion took off.

Summary

Creating solar markets from scratch was not easy. None of the entrepreneurs got it right the first time, and none of them had sufficient resources in the early stages to realize their vision. But they persevered, and the entrepreneurs in all three cases transformed solar diffusion.

These entrepreneurs had a direct impact through what they sold to their customers. But it would prove to be their indirect impact – their demonstration effect for policymakers and other businesses – that would have an even bigger influence on solar diffusion. When competitors followed the entrepreneurs into the market, they brought extra resources to the task of building a market infrastructure. When more banks entered the solar finance business, they brought new capital to the task of making solar more affordable. And when policymakers entered, they designed programmes that gave a further boost to the diffusion process.

Even the entrepreneur in Indonesia, whose business collapsed during the Asian economic crisis, would go on to strongly influence diffusion in other countries through subsequent World Bank projects in Sri Lanka and beyond. We now turn to consider the case of this institution in more detail, and trace how the World Bank learned to accelerate solar diffusion in emerging markets.

The World Bank
on a Learning Curve

We have already seen in the preceding chapters that entrepreneurs were active in lobbying for the entry of the World Bank to support their sales. The view was that if the World Bank entered, they could introduce policies that would lead to a surge in solar sales. But when the World Bank took the bait, and started to develop solar projects, it had no ready template it could implement. Most of its experience was in centralized power plants and large-scale transmission and distribution projects. When it came to supporting decentralized sales and installation of a smaller-scale technology like solar in rural areas, it was initially rather at a loss.

But like the entrepreneurs, the Bank learned how to support solar diffusion. In fact a lot of what it learned came from the entrepreneurs themselves. When the World Bank started off in India, it had little success spurring solar diffusion in rural areas. But those involved learned the lessons from this project and then applied them to Indonesia. And although the project faltered in Indonesia due to the Asian economic crisis, it served as a template for Sri Lanka, where diffusion took off.

The World Bank learned that for solar to rapidly diffuse, it needed to do a better job of supporting the entrepreneurs in the market. This meant Bank staff had to learn the key drivers of the entrepreneurs' businesses – profit margins, cash requirements, consumer finance arrangements – and tailor their policies and lending accordingly. Essentially, the World Bank had to learn how to *see* the market like an entrepreneur. Once it got this right, the World Bank went on to replicate its success in Sri Lanka with even greater effect in countries such as Bangladesh and China.

Ironically, however, the private wing of the World Bank – the International Finance Corporation (IFC) – did not have the same success. In theory, this entity – able to lend directly to the private sector – was well placed to accelerate solar diffusion. But as we shall see, it actually proved less willing to learn and align itself with the needs of entrepreneurs. The several dedicated solar programmes housed within the IFC that were specifically meant to support solar entrepreneurs had much less impact on solar diffusion than the World Bank's country-level programmes.

Forces at Work: How the World Bank Started to Lend for Solar

The World Bank recognized early on that it did not have an answer to universal rural electrification. Its investments in grid extension would have to be selective, since many grid electrification projects would be uneconomic.[1] Furthermore the alternative – isolated micro-grids supplied by diesel generators – proved too costly and unreliable due to costs of transporting diesel oil, availability of spares and so on.[2] Thus by the time solar emerged as a new way of delivering electricity to remote areas, the World Bank was open to alternatives.

But more than needing a solution for rural electrification, the World Bank desperately needed a solution to sustained attacks on its environmental record. As the largest multilateral lender to the power sector, the World Bank started to come under significant pressure in the early 1990s for its environmental impact. Its support of large-scale, fossil-fuelled power plants was accused of exacerbating global warming.[3] Its own internal reports on the handling of large-scale dams found that the World Bank had inflicted a heavy social and environmental impact.[4] In the words of one former Bank staff member, the environment was starting to 'creep into the lexicon'.[5]

When the Rio Summit on Environment and Development rolled around in 1992, the World Bank and other multilateral lending institutions were thus called upon to increase their lending for renewable energy technologies:

> The priorities of international donor agencies must be revised to reflect the opportunities renewable sources present both for social and economic development and for protecting the environment. Renewable energy presently receives too small a share of energy-related assistance.[6]

Sensing an opportunity to improve its record, the World Bank quickly responded with affirmation of the increasing viability of such technologies in the emerging markets:

> The clean, reliable and increasingly cost-competitive characteristics of renewable energy technologies makes them ideal candidates for displacing other conventional energy options in a variety of developing countries in the coming years.[7]

Furthermore, internal changes were made to give the technology more support among its project managers. In 1993, the Asia Alternative Energy Unit (ASTAE) was established to generate confidence among Bank staff in a brand of technology that had hitherto been seen as either an R&D exercise or the sole domain of aid agency demonstration projects.[8] As one staff member noted at the time, it was all about trying to generate a paradigm shift within the Bank.[9]

As we have seen in previous chapters, these events in Washington coincided with more commercial sales of solar in select emerging markets. Kenya received particular attention within the World Bank, given that the private sector had been largely responsible for the diffusion of 20,000–40,000 solar home systems by 1993,[10] an example that was reinforced by private-sector sales, albeit in lesser numbers, in countries such as the Dominican Republic, Sri Lanka and Zimbabwe.

The credibility of solar would then be further enhanced by reports by the Industry and Energy Department, which served as an advisory body to loan officers in the Bank's energy sector.[11] These reports found that under certain circumstances, solar technology was more cost-effective than grid electrification and diesel mini-grids for rural electricity supply. But even with this added credibility, it was only with the advent of the Global Environment Facility (GEF) that Bank staff actually had the funds to make the solar projects viable.

The GEF is a global grant-giving fund established after the 1992 Rio Conference to provide grants to assist in combating climate change, protecting biodiversity and protecting international waters in the emerging markets. Grants for solar came under the climate change programme, where they were justified not solely in terms of directly pre-empting CO_2 emissions that would have otherwise taken place, but also in terms of establishing a longer-term market in which solar and other renewables would continue to be sold. But the GEF could not give its grants directly – it had to work through one of three agencies: the United Nations Development Programme (UNDP), the United Nations Environment Programme (UNEP) or the World Bank.

When it came to renewables, GEF grants could be used by World Bank staff to increase the projected economic returns of projects, and thus enable them to be approved. For example, at the time of the World Bank's solar loan to India in 1994, the minimal internal economic rate of return for electricity sector loans was 12 per cent.[12] Early World Bank assessments projected that without the GEF grant of US$10 million, the rate of return on the solar project in India was too low – only 1.5–3.3 per cent. But after the GEF grant, the rate of return rose to an acceptable 14.0–14.6 per cent.[13]

With the World Bank needing a solution to rural electrification and increasingly needing some environmental cover, with a gathering internal consensus around the merits of solar technology, and now with the necessary grant funds in place, the World Bank was ready to support solar diffusion. But the experience of the World Bank to date had been primarily in developing and lending for large centralized, fossil- or hydro-based power stations, while loans for rural electrification were for conventional grid extension or the development of diesel-powered micro-grids. As such, lending for solar, where power generation, transmission and distribution were now to be located at the level of the rural household, meant that the World Bank needed to find its way. It did not have a ready-made set of policies – rather it had to watch the entrepreneurs then in the market, innovate on this basis, learn from its mistakes, make adjustments and then replicate its success stories. In short, the Bank was on a very steep learning curve.

The India Loan (1994–1999)

The primary lesson from the solar loan to India was that accelerating the diffusion of solar would be a lot harder than Bank staff thought. Specifically, it was not enough to put a line of credit in place for solar customers and hope that the market would somehow work its magic, that entrepreneurs with strong access to capital and good balance sheets would come forward to take the money for their consumers, or that banks would just automatically come forward to take the refinance for their own solar loan programmes. Instead, it became clear that solar projects required more preparation and more hand-holding than Bank staff were used to, largely because everything was 'new': they were trying to attract new businesses, into a new sector, to sell a new technology, to a new kind of customer and find new ways of financing the transaction.

Different stakeholders within the World Bank had long sought to promote a renewable energy loan to India.[14] Staff on the India country desk had already identified a waste-to-energy project with a good economic rate of return, and were on the lookout for other renewable energy technologies to complement this loan and make it bigger. At the same time, the GEF was looking to fund a large renewable energy project, and was particularly interested in supporting solar technology. The GEF was ultimately predisposed to work in India (and not China, for instance), largely due to the Indian Government's long-running support for renewables[15] and its early contribution to GEF funds. So with the help of the GEF, the World Bank's 1994 Renewable Resources Development Loan was launched in India, with a sizeable GEF grant of US$26 million to accelerate the diffusion of both solar and wind energy technologies, of which US$10 million was devoted to solar.

The GEF initially wanted to develop a large utility-scale solar project to capture economies of scale in manufacturing and drive down costs. However, the World Bank's pre-investment studies revealed that such projects were still uneconomic and that India's electricity sector did not yet make provisions for private power generation. Instead, studies found that the most economically and financially viable applications of solar lay in the home lighting sector – for two- and four-light solar home systems, as well as centralized solar stations for around 100 rural households.[16]

But given the inexperience of the World Bank with solar loans, the loan officer in charge did not want to define the solar market ahead of time. Thus the loan was deliberately called the 'PV Market Development Loan', rather than, for example, the 'Rural Solar Development Loan'. Nonetheless, this loan officer was clear about the intentions:

> The conception was that the rural market was where we would find the demand for PV technology and it was in this market that PV technology made the most sense. Solar home systems and solar lanterns, assuming a willingness to pay, were the viable applications.[17]

Moreover, the Bank's studies actually hit the nail on the head when it came to an effective strategy to support the diffusion of solar in rural markets. First, it was recognized that 'because PV systems are characterized by high capital yet low operating costs, financing is a key ingredient in making PV affordable'.[18] Second, the same study saw a need to support the development of a local market infrastructure for solar 'because the industry is still new, marketing networks and support systems for PV are lacking. There is a need to stimulate demand by promoting their availability.'[19] Similarly, the GEF appraisal document stated that 'the solar photovoltaic component has a high potential for replicability ... but it requires the building up of basic market infrastructure'.[20]

So the World Bank and GEF knew what had to be done – at least on paper. But in practice, the preparation of the solar component of the loan would be rushed, as it had to move in time with the waste-to-energy and wind components:

> People say to us that we did not take enough time in developing the PV line of credit. But if we had taken the required amount of time, there would have been no PV component. There would have been no project to attach it to, as the others would have gone through. This is the reality of the situation. We are not working in an ideal world.[21]

Ultimately, the project would not do enough to ensure that the line of credit actually flowed to rural customers. Nor would it incentivize and support entrepreneurs in the market. Basically the two pillars of solar diffusion – affordability through consumer finance and availability through a market infrastructure – would not be effectively established.

The first issue the solar component faced was that the implementing body in India – the Indian Renewable Energy Development Agency (IREDA) – was not particularly excited by the potential for solar in the rural markets. IREDA had been established by the Indian Government in 1987 'to give financial support to specific projects and schemes for generating energy through non-conventional and renewable materials and sources'.[22] More specifically, IREDA was established 'to take greater risks than the commercial banks would. [The commercial banks] simply did not know anything about this emerging technology. They didn't know the products, they didn't know whether there was a market.'[23]

So in theory, IREDA should have been the ideal implementing agency for the World Bank. In practice, though, two years after the loan was sanctioned, while both the small hydro and wind loans under the project were fully taken up, IREDA had not sanctioned any loans under the solar line of credit.[24] Moreover, when the money for solar eventually moved, it ended up going to commercial-scale projects which benefited from a tax incentive from the central government. Although this did not run counter to the intentions of the World Bank, the loan officer nonetheless expressed the view that 'we are still worried about the loan – we are not seeing it move into the rural sector'.[25]

Prior to the loan, a rather hard-hitting study commissioned by a Dutch aid agency found that 'IREDA has done little to help identify and develop sound renewable-energy projects and energy-efficiency projects that are relevant to rural development and the disadvantaged'.[26] As the managing director of IREDA himself later explained, the rural markets were not perceived to be that attractive for financing renewables like solar:

> You can do it, you can reach remote users. But to reach and then recover your money is another problem – the rural credit risk is very high. … Agricultural cooperatives, commercial banks and rural development banks cannot recover their loans for fertilizers, animals, tractors and so on. [Rural people] take all these loans but do not have sufficient income to repay them. We might call this the over-debt burden of the rural person. … This is a major realistic problem.[27]

Thus, from the project's outset, IREDA did not seek to identify, develop and lend to the more viable rural financial channels. Instead, it allowed the market to take its course. When after two years the solar component of the loan was still not moving, it was a foregone conclusion that IREDA would not expend extra effort to develop the rural markets, where the transactions were smaller and the effort required greater. As IREDA staff made clear in 1996 about the prospect of doing more to develop the rural markets, 'We cannot adopt this approach as we have to meet the set project terminal dates – the money from the World Bank lapses in 1998.'[28]

In addition to not being predisposed to on-lending World Bank funds into the rural solar markets, IREDA, and the project as a whole, was not particularly able to support entrepreneurs. A World Bank study midway through the project revealed that though 'there were projects that would lead to PV being placed in rural areas, such as lighting for tea plantations', there were 'none that lead to building rural-sector delivery mechanisms'.[29]

Bank staff *knew* that entrepreneurs would be key to developing these rural delivery mechanisms. As the Bank's loan officer said, 'It only takes an entrepreneur to settle in, to establish themselves and to work with the local people.'[30] But unfortunately, the way the loan had been structured meant that, in the end, the money could not be used by entrepreneurs for such essentials as investing in a market infrastructure. The World Bank and IREDA wanted to 'see' the transaction between supplier and customer, and thus mandated that the funds be used purely for consumer (and not supplier) finance.[31]

In hindsight, this was a major flaw in the project, and a significant learning point for World Bank staff. As the ASTAE adviser to the loan recognized midway through the project:

> The India loan was not well suited to businesses that are selling a product and are concerned about their working capital requirements and cash flows.[32]

Moreover, as we saw in the last chapter, the Indian entrepreneur faced a good deal of scepticism and paperwork when he approached IREDA directly for funds. A World Bank report prior to the loan had found IREDA's procedures were 'long and bureaucratic and that smaller organizations find them complicated and costly'.[33] This would play out in the case of the Indian entrepreneur. But because nothing had been done up-front to ensure that money would flow to start-up entrepreneurs, there was not much to be done – except wait:

> This is difficult, because while a big company has their own legal staff and can handle the documents that IREDA requires, [the Indian enterprise] is not prepared for these requirements. Consequently the loan [to the Indian enterprise] has taken time.[34]

In addition, the Indian entrepreneur's application struggled to meet IREDA's security requirements.[35] As a consultant to the World Bank project commented at the time, 'The borrowers have to be so credit-worthy that they should hardly need to go to IREDA in the first place.'[36] Indeed, the Dutch report mentioned earlier had recognized that 'the continued strict loan requirements tend to bias approvals towards the large-scale and better-established industrial applicants'.[37]

On paper, the Bank had actually put the onus on IREDA to 'offer at its discretion technical and marketing experts to their borrowers to help in product-quality improvement and to establish effective marketing and after-sales service networks'.[38] In practice, however, IREDA offered three entrepreneurial development programmes a year, and even according to its own staff, these were 'just an excuse for a free lunch'.[39]

And so it was that when push came to shove, and IREDA needed to move the solar loan component under the World Bank project, it targeted the commercial solar sector. Here profit-making businesses could avail themselves of Government tax benefits (then 100 per cent accelerated depreciation in the first year for owners of solar systems), as well as a low-interest loans under the World Bank line of credit.[40] Such projects entailed fairly large transactions to help move the money more quickly, and the target customers – corporations – could more easily meet IREDA's security and paperwork requirements.

In the end, the India loan resulted in the installation of 2.5 MW of solar, and IREDA was successful in moving the solar loan component on time. This was no small achievement – the equivalent of 50,000 smaller 50-watt solar systems – but the reality was that little if any of these new solar installations found their way into the huge, nascent rural market in India.

The central lesson Bank staff took away was that solar loans required much more preparation and up-front work – prior to the sanctioning of the loan – to ensure that lines of credit actually flowed to rural customers, and to encourage the entry and growth of entrepreneurs. Fortunately, with the establishment of ASTAE within the World Bank, there was now a mechanism for transferring these lessons to subsequent projects. As the ASTAE adviser commented midway through the India loan and prior to the launch of the Indonesia loan:

> There is a learning curve. We are all trying to learn how best to implement these projects. I have effectively served as a bridge between the India and the Indonesia loan.[41]

The Indonesia Loan (1997–2003)

Unlike the India loan, the push for solar in Indonesia did not come from the GEF to address climate change, but from the Indonesia country desk for rural electrification. The loan officer responsible for the World Bank's second rural electrification loan to Indonesia recognized that even after this loan, 30,000 villages in Indonesia would still be without electricity, and that a lot of these would not receive a connection for 20 to 30 years, if ever. To fill the gaps – what the loan officer described as 'the Swiss cheese effect' – a World Bank mission was sent out in 1995.

During the mission, the team was excited to find the Indonesian entrepreneur, and to discover that he had already, by this time, sold 4000 solar systems on company credit in the first year of operation. According to the World Bank's loan officer:

> At this time it was only [the entrepreneur] who was doing this seriously
> on a private basis. And even he was new to the business. … But after
> seeing his work, the project made sense.[42]

This relates back to our discussion in Chapter 2 of how there can be two-way
feedback between innovating entrepreneurs and policy. The initial success of
entrepreneurs in bringing a new technology to market can serve as an inspiration for policymakers to introduce new policies. These policies in turn feed
back to either nurture or inhibit the diffusion process.

Thus, with the entrepreneur serving as an example of what *could* be done,
the World Bank initiated a US$44.3 million Solar Home System Loan to
Indonesia to support the sale of 200,000 solar systems to rural unelectrified
homes in West Java, Lampung and South Sulawesi.[43] The geographic focus was
not by chance – the entrepreneur in Indonesia had already demonstrated a
clear market potential in most of these provinces. But between seeing the
example set by the entrepreneur and launching the project, World Bank staff
were compelled to spend a full two years preparing it.

This was a long time for a project of this size (relatively small by World
Bank terms), and so there were strong internal pressures on the Bank's loan
officer in charge to 'speed it up'. But the loan officer was clear that he did not
want it to end up like India:

> That is why the solar component of the [India] loan never took off. …
> They are only now awakening to the problems in meeting the require-
> ments of rural areas. … It is a question of pipeline filling and doing your
> homework. In India it was a question of the Bank rushing to get in, and
> then leaving. So it is vital that the Bank does its homework – only then
> can the loan be effective. That is precisely why it took us two years to
> prepare this loan.[44]

The first task was to find intermediaries in Indonesia who would be willing and
able to lend for solar in rural areas. The existing banks of Indonesia were
deemed to be inappropriate intermediaries at this time, as they only offered
short-term loans at high rates of interest for consumer durables. By contrast,
since the entrepreneur in Indonesia had been able to sell a considerable
number of solar systems on company credit, with four-year loans at commercial rates of interest and with seemingly good rates of recovery, Bank staff
decided to make the participating companies themselves the vehicle for delivering finance as well.

This meant investing considerable time in flushing out other businesses
that would also be willing to sell solar on credit. While some were new to the
market, they were selected on the basis that they already operated in related

markets, such as consumer electronics. To ensure that these new entrants could access finance to on-lend to rural solar customers, the World Bank invested heavily in their development. As the loan officer reports, 'This was heavy duty work for us! We literally brought the dealers to the stage and then rehearsed them for their performance in front of the banks.'[45] As recognized by the ASTAE adviser, this contrasted strongly with the India loan:

> In Indonesia it has taken a huge effort, and a huge amount of prepara-
> tory money and work, to get the dealers in place to apply for the loan. In
> India, we had neither the time nor the resources to develop this pipeline
> of borrowers.[46]

In addition, World Bank staff carefully selected four banks that demonstrated a willingness to invest in entrepreneurs entering the market. Unlike in India, the loans in Indonesia could be used to both finance customers' purchases of solar and develop a rural market infrastructure. As the loan officer recounted, in contrast to the India loan:

> In Indonesia, the provision of working capital by the Bank is made
> explicit. The Bank has designated itself in Indonesia as explicitly refi-
> nancing the working capital requirements of Indonesia's dealers.[47]

The four participating banks in Indonesia required security on such loans. However, unlike IREDA, where the security required was for 100 per cent of the value of the loan, in Indonesia the banks were seeking two-thirds collateral, plus one-third equity investment. Because this was still stringent, the World Bank also went to the extent of identifying 'private investors' to take the equity stake, while the remaining two-thirds was to be provided in the form of land, solar panels and, for the banks that agreed to this, accounts receivable on the balance sheet of participating firms.

But more than just preparation, the Bank staff involved with the Indonesia project introduced a significant *policy innovation*, not yet tested. In India the GEF grant was used to buy down the rate of interest to 2.5 per cent. The rationale was that it would then induce customers to take loans for solar. But as we saw, with little money finding its way to rural intermediaries in the first place, the impact of the interest reduction was muted. So in Indonesia, in line with the recognition that more needed to be done to support entrepreneurs in the market and their cash-flow positions, the GEF grant was to be passed *directly* to the firm that sold the solar system, on a basis of US$100 per system installed. It was then up to the entrepreneur to decide how much they retained and how much they passed on to the consumer. Moreover, to administer the grant, Bank staff innovated further. Instead of channelling the grant through a government department or agency, the project would set up an *independent* administering unit to disburse the grant, to uphold basic quality standards in products and after-sales service, and to ensure grants were claimed only for genuine installations.

The 'grant per unit installed' concept was a significant policy development, and it was bold. It was not intuitive that channelling the grant directly to a firm selling a solar system was the best way to use it. It also risked the perception that the World Bank was funding the interests of business, as opposed to the rural consumer. But Bank staff recognized that for any rural customer to receive the option of buying a solar system in the first place, there needed to be a strong market infrastructure in place, and the grant was a way to attract entrepreneurs to the sector and help them build this. Furthermore, it was reasoned that competition in the marketplace would force most of the grant per unit installed to be passed on over time.

At the outset of designing the project, there was only one entrepreneur in Indonesia dedicated to serving the rural market directly – the entrepreneur profiled in Chapter 5. Other solar companies in Indonesia were mainly engaged in serving small government tenders and projects. But by the end of 1996, with the incentive of the grant and working capital loans in place, 14 other firms had come forward to participate under the loan. Moreover, the Bank's loan officer reported that of these, eight had already received approval of working capital loans from the participating banks.

The promise of this project would, however, never be realized. Within days of the loan being signed by the Indonesian Government for 200,000 systems, the Asian crisis struck. With interest rates soaring to prop up the rupiah, the firms that had originally come forward could no longer afford to take their working capital loans. Furthermore, devaluation dramatically increased the local price of solar modules, which were imported and which made up roughly 50 per cent of the retail price of the system in the case of the entrepreneur in Indonesia. The entrepreneur subsequently folded, and the other solar companies, like many businesses in Indonesia, went into a form of hibernation.

It took years for businesses to regain their confidence to invest in Indonesia, both domestically and internationally. Few businesses or banks were now willing to take any rural credit risk in the prevailing market environment, marked by very high interest rates. The few small solar companies who started to sell again were still only willing to cater to the government tender markets, rather than take the risk of developing a market infrastructure and selling on credit terms.

Without either consumer finance or a market infrastructure in place, the World Bank's Indonesia loan languished. While under more favourable conditions, the Indonesia Solar Home System Project could have easily seen the sale of 10,000 solar systems in the first full year of operation, 1998, in that year it achieved only 200. Annual sales under the project would only ever increase to 4000 solar systems in 2003, prior to the Indonesian Government losing faith in the project and cancelling it. Overall, this high-potential project, which could have led to the diffusion of 200,000 solar systems over five years, delivered only 8500 systems by the end of 2003.

However, the hard-won battles within the World Bank to put the Indonesia loan in place would not have been fought in vain. Bank staff did not know it during the darker days of trying to revive the Indonesia project, but they had developed a winning template to help accelerate the diffusion of solar. The template was simple: lines of credit to support consumer finance and business development, a grant per unit installed to attract entrepreneurs to the market, and an independent administration office to safeguard the interests of the project and the solar consumer.

In parallel with the preparatory work in Indonesia, the entrepreneur in Sri Lanka had been lobbying for a World Bank programme in his country. In the same year, 1997, Sri Lanka would pick up where the loan in Indonesia left off.

The Sri Lanka Loan (1997–2002 and 2002–2007)

The same consultant who helped develop the Indonesia project also worked on the Sri Lankan one. He confirmed that the efforts expended by the loan officer on the Indonesia project greatly assisted the Sri Lanka project, not only by providing a template, but by making it easier to secure Board approval in the Bank.[48]

Like the Indonesia project, the Sri Lankan one incorporated a grant-per-unit-installed approach, and made available lines of credit for consumer finance. It also established an independent administering unit (AU), and used the technical standards from Indonesia, albeit slightly modified. The name of the project was the Energy Services Delivery Project (which included a loan of US$24.2 million and a GEF grant of US$5.9 million). Under this project, the World Bank set a target of 30,000 solar home systems to be installed between 1997 and 2002.

But cutting and pasting the template would not work in its entirety. The key problem proved to be that, unlike in Indonesia, the companies in Sri Lanka had already tried to finance their customers, and largely failed. One firm had tried to finance solar on a fee-for-service basis; another offered company credit. But they all found that it was too difficult, too time-consuming and too costly to manage collections from a dispersed rural customer base. They came to the conclusion that they couldn't manage both consumer finance and a market infrastructure to sell solar.[49] As one of the companies reported at the time: 'Building a rural service infrastructure with technicians is a very different business from building a rural credit delivery and collection infrastructure.' And as another said, 'Credit is not [the supplier's] business … it is the business of the microfinance institutions, and the success of credit depends on local connections, knowledge and institutions already in place.'[50]

Thankfully, the project in Sri Lanka had left room for banks to also borrow under the line of credit and pass it on to the consumers. But like the firms selling solar, the commercial banks in Sri Lanka shared the view that financing rural consumers for solar entailed too much in the way of transaction costs and risk. A common refrain from the banks was that because solar was not perceived to augment income, the customer may not have the means to pay for it. At long last one bank did come forward – the People's Bank, the bank with the largest number of rural outlets of any in Sri Lanka. But this bank was Government-owned, and the World Bank had effectively precluded the participation of such institutions, stating in the project document that: 'in order to become eligible to participate in the ESD Credit Program, and to maintain their eligibility, credit institutions must be privately owned and controlled'.[51]

Thus it is not surprising that half way through the project, World Bank staff were quite pessimistic. On 23 August 1999, the World Bank's 'Mid-term status review of the Energy Services Delivery Project' noted, in a rather dejected manner, that since 1997, when the project was launched, only 500 solar systems had been installed against a target of 30,000, and there were only two and a half years remaining. To explain these poor results, the report identified the lack of consumer finance for solar as the main barrier:

> While the project has a number of components, it is facing one major problem in implementation – serious lack of progress in the component that provides financing and grant assistance to permit unelectrified rural consumers to buy an SHS. The challenge to marketing such systems is that the cost of the system is high.[52]

The review went on to explain that participating companies are:

> reluctant to give credit to rural households – they consider repayment risk is too high. Commercial banks are also reluctant to give small consumer loans. They too consider these too risky and transaction costs too high. … Companies who do sell consumer durable goods for credit in rural areas also seem reluctant to enter into the SHS sales business.

So two and half years in, the solar project was going nowhere. The World Bank was in a fix. This would be the third solar project it had launched, and if it also failed, that would be three in a row. It needed a success story.

At this exact time, however, the tide was turning in favour of the project. The Sri Lankan entrepreneur profiled in Chapter 5 had already signed a tentative letter of intent with SEEDS by the middle of 1999. Moreover, with the grant per unit installed in place, Shell Solar decided to make an investment in Sri Lanka by September of that year, and quickly ramp up the business before the World Bank project ended. With this investment, the entrepreneur had the funds at hand to credibly demonstrate to SEEDS that they should get out of the business of selling solar, and focus just on financing it. And to finally seal the deal, and secure SEEDS entry, the entrepreneur agreed to share the grant available under the project with SEEDS. The grant per unit installed turned out to be the carrot not only that attracted Shell Solar's investment, but that encouraged SEEDS to focus on just financing solar going forward.

From 1997 until the end of 1999, the project delivered only 500 solar systems. But in 2000 alone, the project saw the sale and installation of 1891 systems, of which the new Shell Solar venture had an 80–90 per cent market share due to the rapid roll-out of its market infrastructure. And with the grant now in place and SEEDS now in the market, as we saw in Chapter 5, more competition entered. In 2001 the number of systems sold jumped to 10,742 (Figure 6.1).

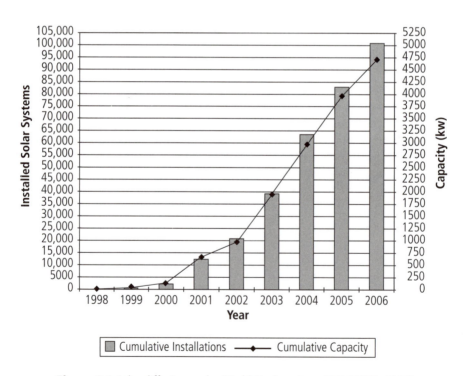

Figure 6.1 Solar diffusion under World Bank projects ESD (1997–2002) and RERED (2003–2007) in Sri Lanka

Source: Renewable Energy for Rural Economic Development Project (2007)

Because the Sri Lanka project got off to a slow start, it could not reach the original target of 30,000 solar systems sold by the end of 2002. But it did reach a figure of 20,953 systems, and because the annual sales had jumped from 1891 units in 2000, to 10,742 in 2001, the Sri Lankan Government and World Bank became convinced of the future potential, and started preparing for a follow-on project.

A key feature of the project, borrowed from the Indonesia template, was the establishment of an independent administering unit (AU) to roll out the project in Sri Lanka. During the darker days of 1998 and 1999, before the project took off, the AU was desperately trying to attract more companies and banks into the market. Once the project took off in 2000, its role as an administering body for the grant and a monitor of performance kicked in.

All product components had to meet the technical specifications laid down by the AU. All documentation relating to the installation of the system would have to be passed through the AU, prior to the participating company receiving their grant. And the AU would make unannounced spot-check visits of customers to discern if the customer did in fact buy a system, that the technical specifications had been adhered to, that the installation was of sufficiently high quality and that the customer was receiving adequate service.

Interestingly, World Bank staff had decided to place the AU within a private-sector bank – the DFCC Bank, a very professional establishment listed on the Colombo stock exchange. The beauty of placing it in a private-sector bank was that there could be total transparency in the use of funds. Moreover, because the World Bank was the contractor, they could demand and expect high levels of performance against agreed targets and deliverables. But what the World Bank could not have expected is that the AU itself would start to take on the role of championing solar within Sri Lanka, attracting the attention of the Government, and helping it to roll out a second, highly successful project.

The first signs of this role emerged in 2001, when, as discussed earlier, the Sri Lankan entrepreneur was successful in convincing the Uva Provincial Council to introduce an extra US$100 grant per unit installed. Eventually the AU and the entrepreneur would be successful in convincing the Government of Sri Lanka to roll out the grant to other equally poor provinces in the north and east, and ultimately countrywide. Moreover, the AU would end up taking on the role of disbursing this additional grant on behalf of the Sri Lankan Government.

Furthermore, the AU would play a key role in helping the World Bank secure rapid approval and support for a follow-on project in Sri Lanka – the Renewable Energy for Rural Economic Development (RERED) project. Having seen that the nascent solar industry could deliver 10,000 systems in one year, this project took on considerably greater ambitions – to ramp up sales of solar to a total of 100,000 by the end of 2007.

RERED retained the grant-per-unit-installed approach, albeit reduced to US$70.[53] With the continuity in the grant per unit installed, and the new additional grant for the northern and eastern provinces of US$100 per system, yet more solar businesses and banks entered the market after RERED was launched. With greater availability of both product and finance, system sales surged to 2085 units per month in 2004 (close to all the systems sold in 2001), and touched 3000 units in June 2004.[54] By the end of 2007, the project had encouraged the entry of a total of 14 firms selling solar and 4 banks financing solar, and the ambitious targets set by RERED had been exceeded: as of the end of 2007, RERED had encouraged 94,242 solar installations. When combined with ESD, this put the cumulative solar installations in Sri Lanka at 115,195 by the end of 2007.[55]

After two cases of projects not succeeding in ramping up rural diffusion of solar – in India and Indonesia – the World Bank finally had a case of success in Sri Lanka. But more than just having good results in Sri Lanka, the World Bank now had a formula which it could replicate in other countries.

Replicating – China

Even before the Sri Lankan project had turned the corner, the World Bank was starting to put in place its next project, in China. The same ASTAE adviser who had advised the earlier loans was advising the Renewable Energy Development Project (REDP) in China. Launched in 2000, this project would channel US$100 million as a line of credit and US$35 million as a GEF grant to support the sale of roughly 350,000 solar systems (as well as solar/wind hybrid systems) for a total of 10 MW. The World Bank was now aiming for higher targets and larger scale.

Before the Bank entered China, there was already an active market for smaller systems, of two or three lights, most often paid for on a cash basis. Very often these systems were plug and play, and mobile. It was already very much like buying a consumer durable product – sometimes they even had the appliance, such as a radio, integrated into the solar product itself. They were particularly popular in the western parts of China, where many people led a semi-nomadic lifestyle and needed to be able to carry their systems up the mountains with their herd of sheep or goats each spring and back down into the valleys in the winter.

When the Bank first began preparing the project, the market for these systems was small. In 1997, for instance, annual sales were estimated to be only 10,000 units per annum.[56] This was a lot more units than in Sri Lanka, admittedly, but relative to China's population, it was still a small market. The aim of the World Bank project was to rapidly scale it up.

Bank staff originally hoped they could prime the solar market with consumer finance. But without a strong history of consumer finance in rural

China, it was decided during the course of the project to focus just on using the grant. Here again, Bank staff innovated. In China they gave the grant on a US$-per-watt basis to enable the customer to effectively choose whichever product size they wanted. Specifically the Bank offered US$1.5 per watt for any system above 10 watts – thus a firm that sold a 25-watt system would receive a grant of roughly US$37.

As in Sri Lanka, the grant was administered by an independent office, which also set and monitored standards of quality. Indeed a large component of the project was dedicated to introducing the concept of product certifications, to improve the quality of manufactured PV panels in China, to improve testing facilities for PV modules and systems in China, and to train technicians in improved installation and maintenance of systems.[57]

The results in China were astounding, and demonstrate the power of a small grant to dramatically accelerate solar diffusion, even without consumer finance. By the end of 2006, the World Bank had essentially met the project target of 350,000 solar systems two years ahead of schedule: 342,000 systems had already been installed for a total of 7.8 MW. Moreover, prior to its completion on 30 June 2008, the project had crossed the milestone of 500,000 solar systems sold and installed, had attracted 28 different firms to the rural solar market, with active retail and distribution networks, and had created an annual market of 80,000–100,000 solar systems per year (Figure 6.2).[58]

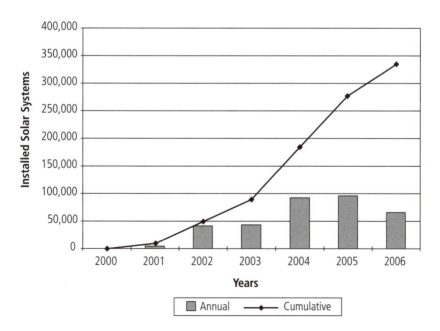

Figure 6.2 Solar diffusion under World Bank project REDP in China

Source: REDP China Office[59]

What is unique about this project is that in the absence of consumer finance, the average system size was much smaller. According to data provided by the REDP project office in China, the average size of each system sold under the project by the end of 2006 was just 23 watts – enough to power two CFL lights and a radio, for instance. But in an interesting development, between 2002 and 2007, the annual average system size increased from 20 watts to 45 watts. This suggests that even in the absence of consumer finance, once the market infrastructure develops, once products improve and once customers find the product attractive and believe in it, they are willing to buy larger systems on a cash basis.

Replicating – Bangladesh

With both China and Sri Lanka showing signs of success, the bank rolled out a 100,000 solar system project in Bangladesh in 2002. Here again, it applied the same template of putting in place a line of credit for customers, as well as a grant per system installed and an independent administering office – IDCOL. However, in Bangladesh there was a chance for the Bank to actually put the model it had envisaged in Indonesia to work. The two largest NGOs in the country – Grameen Bank and BRAC – had adopted the same model as the Indonesian entrepreneur: selling and financing solar under one roof.

As discussed in Chapter 4, in line with solar sales becoming a more commercial activity, NGOs such as Grameen Bank in Bangladesh decided to get into the business of selling solar. Grameen Shakti started in 1996, but with limited funds they could only offer their customers one-year finance, and sales remained low – 20 per month in 1997.[60] Their break would come later in that year, when they secured a line of credit from the International Finance Corporation (IFC) – the private wing of the World Bank – at attractive rates under the latter's 'Small to Medium-Scale Enterprise Programme'. With these funds they were able to offer the customer a slightly better package – either buy on a cash basis and receive a 4 per cent discount, or take one of the following two loan packages: an 85 per cent loan repaid over three years with a 12 per cent service charge or a 75 per cent loan repaid over two years with an 8 per cent service charge.[61] This new scheme had a large impact on sales: from 1997 to 1999, Grameen Shakti's cumulative sales jumped to 1500 systems (roughly 750 per annum), and by 2000 they were targeting 2000–2500 systems per annum.[62]

By 2001, Grameen Shakti was the undisputed leader in the solar market in Bangladesh, with 30 distribution and sales points and cumulative sales of more than 4000 systems. But others had also entered this promising market. An NGO of equal size – BRAC Foundation – had started selling solar, and was also running their operations like a business. Having the two largest NGOs in

Bangladesh now in the solar market was very promising. These organizations brought a huge network of 'branches' that they used to disburse loans and other goods and services from, a huge client database, and a strong competence in managing microfinance.[63] The stage was set in Bangladesh for a dramatic increase in solar diffusion once the World Bank entered.

With the World Bank line of credit in place, Grameen Shakti and BRAC could extended their loans up to three years, with a 'service fee' (as per local custom, interest rates are termed 'service fees') that varied with the duration. If a customer took a three-year loan, for example, the down payment was typically 15 per cent and the service fee typically 12 per cent. Moreover, with the grant per unit installed, the project attracted a host of new players. By 2007, there were more than 15 different entities – mainly NGOs operating like businesses – participating in the Bangladesh solar market.[64]

From annual sales of just 5000 systems when the project was launched in 2002, the market in Bangladesh would ramp up to 37,151 systems per annum by 2006. Of this, Grameen Shakti had 62 per cent market share, and BRAC Foundation 22 per cent. A combined total of 84 per cent market share is not surprising if you consider the strength of these entities' market infrastructure and finance in rural Bangladesh. Today it is estimated that Grameen Shakti has 292 branches selling and financing solar under one roof, and BRAC Foundation has 260.

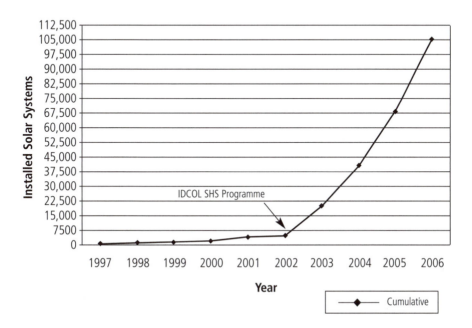

Figure 6.3 Solar diffusion under World Bank project IDCOL SHS in Bangladesh

Source: IDCOL (2007), p3

The original target for the World Bank project when it began in 2002 was 50,000 solar systems over five years. But the project met its target by September 2005, almost three years ahead of schedule and US$2 million under budget. And given the momentum, other donors were encouraged to enter. German aid agencies KFW and GTZ both contributed to the project, helping to extend its run of success.

With these new sources of funding in hand, IDCOL – the agency administering the project – set a new target of a total of 200,000 solar systems by the end of 2009. Again this target was met ahead of schedule: as of May 2008, 211,000 systems had been installed, equivalent to more than 11 MW of solar installations, and 1 million users are now receiving electricity thanks to solar. Today there are more than 16 different NGOs and firms active in the market, and IDCOL has set a new ambitious target of 1 million solar systems by 2012.[65]

A Contrasting Experience in the IFC

As we can see from the early history of World Bank lending for solar, there was an ability within the Bank to learn from early mistakes, adapt, find a successful formula, ramp up solar diffusion and then replicate. Indeed, in Asia, the World Bank would go on to replicate further in the Philippines.[66] And once the pressure came down from the G8 to do more in Africa, the World Bank replicated in Uganda (Energy for Rural Transformation) and Tanzania (Energizing Rural Transformation), the former envisaging the sale of 90,000 solar systems (6.3 MWp) and the latter 140,000 solar systems (9 MWp).[67] Essentially, the World Bank would stick to its formula of lines of credit for finance, a grant per system installed and an independent agency to monitor, albeit with some variation and innovation along the way.

But not all parts of the World Bank were able to demonstrate the same degree of learning in support of solar. The private wing of the World Bank – the IFC – should have been the ideal body to drive solar diffusion. In theory, because it could lend directly to entrepreneurs and businesses, it was better suited to move more quickly than the country desks in the World Bank. After all, country-level programmes took two to three years to develop, and then once it was on the ground they generally took two to three years to have a meaningful impact on solar diffusion. Moreover, because the IFC was the private wing of the bank, it should have been even better able to understand and address the barriers that entrepreneurs were facing in the market. But interestingly, the IFC proved not to be as successful as the core operations of the World Bank.

During the mid 1990s, a host of programmes were launched within the IFC that supported solar. Some of them had solar diffusion as their core mandate, such as the Photovoltaic Market Transformation Initiative (PVMTI) and the Solar Development Group (SDG). Others incorporated solar among other renewable energy and clean-tech innovations to be supported – the Renewable Energy and Energy Efficiency Fund (REEF) and the Small to Medium-Scale Enterprises (SME) fund. Essentially, in one way or another, they were all debt and equity funds that could support solar entrepreneurs.

Given that many of the early entrepreneurs in the solar market lacked capital to invest in growing their businesses, these programmes held out great promise when they were introduced in the late 1990s. Indeed, in one or two cases, such as the loan to Grameen Shakti, we can see the IFC fulfilling this potential and seeding a local solar market. But largely, these IFC programmes exacted terms that were not in line with the still nascent development of the rural solar markets and the entrepreneurs' stage of growth. The IFC would prove less flexible than the World Bank's country desks to adapt to those realities. Instead it would hold firm to its position that the rural solar markets should develop along more 'commercial' lines, and the funds would by and large not meet their objectives.

The REEF and the SME fund

In the late 1990s, the IFC established the REEF to offer both equity and debt financing to commercial enterprises for a range of renewables, both on and off grid. By November 2001, US$65 million of equity plus debt had been placed with the REEF. Of this, the IFC stipulated that 20–30 per cent should be invested in the off-grid sector, of which 20 per cent should be in deals under US$5 million, and that no proposal would be too small to finance. In the rural solar sector, the REEF's investments were intended to reach businesses who wanted 'to expand their businesses' and support 'consumer financing schemes'.[68]

Because many investments in the off-grid sector, which included solar, would be of US$1 million or less, and because the returns would be low – not above 10 per cent[69] – the GEF approved the allocation of US$30 million. This was to enable the REEF 'to consider opportunities that are not receiving attention from international investment funds, such as smaller or more complex, leading-edge projects with proportionally higher transaction costs'. Even with these funds in place, however, it was felt that the returns on solar loans might not even cover the transaction costs of negotiating the investments.[70] The cost structure of the REEF was too heavy for the rural solar markets, and it generally failed to deliver its objectives before it was closed in 2003.

By contrast, the IFC's SME facility had more success in finding solar investments. This fund also used GEF funds – US$20.8 million was provided as debt and equity to the companies. By 2000, the SME facility had invested roughly US$1.6 million in solar companies as debt, equity and even partial guarantee (for banks). The three transactions that made up this amount were with the American entrepreneur's firm in Vietnam, Grameen Shakti in Bangladesh and the fee-for-service business in Central America (as profiled in Chapter 4). But of these businesses, only Grameen Shakti would have a sustainable impact, and here, as we have seen, it was a small loan. It was not sizeable enough to have the same impact as the line of credit and grant the World Bank later put into the country.

The PVMTI

The PVMTI began its life as a GEF initiative designed to operate much like the US Environmental Protection Agency's awards to US companies that successfully developed more energy-efficient appliances. The GEF sought to provide grants directly to businesses that developed new delivery channels to reach solar customers, and dramatically reduced the cost of manufacturing solar modules. It was an innovative and bold proposal, and the GEF allocated a grant US$30 million to the PVMTI, to be managed by the IFC.

But the IFC did not like the idea of handing out grants of this size directly to businesses. So somewhere during the process, it was converted from being a full grant-giving initiative to being an initiative that provided only 10 per cent grant to businesses as part of a total package of debt or equity loans. The objectives were now sounding far from 'transformational': 'to provide successful examples of sustainable and replicable business models that can be financed on a commercial basis'.[71]

The PVMTI selected three high-potential countries – India (US$15 million), Morocco (US$5 million) and Kenya (US$5 million). The remaining US$5 million presumably went to administration of the PVMTI facility over a 10-year period. In a way it was promising: the PVMTI intended the funds to be used not for manufacturing or large solar installations, but for extending sales, distribution and service networks, expanding the assembly of systems, and developing consumer finance packages. But the IFC's terms were too tough. The IFC wanted leverage of private capital against PVMTI funds to be 3 to 1 in India, 2 to 1 in Morocco and 1 to 1 in Kenya. That meant that an entrepreneur in India would have to put up $3 for every $1 that the PVMTI would offer. If we think about how little equity the early solar entrepreneurs had to offer, this simply was not realistic.

So not surprisingly, the PVMTI funds went to the bigger companies, which could put up more of their own equity capital. For example, in India, in the initial round of funding in 1999, the successful applications were a big finance house that raised $3.5 million as loan and grant from the PVMTI, an LPG company, and Shell Solar, which each realized $2.2 million as loan and (minimal) grant. It would take another four years for the entrepreneurs in India, profiled in Chapter 5, to raise just $1 million in loan and grants.

By 2008, PVMTI investments targeted 11.5 MW in India, 3.1 MW in Morocco and 1.75 in Kenya – a total of over 16 MW. But best estimates are that the Shell Solar investment led to 1 MW, and since the time the investment was made to the entrepreneurs in India, possibly another 1 MW has been added. All the other deals led to very little. This is a long way off the stated goal of 11.5 MW in India.

So why did the IFC not learn from the examples of Sri Lanka, China and Bangladesh? Once it saw that the PVMTI was not moving as quickly as hoped, why did it not convert the $30 million in GEF grant money to a $100 grant per system installed? This would have equated to 300,000 solar systems and, assuming an average of 50 watts per system, delivered 15 MW (essentially meeting the PVMTI's targets). Moreover, the grant per unit installed could have been reduced over time to deliver even more MWs of solar. Any company which could show an investor US$100 grant per system installed would have found it much easier to raise equity or debt capital in the private markets, instead of turning to the PVMTI for such funding. And as demonstrated by the entrepreneur in Sri Lanka, part of the grant could have also been used to leverage the interest of banks and microfinance partners to start offering solar loans to consumers.

Unfortunately, however, even as the PVMTI showed signs of underperforming, the IFC did not restructure it. This tendency to stick by its guns and seek more commercial terms would play out again in the case of the Solar Development Group (SDG).

The SDG

The SDG was spearheaded by several US foundations and was picked up on and supported by the then president of the World Bank, James Wolfensohn.[72] From the very beginning, the SDG was set up to provide support to entrepreneurs who were engaged in either selling or financing solar.

The support was to come in one of two ways, either through the Solar Development Foundation (SDF), which was established to provide grants, soft loans or both, and the Solar Development Corporation (SDC), which was established to provide equity and debt at commercial rates to more advanced solar businesses operating in the rural areas. The SDF was founded with about US$19 million as a non-profit foundation, and the SDC was established as a 10-year fund with US$28.75 million.[73]

The SDG was set up to operate as an independent, separate holding company, with a separate management structure. But in its day-to-day affairs, it received guidance from the IFC, some of whose staff sat on the board of the SDF and the SDC. Furthermore, the IFC also represented the interests of the GEF on the SDC.

By the end of 2003, the SDF had only disbursed about $2.5 million in deals for NGOs, manufacturers, distributors, financiers and retailers of solar across about 40 projects in 19 different emerging markets.[74] Although there was much hope that the SDC would find many entrepreneurs to invest in on commercial terms, the SDC would ultimately find *many* reasons why its original mandate to support solar entrepreneurs would not work out. It listed down its reasons in 2003: margins can be thin in rural markets relative to the effort to reach customers; operating costs are high, because the market is where the grid does not go; each sale is difficult, because it is a very large investment of a rural household's annual income; it is not easy for entrepreneurs in emerging markets to prepare their business plans and accounts in a way that meets the expectations of an international equity fund; owner-managed businesses in solar are poorly capitalized; it is difficult for the SDC to make a large invest-ment without taking a dominant stake; and small investments have high transaction costs.[75]

But in fact, a lot of the problem stemmed from the fact that the SDC sought returns that would have been in line with the IFC's requirements, but were not commensurate with the nature of the business. Several entrepreneurs complained that the SDCs expectations of 20 per cent returns per annum over a five-year period simply were not realistic. The SDC originally started off trying to make a few large investments in the market leaders, to secure the returns that it expected and to limit its transaction costs. But by 2003, it felt that a more appropriate approach, in line with the market, was to try to make more, smaller investments across a broader range of entrepreneurial compa-nies, using, as it described, a 'more flexible range of financial instruments'.[76] In the end, however, it would prove to be too late. Too much of its funds were expended in administration, and faith in its ability to deliver was lost. It was shortly wound down and dismantled.

Summary

The World Bank had a need for solar – to add to its portfolio of solutions for rural electrification and to help to respond to outside pressures for more lend-ing for renewables. With the advent of the GEF in the early 1990s, the World Bank also had the requisite grant funds to do more for solar in emerging markets.

But solar was not a natural fit for the World Bank. It was a small energy technology, decentralized in its application – totally different to the large-scale, centralized power plants it was used to funding. So it was clear that on day one the Bank would not have all the answers – it would have to stumble, grope and find its way towards the best means of supporting solar diffusion.

But to the World Bank's credit, it did just this. The establishment of ASTAE in 1993 was an important decision, as it established a centre of excellence concerning renewables, and solar in particular, that could assist the loan officers in the Bank and apply the learning from country to country. As we saw, the World Bank failed to reach the rural solar markets in India. But Bank staff learned from this experience that they needed to do a better job of supporting entrepreneurs in the market, and needed to take more time to prepare each loan.

Applying these lessons to Indonesia, the Bank set out to explicitly support entrepreneurs and new entrants to the market with working capital loans and with grants, so as to encourage their growth and success. They took their time to ensure that these players were all lined up, and pre-approved for funding. And they innovated with a grant-per-unit-installed approach that would prove to be a mainstay for future projects.

Although the World Bank was thwarted in Indonesia by the Asian crisis, a template had emerged that it would subsequently apply in several other Asian countries to dramatic effect – in Sri Lanka, China and Bangladesh. These three countries alone would, by mid 2008, be responsible for more than 800,000 new solar installations. It was a significant achievement.

Yet, whereas the country desks in the World Bank proved to be flexible and able to learn, the entity that should have in theory been best suited to the task of supporting solar entrepreneurs – the IFC – was less so. Despite the willingness of the GEF and others to provide grant funding direct to entrepreneurs as an incentive to scale up their businesses, the IFC sought to apply more commercial criteria than the entrepreneurs and the market were ready for. In contrast to the World Bank's successes in ramping up diffusion in rural solar markets, the IFC's impact would remain muted at best.

As we turn to the third and final part of the book, we will become more prescriptive and forward-looking in our approach. In what follows, I seek to apply the lessons learned from a review of the case studies in Part II to the challenge of how to further accelerate solar diffusion throughout the emerging markets.

Part III

Policy and Conclusions

7

Policy Guidance:
Seeing it Like an Entrepreneur

Policy has had a powerful impact on solar diffusion in emerging markets, not just by helping pioneering entrepreneurs sell more solar systems, but by attracting a host of new players and more resources to the market. But it was not all one way. Policy was often inspired and influenced by the entrepreneurs themselves. As discussed in Chapter 2, there was a two-way relationship between the actions of the entrepreneurs and the policies that emerged to support them.

In light of the power of policy, I use this chapter to prescriptively review and recommend which policies work and which do not in driving solar diffusion in emerging markets. The overarching message to all policymakers, whether international or national, is that to effectively ramp up solar diffusion, you need to be able to *see* the market like an entrepreneur.

We postulated in Chapter 3, and saw in practice in Part II, that there is not a demand issue for solar in unelectrified areas of emerging markets. Living without the grid and relying on inferior fossil-fuel substitutes, customers are very interested in the clean, convenient and less costly advantages of solar. The key is that someone needs to make the product and service available to them, and someone needs to make the product more affordable with finance. Once you arrive at this conclusion, the natural challenge for the policymaker becomes how to attract more entrepreneurs to the market and assist their growth so that they remain engaged and continue to service the customer demand. Again, to do this, a policymaker has to be able to see the market like an entrepreneur.

That is our general theme for Chapter 7. The specific policy prescriptions that flow from this theme and from our case studies are summarized below in a list of eight policy recommendations.

As we run through this list, we will refer back to the supporting evidence in earlier chapters. We will also bring in one or two new stories, such as the failed case of fee-for-service in South Africa. Such additional case material serves as an important point of contrast for the policies that we will go on to recommend.

Policy Recommendations

1   Do not create parallel government-driven markets
2   Make foreign direct investment and direct selling easy
3   Do not apply import duties and sales taxes
4   Deploy a grant per unit installed on a consistent basis
5   Facilitate lines of credit to rural finance institutions
6   If there is no rural finance, do not do fee-for-service
7   If there is no rural finance, target smaller system sales instead
8   Establish an independent agency and monitor

Do Not Create Parallel Government-Driven Markets

The first step in forming a positive policy framework for solar diffusion is to decide as a government that 'we will not set up our own parallel, tender-driven, subsidized market'. If a government can fully subsidize every household in its country, then there is no issue. As the solar system is virtually free, diffusion of solar will happen quickly, provided the government can build or tap into a market infrastructure.

But the fact is that most, if not all, emerging markets have neither the will nor the ability to pay for universal electrification with solar; nor do they have such a ready-made market infrastructure at their disposal. Instead they must rely on the purchasing power of their populations to buy a system, and private-sector capital to set up a market infrastructure to deliver it. Therefore policy needs to nurture this process, and not run against it.

We saw in Chapter 4, however, that countries such as India and the Philippines took a different approach. They sought to tender for solar systems, subsidize them heavily and even directly distribute them. The downside of this approach was that the private sector became complacent – sitting on the sidelines and selling into the more convenient, easier to influence tender markets. The companies were not in any way incentivized to go out and invest in and establish a market infrastructure to sell and service the customer, because, in the end, somebody else was doing that work for them – the government. Moreover, who could compete with the government's prices in the market anyway?

As the World Bank recognized at the outset of its loan to India, such policies conflict with creating a market for solar:

> Currently, PV systems are distributed through an [MNES] administered programme, where the sales are subsidized. Operating the [MNES]

demonstration programme in parallel with the market development programme will send conflicting signals to the market.[1]

If we consider the case of Gujurat, in northwest India, for example, the World Bank would seem to have had a point (Table 7.1). On the supply side, even if entrepreneurs were interested in serving the Gujurat market, they would not invest to sell solar at commercial prices of US$445 if the government agency could undercut them by selling at US$7.75. On the demand side, imagine that there was only enough money in the annual budget for 1000 households in Gujurat to receive a solar system priced at US$7.75: it is clear that the 1001st customer in Gujurat will not buy a system for $445 if all of their neighbours have been able to buy at $7.75. Instead that person, and the rest of the pending market, will simply wait until the next year's budget and buy then. This is not the way to arrive at a self-sustaining, accelerating mode of technology diffusion.

Table 7.1 Breakdown of cost sharing for solar system in Gujarat, India

Total cost of SHS	Central govt subsidy	Nodal agency subsidy	Total subsidy	Consumer payment
US$445.39	US$174.28	US$263.36	US$437.64	US$7.75

Source: Shah et al (1993), p207

Returning to the entrepreneurs in India, the main reason they could gain a foothold in the market was because Karnataka was not running a heavily subsidized programme like the other states. As an MNES official noted about the entry of the entrepreneurs in Karnataka:

> In states where there is a strong state network, it will be difficult for [the enterprise] to initiate its schemes. ... The only reason that the entrepreneur was able to set up in Karnataka and convince customers to buy from him was because the nodal agency there had taken the decision not to start selling solar home systems directly themselves into the rural market.[2]

The head of the Karnataka nodal agency was seen as something of a renegade at the time. He had taken a deliberate decision not to go with a heavily subsidized government programme: 'Right from the beginning it was decided that we do not believe in subsidies. We were the first to approach the MNES and force them to remove subsidies on solar hot-water heaters.'[3] His rationale was that under a subsidized distribution programme, both manufacturers and users 'become complacent, resulting in pervasive inefficiency'. In the case of solar hot-water heaters, once the subsidy was removed he found that 'manufacturers now had an incentive to improve the quality of the systems'. Moreover, he notes that without a subsidized distribution programme, there was no government competition to the entrepreneurs: 'There are no offices, no ventures, so for [the enterprise] there is no competition from us.' And by way of conclusion he said, 'You cannot have parallel markets – that is why [the Indian entrepreneur] has been successful in this state. It was left open for him.'

If we compare the results of Karnataka with the MNES schemes that have operated throughout the country, we see that the head of the nodal agency in Karnataka was right to hold back. The MNES programmes have been running for roughly 20 years, across all the states of India. As of the end of March 2007, the MNES recorded a total nationwide result of 313,859 solar 'home lighting' systems.[4] If we break that down across 26 states and over 20 years, that implies only 600 systems sold per state per annum. Now compare these results with private-sector sales from just one state in India – Karnataka. As of the end of 2007, an estimated 100,000 systems had been sold by private-sector entities in 11 years – an implied rate of 9000 systems per state per annum, or roughly 15 times faster than the Government's parallel market.

Based on the strength of these results, we must conclude that governments will always do better to get out of the way of entrepreneurs and let them directly serve the rural solar markets. Once it is accepted that the aim is to foster and nurture private-sector entrepreneurs in these markets, rather than do it through government channels, then the next step is to facilitate the flow of a lot of capital to these ventures.

Make Foreign Direct Investment and Direct Selling Easy

As we saw in Part II, many of the early entrepreneurs either came from abroad or were accessing capital from abroad. If we look at the impact that foreign capital had on diffusion in India, Indonesia and Sri Lanka, it is clear that a government should not be afraid of foreign investment, but should rather embrace it.

The first step for some emerging markets would be to enable 100 per cent foreign ownership of local solar companies. Policymakers need not be concerned that solar companies without foreign investment cannot compete. For example, as we saw in Chapter 5, Shell Solar acquired a local solar firm in Sri Lanka and owned it 100 per cent. Immediately following the acquisition, Shell Solar's market share was as high as 90 per cent. But by 2006, the local competition in Sri Lanka had eroded Shell Solar's market share to less than 30 per cent, and in that same year the company exited the market.

We also saw in Chapter 5 how delays in arranging for foreign ownership of the Indian firm delayed the inward remittance of essential capital and diffusion. By contrast, in Sri Lanka, the Board of Investments (BOI) gave swift approval for the acquisition of the local solar company. The only criterion was that a certain amount of money needed to be invested as equity into the company over a certain amount of time. Because the transaction happened smoothly and quickly, the entrepreneur in Sri Lanka could start to build the market infrastructure weeks after the deal was signed. This, in turn, would assist in closing the deal with SEEDS and setting in motion a rapid increase in solar diffusion.

But it is not enough to enable 100 per cent foreign ownership if foreign retailing in the country is prohibited. This is often known as a 'retail law', designed to ensure that local dealers are involved in the retail process.[5] The motivation is clear and understandable – a government wants local retail outlets to have a cut of the value chain. But the problem is that by applying it to the solar sector, a policymaker has inadvertently stopped foreign capital from more fully flowing into the growth of a local market infrastructure for solar.

It is not that using dealers, instead of selling directly, cannot eventually work. But it is better to leave this to individual entrepreneurs and companies to decide, rather than mandating it. First of all, identifying dealers to enter a market that hardly exists yet is not straightforward. We saw in the case of Sri Lanka that Singer's dealers simply were not willing to devote time and money to building the solar market early in its development, because they did not yet believe in it. Moreover, many smaller, local dealers in rural areas will not have the working capital to finance the heavy inventory and receivables that will accumulate, especially when solar sales start to grow.

To create a solar market in unelectrified areas of a country, where none exists today, is obviously not easy. We saw that in Chapter 5. The priority for a policymaker needs to be attracting entrepreneurs to this difficult sector, and enabling them to quickly put capital to work to serve the people. Whether the salespeople and technicians work for a local dealer or for a foreign company should be an issue of lesser significance to policymakers.

Having arranged for capital to flow easily to the solar market, policymakers then need to think about how to make the rural solar markets more attractive to investors. The first step in doing this is to avoid taxing solar with import duties and sales taxes.

Do Not Apply Import Duties and Sales Taxes

Today many emerging markets levy both import duties and sales taxes on solar. Even more counterproductive is that they tax solar while subsidizing kerosene. This occurs in many emerging markets, because kerosene is a staple for cooking. But as we saw, kerosene is also used for lighting. If a policymaker's objective is to ensure that more people have access to high-quality lighting, and it is politically impossible to remove subsidies for kerosene, then at the very least, solar should not be taxed.

Import duties and sales taxes have the same effect – they raise the cost of solar compared to the alternatives. Although in theory an entrepreneur can always pass on these taxes to the customer, in practice entrepreneurs, such as the Indian entrepreneur, may not feel they are able to do so, and their margins will become unduly squeezed.

In Indonesia, the entrepreneur was able to work with very low import duties. Indonesian officials were clear that while they desired in-country manufacturing of solar, they were not prepared to tax the solar module with an import duty:

> We have been proposing a reduction in the tariff since 1991. So far we have managed to have it reduced from 5 per cent to 0 per cent on the cell and from 15 per cent to 5 per cent on the module. We are still pushing for 0 per cent on the panel.[6]

Partly as a result of his component selection, and partly as a result of facing lower duties, the Indonesian entrepreneur's margins were 30 per cent, and his system price was 15–20 per cent lower than that of the entrepreneurs in India, for example.

In Sri Lanka as well, with BOI permission, the Sri Lankan entrepreneur was able to import solar systems on a duty-free basis for a prescribed period of time. Here the entrepreneur's margins were also more than 30 per cent. But as we saw in Chapter 5, the entrepreneurs in India struggled with higher import duties. Because the Indian entrepreneur felt restricted in how high he could price the product, he was operating with just 10–12 per cent margins. Let us look a little more closely at this example in India, because it is instructive on why import duties should be brought down.

When solar photovoltaic technology was singled out by the Indian Government for support in the 1970s, India already possessed a strong science and technology base, which allowed for its indigenous manufacture. But, in reality there was no other option but to manufacture PV in-country:

> At this time, the general policy throughout all sectors was one of indigenous development. If you wanted a wristwatch, you didn't buy it from Switzerland, you made it yourself. This was the kind of era into which PV was introduced.[7]

In the early 1970s, an indigenous public-sector electronics firm was put in charge of developing solar cell technology in India, but found that they lacked the necessary experience. To remedy the situation, the Government established a small laboratory in 1976, and by 1980, solar cells were being manufactured in India. In 1985, two more manufacturers joined the PV market, one which produced semiconductors and 'wanted a piece of the Government projects' and the other a further public-sector electronics manufacturer.[8] To nurture this fledgling industry, the Government established procurement programmes, both inside the MNES and in other ministries – such as the railways ministry – and it put up import duties to protect the industry from outside competition.

Even after economic liberalization in India in 1991, the duty on solar PV modules was 110 per cent, unless a user certificate was received from the MNES, which would allow for duties of 69 per cent on modules and 80 per cent on complete systems.[9] By 1996, when the entrepreneurs were trying to grow their sales in India, the duties had come down. But they were still high by international standards, at 30 per cent. Whereas international prices for solar modules were US$4–4.5 per watt in 1996, the entrepreneurs were paying US$6.9 (at the 1996 rupee rate). And just as damaging were the duties on batteries – the entrepreneurs in India were paying US$129 for deeper-cycle batteries well suited to solar, while international prices were roughly half this amount. By 2005, the duties in India on solar modules had come down to zero under a more enlightened approach. Had the entrepreneurs been able to bene-fit from this policy then, their margins and cash position would have improved dramatically, and consequently so would have their early efforts to diffuse solar.[10]

In addition to import duties, governments have tended to directly tax solar with sales taxes. This is because solar gets caught up in a government's more macro-level policies on tax. But the net effect is the same as a duty: it raises the cost of solar to the consumer and, if an entrepreneur feels they cannot pass on this cost, it reduces the entrepreneur's margin.

For example, between 1999 and 2002, the Government in Sri Lanka charged a defence levy (to finance the war in the north) and general sales tax that resulted in roughly an additional US$45–50 per 50-watt system. In the end, because there was a grant of US$100–120 per system in Sri Lanka under the first World Bank programme at the time, such taxes did not have a major impact on entrepreneurs' margins. But, first of all it seems slightly odd to give a grant only to tax back 50 per cent of it. Second, without such a grant in place, such taxes run the risk of squeezing entrepreneurs' margins if they cannot pass them on to the consumer.

It may seem strange for policymakers to be worried about the margin entrepreneurs earn on a solar system. But in order to attract entrepreneurs to this segment, for them to build a market infrastructure and for them to endure, policymakers will need to concern themselves with this fundamental issue. Of course, what a healthy margin is will depend on the operating costs in the country, and so will vary. But a margin of 30 per cent (including all direct sales costs but not including overheads) is a number to keep in mind. Below that it's not clear that entrepreneurs will be interested in the market or, having invested, be able to sustain the investment in the market infrastructure required for diffusion to accelerate.

The added virtue of eliminating all taxes and duties on solar is that entrepreneurs may be able to earn a better margin, and customers receive a better price, without policymakers offering further grants. That said, our case studies in Part II revealed how powerful a grant per unit installed can be.

Deploy a Grant per Unit Installed on a Consistent Basis

Most, if not all, rural electrification programmes around the world have been funded through subsidies, often cross-subsidies from segments of the population who pay a bit more for electricity than rural inhabitants. The rationale for having to subsidize is quite clear, as World Bank studies have recognized:

> This is because rural settlements are among the most expensive to serve by traditional grid extension, often containing the smallest individual loads, and customers are least able to pay – low projected sales and high expected costs make for poor business prospects.[11]

The same logic applies to the sale of solar in rural areas of emerging markets: selling solar in remote places, where customers are often dispersed and have limited purchasing power, is not intuitively an ideal place for an entrepreneur to earn a return. As we have seen, to sell solar in this environment, entrepreneurs will need to invest in training staff, establishing networks of salespeople and technicians, vehicles, mobile phones, and so on. The only reason significant capital will flow to this sector is if entrepreneurs can show that it is possible to earn a return on investment by doing so. Subsidies need to be designed to fundamentally convince entrepreneurs that there is an attractive opportunity in investing in, developing and remaining in this market.

A grant per unit installed, channelled directly to entrepreneurs, provides an excellent incentive. By improving the margins that a firm can earn on each solar system, this grant not only makes it more attractive for entrepreneurs to enter the rural solar market and develop the market infrastructure more quickly, but it enables them to do so with a better overall profit and cash position; thereby ensuring some degree of financial sustainability. We have seen in the case of Sri Lanka how it provided an incentive for the eventual entry of 14 different firms, all actively selling solar and driving diffusion. Equally, we saw in the case of Bangladesh how it led to the entry of 16 NGOs and firms, which, in addition to selling solar, were driving diffusion even faster by offering in-house finance.

As discussed in Chapter 6, the idea for a grant per unit installed came from within the World Bank when preparing the Indonesia loan. It was not intuitive, because many, not least within the World Bank itself, would have described it as a 'sop' to business. Indeed, we saw, for example, how the IFC was not in favour of disbursing GEF grants directly to entrepreneurs – and this stance is largely why programmes like the PVMTI and SDG did not have the same impact as the World Bank's country-level programmes. But it was not only the correct policy innovation, it was also bold, because it would have faced resistance.

How the grant works is straightforward. It is channelled directly to the firm that invoices the final customer, with no mandates for how much is passed on. It is up to the firm to decide whether to use the grant to reduce the price or to strengthen its margins, but, by and large, over time the grant will get passed on simply because there will be more and more competition in the sector.

In terms of the amount of subsidy that has tended to be deployed under this approach, experience suggests that an effective starting point is roughly 20 per cent of the system price. For instance, under the first World Bank programme in Sri Lanka (the ESD project), firms received a maximum grant of US$120 at a time when the average retail price for a 50-watt system with six lights was US$530 (after the grant). Firms were using the grant partly to reduce the price and partly to improve their margins. Later, as the grant declined, and as costs of some components went up, so the price went up. For instance, under the second World Bank project (RERED), the grant was reduced to US$70 and the retail price of the 50-watt system described above rose to US$650.

However, it is worth taking a minute to consider what happened under the second World Bank project in Sri Lanka, as it shows the dangers of *discontinuity* in the grant-per-unit-installed policy. Under the second loan, the World Bank mandated that from July 2004, the grant of US$70 would only be available for systems of 40-watts or less. And after 2006, it was envisaged that the grant would only be available for the smallest systems, of 10–20 watts. The rest of the systems would not be given any grant whatsoever.

Table 7.2 Grants based on size of solar system in Sri Lanka

Solar system capacity	Oct 2002–June 2004	July 2004–Dec 2005	2006–2007
10–20 Wp	$40	$40	$40
21–40 Wp	$70	$70	0
41–60 Wp	$70	0	0

Source: Finucane (2005), p8

Figure 7.1 Example of a small solar system (10 watts) installed in Sri Lanka

The overall objective of this policy was 'poverty alleviation'. The World Bank staff made it clear that the only way they could secure a second follow-on project was to demonstrate to the World Bank's Board that the second project would not only address solar diffusion, but poverty alleviation as well – by reaching poorer and poorer homes. As we will see, this confusion of objectives, to which we will return in Chapter 8, actually led to a distortion in the market-place that would not serve the interests of long-term solar diffusion.

As reported by a World Bank consultant to the project, the effect of this change in policy was to shift most sales to smaller solar systems:

> With the removal of the $70/Wp grant for systems larger than 40 [watts], the distribution of the products sold changed dramatically. Based on the available sales reports, sales of systems [of] 40 Wp capacity and smaller had taken, on a monthly basis, 78 per cent of the market by March 2005.

Before this shift in policy, sales of systems of 40 watts and less represented only 40 per cent. The consultant's study goes further to cite 'reports of the companies' sales staff that the higher-income-profile customers, who could have afforded a bigger system, were also shifting to the 40-watt capacity systems' (see Figure 7.1). This was subsequently bolstered by a detailed market research study, based on which the World Bank consultant concluded:

> In terms of household ownership of assets, income and expenditures, the results appear on balance to support a conclusion that better-off customers have migrated from the 50–60 Wp to the smaller 35–40 Wp systems.[12]

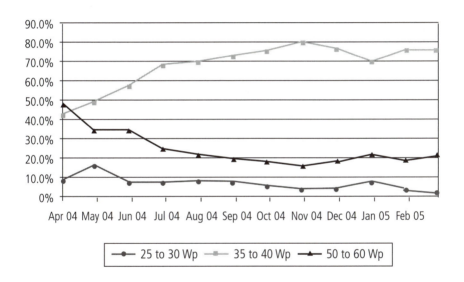

Figure 7.2 Size of solar systems installed in Sri Lanka over time, as a percentage of total market

Source: Finucane (2005), p9

This policy step would have unduly impacted the quality of the Sri Lankan customers' experience. Because customers were encouraged to buy smaller systems, they were buying systems that may not have fully met their needs. Many customers will not have understood that buying a 40-watt system with four lights, as opposed to 50- or 60-watt system with five or six lights, will mean that they cannot use much radio or TV in addition to their lighting needs. And this will have been problematic, as customers in Sri Lanka generally wanted to run all these loads on their systems. This policy measure therefore created a risk of customers overusing the system, widespread customer dissatisfaction and potentially negative referencing that would damage the interests of longer-term diffusion.

In addition, the fall-off in sales of solar systems of 40–60 watts (or more) from 50 per cent of the market to just 20 per cent would have seriously damaged the margins and earnings of all the solar companies active in the market. Smaller systems do not have the same overall margin associated with each sale. So a company must sell many more of these systems just to keep up. Furthermore, there were other factors in the market that would have resisted the necessary up-tick in sales, such as delays in processing by SEEDS and other banks, and the lack of availability of small modules in the global market at affordable prices. And so the net result would have simply been a reduction in earnings, with an overall impact on the strength and durability of the country's market infrastructure.

Moreover, with the impending removal of the grant for even 21–40-watt systems, things were going to get worse. The same World Bank consultant referred to earlier did an analysis of a firm's earnings on a 40-watt system and arrived at the results presented in Table 7.3.

Table 7.3 Estimated monthly profit of solar company in Sri Lanka with and without grant on a 40-watt system (US$)

	With grant	Without grant
Unit sales	350	350
Unit price (SLR47,000)	452	452
GEF grant	70	0
Sales, value	182,673	158,173
Cost of goods	138,796	138,796
Estimated gross margin	43,877	19,377
Operating costs	9784	9784
Operating profit	34,093	9593
Break even, units	78	177
Short-term finance costs	8750	7829
Depreciation	2083	2083
Long-term finance costs	2000	2000
Profit before taxes	21,260	−2319
Gross margin	**24%**	**12%**
Net profit on sales	**11.6%**	**−1.5%**

Source: Finucane (2005), p15[13]

Thus it was the consultant's conclusion that the RERED should continue with grants for systems up to 40 watts, and should even reverse the decision to eliminate subsidies for 60-watt systems. Instead of pegging the grant to a particular system size, the study recommended 'lowering the grant to $60 at the end of 2005, and then $40 at the end of 2006' on all systems, regardless of size.[14]

Thus, based on this experience in Sri Lanka, we should note that a key feature of the grant per unit installed is that it must remain *consistent* in its disbursement. Policymakers should avoid an overnight elimination of the grant based on, for instance, the size of the system. An alternative route is to instead gradually reduce the grant for *all* systems, bearing in mind that it might not be advisable to eliminate the grant entirely.

Unlike Indonesia or Sri Lanka, Bangladesh took the measure of *determining* how much of the grant would be passed on to the customer, and how much could be retained by the firm as an 'institutional development grant' to build capacity. Although it is by and large preferable for a business and the market to be left to decide on this matter, this aspect of the grant programme has not seemed to unduly diminish its success.

Moreover, because the Bangladesh programme envisaged the ultimate 'commercialization' of solar in the country, it has sought to eliminate the grant over time. But it has not done this by tying it to the size of the system for poverty alleviation reasons, or stopping it overnight. Rather, as Table 7.4 shows, it has sought to gradually reduce it in a phased and consistent manner over the process of selling and installing 200,000 systems.

Table 7.4 Gradual decline in grant under Bangladesh programme

Item	Total grant	Buy-down grant	Institutional development grant	Grant provider
First 20,000 systems	US$90	US$70	US$20	World Bank
Next 20,000 systems	US$70	US$55	US$15	World Bank
Next 30,000 systems	US$50	US$40	US$10	World Bank
Next 28,000 systems	€38	€30	€8	GTZ
Next 30,000 systems	€38	€30	€8	KfW
Next 35,000 systems	€36	€30	€6	KfW
Next 35,000 systems	€34	€30	€4	KfW

Source: IDCOL (2007)

This would seem to be more effective than the approach in Sri Lanka: in Sri Lanka, after the introduction of the new grant policy in 2004, annual sales started to drop off (Figure 7.2), while in Bangladesh they have simply continued to rise.

However, it is worth reflecting on whether solar diffusion will ultimately benefit from an elimination of the grant and *full* commercialization. In some ways this would be better, as it ends a dependence on the government and a lot

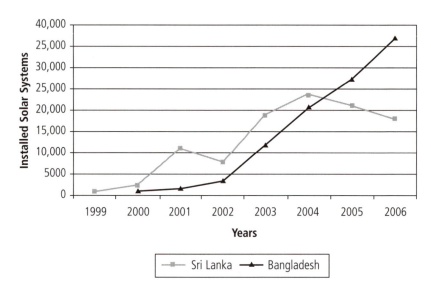

Figure 7.3 The adverse impact of policy decisions on diffusion in Sri Lanka compared to Bangladesh (annual installations)

of administration for a firm. But it is not clear that the rural solar market is yet able to take it.

There has been a lot of talk of so-called 'smart' subsidies, by which is meant subsidies that exist only for a limited programme duration and are self-eliminating. The idea is that, with volumes of transactions growing and with businesses becoming more efficient, prices will decline and grants can be gradually reduced.[15] But in the case of rural solar, it may be that after reaching the more accessible customers who can afford to buy, grants will still be required to reach the poorer, more remote segments of society. It is not clear that a grant can eventually be eliminated.[16]

Ultimately, there is a reason why more firms have not already invested more money into the rural solar sector of emerging markets. There is a perception that the costs are high and the rewards are low, relative to the risks and hassle. Recall what the general manager of a PV module manufacturer in India thought of serving the rural markets:

> The rural markets are dispersed – here the problem is 'How do I reach them?'. The reach is where the costs come in for us. You need many of these little, little, little centres, and then one needs to manage these centres, and they will grow and then there is the problem of how to orchestrate them. Suddenly, when you have one hundred of them, it becomes a difficult task. That is where the costs enter in.[17]

Although entrepreneurs with an all-consuming vision were willing to invest early in these markets, a government cannot dramatically accelerate solar diffusion on the back of pioneering entrepreneurs alone. It is critical to attract and retain a host of firms that are willing to sell solar in the rural markets. The grant per unit installed is a key policy tool for doing so.

In parallel with using a grant to attract and retain interest in the rural solar markets, a government needs to consider how to make the product more affordable. The key is to encourage finance institutions to start to offer loans to solar customers. Without some kind of consumer finance mechanism, those selling solar will struggle to sell in sufficient volumes and generate a sustainable business.

Facilitate Lines of Credit for Consumer Finance

All our case studies demonstrated the power of consumer finance to open up rural markets for solar. We saw from earlier chapters that although solar technology was already intrinsically competitive with the alternatives, 75 per cent of its lifetime costs are loaded up-front, and therefore consumer finance becomes critical to making it more affordable. The trick for the policymaker is how to make consumer finance for solar as prevalent and accessible as possible.

It is ideal if the rural banking sector can be encouraged to enter the sector. We saw in the case of the Syndicate Bank in India how powerful a role such institutions can play. That said, in other countries, the microfinance institutions (MFIs) – such as SEEDS in Sri Lanka – might be stronger and/or better suited to the task than the formal rural banking sector. But whether it is the banks or the MFIs, the virtue of bringing existing rural finance players into the market is that they will already have established networks of branches, field staff and procedures geared for doing rural lending. Having this infrastructure in place will make them better able to handle the surge in solar loans that will come, provided they have sufficient liquidity.

Very often banks or other finance institutions might be reluctant to enter the solar market. Certainly for many years this remained the case. For example, in Sri Lanka throughout the 1990s, the Sri Lankan entrepreneur was unable to encourage them to enter the market. The same applied to Indonesia, where the entrepreneur was also unable to convince the banks to enter. How then to encourage the rural banking sector to enter and start to lend for solar?

One way is with a default guarantee – for example a guarantee to cover a small percentage of the overall defaults that an institution incurs. The problems with this approach are that it tends to entail a lot of transaction costs (for example, paperwork and negotiation on a bank-to-bank basis) and it does not tend to put the risk where it belongs, with the finance institution deciding on the creditworthiness of the customer.[18] It is much easier to introduce a small grant per unit financed as a carrot to encourage entry of participating finance institutions, and then ask them to take the full credit risk – the latter can then decide if they want to set aside some of the grant to cover possible defaults, or instead invest it in the solar lending business.

In Bangladesh we saw how under the World Bank programme, IDCOL gives a grant for 'institutional development' only to those entities who are willing to finance solar. If the system is a 'cash' sale, then there is no grant for institutional development. It is not necessarily recommended to limit a grant in this way, but the point stands that offering a grant per customer financed is an attractive incentive that worked well in encouraging consumer finance in Bangladesh. This approach was also used by the entrepreneur in Sri Lanka, where he offered to share the grant per unit installed with SEEDS in the initial stages of growth – an offer that helped convince SEEDS to stop selling solar and fully focus on financing it on a larger-scale basis. And it is important to note that this amount need not be much. As we saw earlier in the chapter, in the case of Bangladesh, the grant started at US$20 per unit financed, and eventually will ramp down to just €4 per unit financed by the sale of the 200,000th system (over roughly five or six years).

Having encouraged the banks to enter, the trick for the policymaker is to ensure that the participating finance entities can access sufficient funds. The following is an example from the Philippines of why it is important to have sufficient funds in place.

In the Philippines it is estimated that 20 per cent of the unelectrified households spend US$6–7 per month (assuming $1 = 50 pesos) on energy for lighting and other electricity-consuming devices. These households are estimated to have an average annual income of roughly US$2000.[19] In this market, Shell Solar introduced a lower-cost 50-watt system, thanks to a grant from the Dutch Government – the price to the customer was roughly US$400. But it was not until rural banks and MFIs could be encouraged to enter that the project started to move. These entities offered loans to solar customers with a 15 per cent down payment, repayable over three years; which meant US$60 down and roughly US$11–12 per month. If we consider the estimated 22 per cent who spend US$8 per month on inferior services, this works out as a market size of 550,000 unelectrified households (of a total of 2.5 million). So not surprisingly, once these facilities were put in place, the monthly sales jumped from just 100 to 400 units over just two months.

The only problem in the case of the Philippines was that the rural banking network and MFIs were quite illiquid by international standards. As demand surged, there was a liquidity crunch that kept them from keeping up with the demand, and shortly thereafter, with key finance institutions running short on funds, the sales under the Shell Solar project fell back down again to 100–200 units per month.

Figure 7.4
Solar home
in remote valley
in the Philippines

Figure 7.5
Customer enjoying
his solar home
in the Philippines

Figure 7.6 Mother and child outside solar home in the Philippines

Figure 7.7 Solar light
in typical kitchen
in the Philippines

Figure 7.8
Solar-powered television in the Philippines

Therefore policymakers must put in place lines of credit that can be easily accessed by participating finance institutions so as to be able to sustain the surge in demand that will follow. Moreover, the rate of interest on the available funds must be low enough to enable the finance institution to earn a sufficient 'spread' between the rate at which they borrow the funds and the rate at which they on-lend them. The spread needs to be enough to cover all their cost of operations, their defaults and, if they are profit-making entities, their profit for shareholders.

Take the case of Bangladesh: as the administering entity, IDCOL offers a soft loan of 10-year maturity with a 2-year grace period at 6 per cent interest per annum to the participating finance institutions. IDCOL generally does not require collateral or security for the loan, except for a lien created on the project accounts. Until such time as the participating entity defaults on payment to IDCOL, they are authorized to operate the project account on their own. IDCOL will not, however, release the funds until it carries out an inspection of the system (not longer than 21 days from receipt of a disbursement request). Furthermore, the refinance amount will not exceed US$230 per system in local currency.[20]

In turn, the participating organizations will take the money lent to them and pass it on to the consumers. So again, in the case of Bangladesh, Grameen Shakti and BRAC Foundation offered customers loans for up to three years at 12–13 per cent interest. It is in the difference between the refinance amount of 6 per cent and the retail interest rate of, for example, 12–13 per cent that these finance organizations make their money.

In Sri Lanka, it was much the same process. The administering unit (AU) worked through the DFCC bank, which passed on funds at roughly 11–12 per cent. Participating finance entities such as SEEDS then on-lent the money at higher rates of roughly 24 per cent. With a healthy spread on its loans, and with sufficient funds in place under the World Bank's ESD and subsequent RERED projects, SEEDS was able to radically scale up their financing of solar between 1999 and the end of 2007, by which time they had lent for 69,599 solar systems.[21]

SEEDS then set an example to the rest of its industry. In 2004, SEEDS was executing 1200 solar loans per month on average, with 90 per cent market share. But then other finance institutions entered, such as Lanka Oryx Leasing Company (LOLC), Ceylinco Leasing, Alliance Finance and Sanasa. By 2005, SEEDS's market share had reduced to 50 per cent. But even then it was doing more solar loans per month than all the other finance institutions combined.

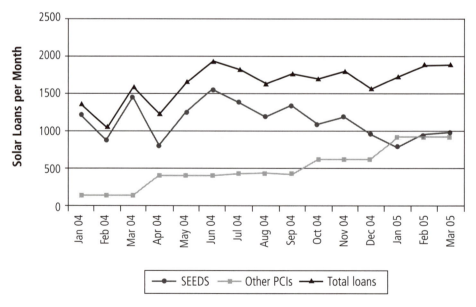

Figure 7.9 SEEDS concedes market share in Sri Lanka to other PCIs

Source: Finucane (2005), p19

It is important for policymakers to note, however, that if not executed well, lines of credit can get blocked. This comes down to the selection of the agency responsible for disbursing the funds and the criteria they adopt for disbursement. By and large, it is best if the agency is independent (for example not part of a government ministry or owned by the government), such as the DFCC Bank in Sri Lanka, which housed the AU. It is also important that a policymaker scrutinize and decide upon the criteria that will be used in assessing the participating finance institutions. If these are too rigid and conservative, they will limit the flow of funds and overall diffusion. As we saw in the case of the World Bank loan to India, because IREDA was not predisposed to lending to rural finance institutions for solar, and because their procedures and criteria were quite restrictive, the money never reached the rural markets. Instead it went to the commercial sector, which had a perceived lower risk of default and could better meet the paperwork and security requirements.

Having established a viable line of credit to participating finance institutions, how important is the rate of interest that customers bear? Should this be lower than the prevailing rates to incentivize diffusion?

The rates in Sri Lanka, at 24 per cent, were not low. They were even higher in the case of the Indonesian entrepreneur, at 30 per cent. But as the latter reasoned, it was possible to charge higher rates of interest provided the actual monthly amount the customer paid was no more than roughly US$10. To achieve this target figure, he offered his loans over a longer period of time (four years) than the existing rural banks in Indonesia were offering (just two years). The same was achieved by SEEDS, which initially offered their loans for five years. In both cases, with longer-tenure loans, we saw very high rates of diffusion. This is a key lesson for policymakers trying to encourage more finance for solar: do not focus on the interest rate, focus more on the duration of the loans. Finance institutions can charge a high rate of interest (to cover their costs and their risks) provided they can offer longer-term loans.

To further reinforce the message that high rates of interest do not necessarily restrict a rural solar market, we can point to a study from Kenya which found that the interest rate was more important to those who already had access to finance than to those who did not. Prospective customers who were part of a cooperative, and used to getting loans at 12 per cent, did not want to pay more than 12–14 per cent over two years for solar. Those in a very different setting, where there were no other formal credit routes, were willing to take on loans at 20 per cent over two years, which starts to approach the commercial rates in Kenya of 25–30 per cent.[22]

On the other hand, as discussed in Chapter 5, the case in India was rather different. In 2003 UNEP and the Government of India introduced a scheme whereby households in the state of Karnataka were able to buy a system at a reduced rate of interest, reduced from 12 per cent to just 5 per cent per annum, from two public-sector rural banks with extensive branch networks – Syndicate Bank and Canara Bank. This rate was subsequently gradually increased to 7 per cent, then to 9 per cent, and finally it returned to its original 12 per cent.

In this case, however, there was *already* a widespread network of rural banks engaged in financing solar at 11–12 per cent interest, and there were already several firms actively selling solar through this banking network. In this situation, it is not clear that reducing the interest rate had a terribly big effect on affordability. But it did have a psychological impact for the customer, giving the feeling of getting a better deal. Customers had already become familiar with offers from companies and participating finance institutions of 12 per cent – so when the opportunity came up to buy at 5 per cent, it created a stimulus that helped to accelerate diffusion, until, that is, the funds ran out.

So the conclusion must be that high rates of interest are not necessarily a deterrent, provided the duration of the loan is sufficiently long to compensate. And it is better to have high rates of interest than no finance at all for solar. That said, if there is an existing market for solar, and a well-established rate of interest that customers know, then a useful stimulus can be a low-interest loan scheme to excite demand. But it is important that, if such a stimulus is used, there be sufficient funds to sustain the scheme over a long period of time, for example 10 years, with interest rates gradually approaching market rates over that period.

Finally, what of those cases where no rural banking infrastructure exists? There are countries where the rural banking infrastructure is extremely weak, and where there just might not be any banking partners of MFIs to encourage to enter the market. Indeed, it is because some analysts have been faced with these situations – a total absence of rural lending – that they conclude:

> The prospects for consumer credit are very specific to cultural, legal and financial factors in each country. The Sri Lanka micro-credit model appears sustainable, but perhaps only because Sri Lanka has a strong and long-standing microfinance culture and set of institutions in rural areas, along with a well-developed commercial banking system.[23]

Given the strength and reach of the microfinance industry throughout the emerging markets, it is hard today to conceive of a country that does not have *any* rural finance in place. But, assuming it's simply not possible to use a grant and lines of credit to encourage the entry of any finance players into the rural solar market, what should a policymaker do?

In some countries, entrepreneurs and policymakers have tried what is called 'fee-for-service' as a way of financing solar and ensuring customers had access to an ongoing service. Fee-for-service describes a situation in which a business retains the solar system on its own balance sheet as an asset, and then installs it in the home of a rural customer, charges a monthly fee, provides free replacement of parts, and hopes that the customer will pay on time and that their asset will not disappear. It is essentially a 'rental' model. Because it was deemed to have so much potential when launched at the end of the 1990s, the following section takes some time to review why it has generally failed. Specifically, I refer to the high-profile example of South Africa to substantiate why it is better to avoid a fee-for-service model.

If There is No Rural Finance, Do Not Do Fee-for-Service

From a policymaker's point of view, fee-for-service can sound ideal. A customer can access a solar system for a fraction of the price they would otherwise pay. Instead of paying on a cash basis, or taking out a loan, a customer simply pays a monthly fee. This fee is intended to cover the cost of the solar system, as well as regular servicing and the replacement of essential components such as batteries and electronics. It seems an ideal customer offer, with the potential for high rates of diffusion. But in line with the theme of this book, the more worrying question is whether it can ever be successfully executed by entrepreneurs as a business model.

This gets back to our emphasis on agency in Chapter 2. It is not enough for solar to be made affordable and for service to be made available (fee-for-service will certainly do that): an entrepreneur must also be able to bring the capacities and resources together and deploy them in a profitable manner. If a strategy is so taxing that entrepreneurs and their businesses fail, then this leads to a delay in diffusion of the technology.

Various studies have found that, while a cash and credit set-up can serve up to 25 per cent of the rural unelectrified market, to get to 50 per cent you will need a fee-for-service approach (see Figure 7.10). For example, a study carried out in the Eastern Cape in South Africa found that very few people could afford the up-front costs of a PV system on a cash basis, but that roughly 50 per cent of the rural unelectrified population could afford 47 rand per month (US$7).[24]

Seemingly responding to such studies, the South African Government put in place a programme that charged the customer just US$25 at the time of installation and US$7 per month for as long as they used the system. All replacement costs – for example electronics and batteries – were to be included in the monthly service fee. If we compare this to the credit schemes we reviewed in Indonesia, for example, where customers paid $100 up-front and $12 per month for four years, we can imagine that fee-for-service would lay the foundations for a rapid diffusion of the technology. Moreover, in

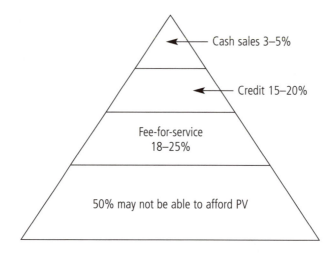

Figure 7.10 The theory behind fee-for-service

Source: Eckhart et al (2003), p12

Indonesia, and the other countries profiled, customers were responsible for paying for their own battery replacements outside of warranty. So clearly the South African Government's scheme was a pretty good deal for the customer, and should have led to rapid diffusion.

This proved to be the case – at least initially. Under the South African programme, an Eskom–Shell joint venture took only three months to sell and install 6000 solar systems in 1999 – a truly unprecedented rate of diffusion. But by 2004, when Eskom and Shell exited, the number of customers served still stood at only approximately 6000. Other companies had also commenced operations under this programme, but by the end of 2006, none of these companies had significantly exceeded a cumulative base of 10,000 systems installed (compare this to Grameen Shakti in Bangladesh, which exceeded cumulative sales of 120,000 solar systems by mid-2008).

On the surface, this shouldn't happen. If a customer is paying a much lower down payment and monthly amount for a solar system, as in the case of fee-for-service, solar sales should ramp up very quickly. But this was not an isolated instance of slower than expected sales under fee-for-service. In the Dominican Republic and Honduras, for example, one of the early pioneers profiled in Chapter 4 deployed a fee-for-service model requiring the customer to pay US$15–20 per month, depending on the size of the system. Under this programme, 1500 systems were installed in the Dominican Republic and 2000 systems were installed in Honduras over approximately four years.[25] But given that the aim was to quickly scale up to 25,000–50,000 households, diffusion was clearly moving slower than expected under the fee-for-service model.

Around the same time, a company in Morocco launched a similar fee-for-service business. Under the first scheme of its kind in Morocco, the company received exclusive rights from the Government to service customers in its designated territory using a fee-for-service approach. But after four years of doing business, the firm had reached only 4000 customers and was consumed with just trying to make an operation of this scale work – there was no commercial basis for increasing the number of installations beyond this level.

The American entrepreneur profiled in India also launched a subsidiary in Sri Lanka. Initially this firm had ambitions of doing fee-for-service, but after a trial run, the local team pulled the plug. Similar fee-for-service programmes in Cape Verde and Argentina, which the World Bank was at one point interested in supporting, also failed to take off. For example, in Argentina it seems that the number of systems installed between 1995 and 2002 under a fee-for-service programme was only 700 out of a total unelectrified market of 66,000 households.[26]

It has clearly been hard to make fee-for-service work, and the reason for this starts to emerge if we consider a few articles on the subject. For example, in an insightful article called PV 'power and profit?', it was questioned whether anyone doing fee-for-service in South Africa could ever make any money:

> The companies will need to keep a real presence alive in the rural communities, and of course manage revenue collection – all in remote areas, far from major centres, and with poor road and telecommunications infrastructure. The service must be delivered at a fee affordable to the poor, yet sufficient to generate adequate returns on investment for the investors.[27]

And an article on 'lessons learned' by the World Bank concluded about the entrepreneur's efforts in the Dominican republic and Honduras that 'the firm is attempting to scale up the business model to 25,000 systems, but recurring overhead costs and slim profits make the expansion difficult.'[28]

Similarly, the findings from Sri Lanka were that 'one firm tried to operate a [fee-for-service model] for a while, but found the costs of monthly collections among the highly dispersed and remote populations to be high', and so they stopped doing it. Specifically, the firm had offered 140 systems on a fee-for-service basis, but as the organizer of the scheme confirmed:

> Collection costs were eating up our entire profit margin. ... You need a strong fee collection system with good timing, otherwise customers will spend the money on something else, if your timing is off, and default. Or they will pay next month and ask us to wait, or cite poor performance. It's a continuing problem. Also, we found that if customers don't own the system, they won't take proper care of it and this increases our costs.[29]

When one steps back from it, the very idea of renting out high-cost equipment in difficult rural environments, and providing free replacement components for a monthly service fee, was a business model always bound to incur more costs. The 'cost' of running this business model is higher than selling on a cash basis, or even on a company credit basis. An entrepreneur will labour, and in most cases fold, due to six sets of costs that are higher under a fee-for-service model:

1 the cost of anti-theft, anti-tampering and meter-reading electronics;
2 the cost of theft of systems from customers' homes;
3 the cost of replacing components that customers tamper with or overuse;
4 the cost of regular follow-up to collect monthly dues;
5 the cost of churn, when customers stop paying and the system is removed; and
6 the cost of financing the higher capital needs of the business.

Many of these higher costs (points 1–5) come from the fact that what an entrepreneur is running is a *rental* model, where there is no ownership of the solar system by the customer in both a literal and metaphorical sense. Under a fee-for-service arrangement, a customer will have less incentive to prevent theft, or may even collude in theft; less incentive not to tamper with the system; less incentive not to overuse the system; and less incentive to make payment on time, or at all, because if the system is removed, the equity lost is less. Without customer ownership, it becomes a lot harder and more costly for an entrepreneur to manage the business.

Furthermore, point 6 above represents a large and fundamental cost. Any business that receives less cash from a customer up-front will have much larger capital requirements. In simple terms, if a business sold a 50-watt solar system outright to a customer, it might charge $600 as an installed price. In that $600 revenue would be enough to pay its suppliers, cover its operating costs and give a return to investors on their investment capital. But if the same company now only takes $25 up-front for the same system, that means that less than 5 per cent of the required revenue comes in on day one – the other 95 per cent needs to be financed.

As we have seen, it has not been easy for entrepreneurs to raise sufficient capital in the early stages of growth. This was the case even for the entrepreneurs in India and Sri Lanka, who took the decision not to finance the system themselves. Now consider that, in addition to financing the establishment of a market infrastructure, an entrepreneur must finance 95 per cent of the solar assets he or she is putting in the field, and you have a very capital-intensive business. That is not necessarily a problem if there is a good return to be made on the capital. But as we have seen, fee-for-service proves to be a more costly business model to run in practice. Therefore, the proposition to investors is doubly worse – more capital but lower returns – with the net result that entrepreneurs find it even harder to raise the capital and diffusion will be delayed.

Once a government gets involved in mandating and supporting a fee-for-service programme, such as in South Africa, it will find itself subsidizing these higher costs. And in the case of South Africa, which I consider in detail below, this higher subsidy led to delays, ambivalence and ultimately a distancing of the government from this showcase project.

South Africa case study: Fee-for-service

In February 1999, Nelson Mandela, then the President of South Africa, launched in the Eastern Cape what was proclaimed to be 'the world's largest commercial solar rural electrification project'. The aim was to reach 50,000 unelectrified homes with solar in the Eastern Cape in just three years. The implementing business was a joint venture between Eskom, the national utility, and Shell. In theory it was the ideal combination of a utility with strong clout and local market knowledge and a large corporation with solar module manufacturing, capital and strong management skills.

But Eskom and Shell were part of a much bigger Government initiative. As early as 1997, the Department of Minerals and Energy (DME) had identified a number of unserviced areas for off-grid electrification of 300,000 rural dwellings.[30] At this time roughly a third of the population – 15 million people – still had no access to electricity. The Government's target was to ensure that by 2010 it had achieved universal access to electricity, and solar took on a 'saviour-like status as the perfect solution for ensuring that electricity would be available in areas where the grid would not'.[31]

In January 1999, the Government put out a call for proposals, and six concessionaires were chosen to implement the off-grid solar programme. Each selected concessionaire would in theory have a 20-year concession, including a 5-year exclusive right to sell up to 50,000 solar home systems in their area. The chosen concessionaires included an impressive line-up of local and international players: the Eskom-Shell joint venture; Nuon RAPS, which combined a Dutch utility with a local South African company called Renewable Area Power Systems; Électricité de France (EDF) and Tenesa, a local module manufacturing company; Solar Vision, a local solar player supported by SolEnergy, a Norwegian module manufacturer; Renewable Energy Africa, a local solar company still looking for a partner; and BP, which later pulled out of the programme before it commenced.

All the ingredients for rapid diffusion were in place. The Government had succeeded in attracting big players for investment in a rural market infrastructure to deploy solar in remote areas, and it was putting in place significant subsidies to make systems affordable to the customer. The implementing firm was to receive R3500 per system (roughly US$500 at the time the project commenced) as a grant to cover the capital costs of the solar system, the rationale being that with the capital costs of the solar system largely paid for, the business could then survive on collecting a much lower monthly rental. The designated monthly rental was R58 (roughly US$7) – significantly lower than, for example, the unsubsidized programme in Honduras, where customers paid up to $20 per month. With strong private players, a low monthly fee and provisions for after-sales service, large-scale diffusion looked to be assured.

But the reality proved to be very different. By 2002, just over 7000 systems had been installed, including 6000 by Eskom-Shell prior to the official launch of the programme.[32] By 2004 this had gone up, but not significantly: to 19,000 solar systems. But questions were now being asked about the viability of the programme. In the *Johannesburg Business Day*, a headline read, 'Lights go out for off-grid energy projects'. And DME officials were now publicly backing away from the 300,000 target: 'We are no longer married to the number.'[33]

So what happened? Why did a project that was once the pride of the South African Government, deteriorate to such an extent?

There was, of course, a strong sense of needing to correct past injustices in South Africa, and solar was initially seen as a means of doing so when it came to rural electrification. As such, the Government tried to ensure all rural customers would be served as quickly as possible, and that all of them got the best deal possible. Although understandable, the Government was trying to shoot the moon.

First, to ensure that more homes received service more quickly, the Government took the step of carving the country into concessions. The idea was to give the private sector a monopoly to encourage it to enter and to invest heavily in serving the population. But inevitably, once the Government took this step, they had created a monopoly that needed to be regulated. And once it was regulated, it inevitably meant the project would become politically charged, with the private-sector operators and Government officials regularly butting heads throughout the process.

Second, because the Government was seeking the best deal possible for its people, it sought to control the prices and keep them low. As we saw, it set them considerably lower than, for instance, a private-sector fee-for-service initiative in Central America. But once it did this, it essentially meant that a very high subsidy had to be offered to facilitate these prices. Because the subsidy was so high, and because that subsidy even increased as the project went along, it made businesses highly dependent on the Government's every move. And because the subsidy was high, the programme became highly politi-cized, with considerable internal squabbling, making the Government less able to provide a clear and consistent policy framework.

From the announcement of the project in 1999, it would take nearly three years for the formal contracts to be signed with the concessionaires. During this time there was intensive wrangling, because the rand had devalued, and the original subsidy amount of R3500 was worth less in US dollar terms – only US$292 at the worst point in the rand's fortunes, compared to the intended amount of US$500. Whereas the subsidy was meant to have covered the capital cost of the solar system, now firms were left covering some of the capital costs in addition to their operating costs.[34]

With pressure from the implementing firms for a higher subsidy, officials within the DME started to become irritated with the perceived intransigence of the private sector, and started to question the project – was it worth the high subsidy and the hassle? In the end, instead of offering a contract for 10 or 20 years, the DME offered an interim contract for 18 months – from mid 2002 to the end of 2003, later extended to the end of March 2004. While this provided short-term relief, it was far from the clear, long-term policy framework to incentivize significant investment from the private sector in their concessions. How could a business invest in the infrastructure, the inventory, the receivables and so on if it did not know whether there were sufficient subsidies to continue the business beyond two years?

Further in-fighting then occurred between the National Electricity Regulator (NER) and the DME.[35] The result was that the NER placed a cap of 300 systems per month until the end of March 2004 across all the concessions. After complaints by the concessionaires, the NER managed to find some interim funds to keep the programme going, but further damage was then done when, in January 2004, the DME announced that once the NER money was exhausted, there would be no further subsidies from March 2004 onwards, until a review of the off-grid solar programme had been completed.

Adding yet further uncertainty was the parallel political issue that the monthly service fee of R58 per month (US$7) was no longer politically viable. Under a broader measure, the Government announced that all consumers of electricity would receive the first 50 kilowatt hours (kWh) of electricity for free. This made the position of the solar programme untenable, as customers were receiving only 6 kWh per month for R58.

So in July 2002, the DME announced that, in addition to the existing subsidy of R3500 per system, a further subsidy of R40 per month would be added to reduce the monthly costs paid by each customer – so that customers would only pay R18. But again, this proposal was riddled with uncertainty. The DME asked the concessionaires to do this on a pilot basis, but of course this had huge risks. How could a business reduce the price to R18, on a pilot basis? Once reduced by such an extent, customers would not easily allow a business to increase the price back to R58 once the pilot was over.

Moreover, it was not clear that this subsidy would actually be made available, as under constitutional reforms on decentralization of government, the concessionaires now would have to go to multiple municipal governments to collect this operating subsidy, rather than to one point (the DME). These municipal governments, newly formed, were not even clear on the number of customers in their region with solar, let alone supportive of solar in the first place, largely preferring their electorates to have the grid.

With such uncertainty and lack of clear policy direction, Eskom exited in 2004, followed by Shell Solar. The other concessionaires remained, but it was now largely down to three players – NuRa (Nuon RAAPS), EDF and Solar Vision. They continued, and persevered, but by the end of 2006 they were still facing an uncertain subsidy environment, and their numbers of installations were far from the target of 50,000 systems per concessionaire over five years (Table 7.5).

Table 7.5 Annual solar systems installed by company under South Africa's fee-for-service programme

Year	1999	2000	2001	2002	2003	2004	2005	2006	Total
Eskom-Shell	5000	500	500	200	300	**Exit**			**6500**
NuRa				410	2668	1619	3913	1894	**10,504**
EDF				300	2300	2600	4500	300	**10,000**
Solar Vision				600	2800	2300	3500	1200	**10,400**

Source: Author's correspondence[36]

The best estimate is that only 37,000 systems were installed under the fee-for-service approach in South Africa between 1999 and 2006. If we compare this with Sri Lanka's achievement of 100,000 systems sold and installed in eight years, or Bangladesh's achievement of the same number in just four years, we see a big difference.

Moreover, the subsidy per system installed was high. For just 37,000 systems installed over 10 years, South Africa will have borne a subsidy burden in excess of US$18 million (more than US$500 per system). Compare this to Sri Lanka, where best estimates are that the country achieved 100,000 for roughly US$12.5 million in subsidy ($125 per system), or Bangladesh, where the figures are estimated at only US$6.4 million for 100,000 systems ($64 per system).[37] The net result is that fee-for-service ends up costing a government more for less diffusion (Figure 7.11).

Thus it is not surprising that, as the programme progressed, the DME started to dither, and ultimately started to divert the funds intended for off-grid solar to normal grid electrification. It was clear the DME felt they were not

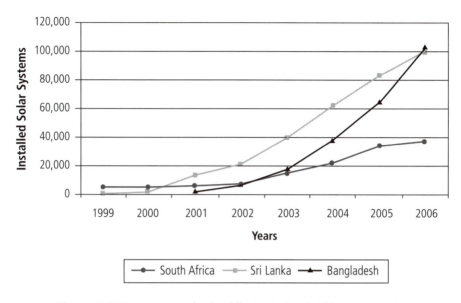

Figure 7.11 Lower rates of solar diffusion in South Africa compared to Sri Lanka and Bangladesh (cumulative installations)

getting value for money: 'The level of subsidy cannot be supported by our budget process,' said the DME official in charge, 'and let's face it, solar home systems only provide four hours of electricity per day.'[38]

Of course, to blame the technology is absurd – South Africa could have implemented the programme very differently. As we have seen, in the absence of an electricity grid, rural homes do not hesitate to invest their hard-earned savings in a solar system and own it, rather than rent it. It was estimated in 2000 that South Africa already had a relatively mature solar industry, with two module assembly plants, several wholesalers of solar modules, and approximately 40 distributors and solar system providers.[39] The question is why the Government did not simply encourage these entities to establish a market infrastructure and sell solar to rural customers directly, and in parallel, encourage the extensive banking network in South Africa and the MFIs to enter the rural markets and finance solar sales.

Of course, under a consumer finance approach a customer will pay more up-front than fee-for-service. This is a concept that may have been difficult for policymakers in post-apartheid South Africa. But as difficult as it may have been, it would have been far better for solar diffusion to have first enabled the growth of a viable, profitable market infrastructure, and then later to have built on that infrastructure with specific poverty-alleviating measures. In the end, the South African Government wanted to be able to get to the poorest elements from the outset, and so mandated a very tough business model and subsidized it heavily. But not only did this result in slower diffusion, but those who were signing up for the programme were still the relatively well off in rural areas, and not the poor.[40]

Given the extent of the grant the South African Government was willing to offer, it is hard to imagine they could not have coaxed the existing MFIs and banks to start to lend for solar in rural areas. But assuming that this was not possible, and there simply was no finance institution willing to lend for solar in rural South Africa, a more viable alternative to fee-for-service would have been to subsidize the sale of smaller solar systems on a cash basis.

If There Is No Rural Finance, Target Smaller System Sales Instead

Financing solar remains the ideal, because it allows customers to buy bigger systems that meet more of their energy needs. Finance takes a bigger solar system, and breaks it into smaller, more affordable chunks, paid for over time. It's a bit like buying a bigger house in a better location with a mortgage, rather than buying a house on a cash basis and living in something very small and far away from the action.

But there are some emerging markets where it would appear that no banks or MFIs are willing to finance solar. In such cases the trick for the policymaker is to make the product more affordable by making the product offering *smaller*. This is not always ideal from the customer's point of view, because they would always prefer a larger system that can provide more power for lights, radio and possibly a television. But in the end, a policymaker wants to ensure that unelectrified households receive, at a minimum, a modicum of light.

As we have seen, Kenya received a good deal of donor support to kick-start solar diffusion. Although a lot of the donor programmes left systems without adequate after-sales maintenance, meaning they consequently failed, they also served to train many local technicians and would-be entrepreneurs in the technology. When the donor funding dried up, these individuals went on to work for and establish their own companies to sell and install solar on a commercial basis.[41]

By the end of the 1990s, there were said to be ten solar module distributors, and at least five companies manufacturing the other components in the system.[42] In many parts of Kenya customers could now find shops stocking components of solar systems, and many live demonstrations of solar systems in market towns. Despite the lack of finance from banks or microfinance institutions, this strong market infrastructure led to between 120,000 and 150,000 solar systems installed by 1999. Furthermore, annual sales were estimated at 15,000–25,000 systems per annum in 1999, with estimated growth rates of between 10 and 25 per cent per annum in the 1990s.[43]

In terms of the amount people paid, historically the prices in Kenya have been some of the highest in the global market for solar systems – as high as US$26 per watt in the mid 1990s, roughly twice the price in Sri Lanka. So it is not surprising that customers in Kenya would have preferred a finance option. For example, when offered a trial scheme of 25 per cent down payment and 12–18.5 per cent interest over just two years, rural customers still gladly signed up. The conclusion of the scheme was that:

> The desire to have access to electricity is so deeply rooted that house-holds that have a chance to obtain a loan to acquire a solar electric system will do so.[44]

Recently there has been some talk of commercial banks in Kenya entering the loan market for solar. But historically, customers in Kenya have had to fend for themselves. Some dealers offered some credit schemes or lay-away plans, but by and large, it has been a cash market.

So in this situation, customers cut corners to make solar affordable. The vast majority of systems sold in Kenya have been the small 10–20-watt variety, enough for one or two lights and maybe a little bit of radio. Often customers bought these systems gradually, component by component; installed them themselves and did not invest in a charge controller to help them regulate the flows to and from the battery. Moreover, with smaller systems and little or no servicing, many customers experienced failure in their system. So in what way does the Kenyan example provide us with a model for policymakers of any kind?

Kenya actually served as a model to many policymakers in South Africa of how they did *not* want to do things, which is ironic, because if they had followed this model, diffusion would have been better off. What Kenya demonstrates is that when faced with a situation of no finance, customers are willing to pay commercial prices on a cash basis for small systems. This is some-thing powerful that a policymaker can build upon, rather than tearing it down by putting in place a fee-for-service programme.

How would a policymaker build upon such a market? First of all, as per our earlier discussions, a grant per unit installed could be offered to the sellers of solar systems. This would catalyse the industry to push out, build its rural market infrastructure and sell more. With increased competition and aware-ness of the programme, the sellers would inevitably be forced to pass on more and more of the grant to the customer over time. And with a grant now in place, policymakers would gain some leverage over the firms selling solar in terms of quality of components and service delivered. This is precisely what the World Bank did in its China project.

We saw in Chapter 6 that the World Bank's project in China was not able to put a line of credit to work for solar. This is not surprising, as there was, and remains, little in the way of rural banking or a microfinance tradition in China. But in this respect the solar market in China was already ahead of the World Bank.

Like Kenya, those selling solar had already accommodated for the fact that there was no finance, and were selling small 10-, 20- and 30-watt solar systems with one or two lights. Indeed this market infrastructure was already quite developed in the northwest provinces and autonomous regions of Qinghai, Tibet, Inner Mongolia, Xinjiang and Gansu, as well as in Sichuan and Xining. For instance, in Xining you will find a street lined with solar shops, all selling very different types of small solar systems. So, in the absence of any viable finance route, the World Bank focused on using its grant per unit installed (determined by the watts in the system) to accelerate and excite the market, and to build in higher quality standards.

The Chinese Government also built upon the approach of selling smaller systems in the absence of credit. They took the position that they wanted to heavily subsidize the sale of these smaller systems in certain provinces to reach unprecedented levels of market penetration. The name of the overall umbrella programme this approach fell under was the 'Brightness Programme', designed to bring electricity to 23 million people in the western provinces estimated to be without electricity.[45] An example of a project that fell under this initiative was the 'Silk Road Project', implemented by Shell Solar and a local Chinese partner and supported by a 14 million euro grant from The Netherlands. The aim of the project was to sell and install 78,770 solar systems of 25 watts and two lights among a mainly semi-nomadic population of 300,000 unelectrified households in Xinjiang. This was a tall order – attempting to reach 25 per cent market penetration. To do it, the Chinese Government decided to apply extra subsidies.

A typical two-light solar system at this time, without subsidy, cost RMB2000 (roughly US$250 at the time of the project). The Dutch subsidy helped to reduce the price by 60 per cent of its normal level – to RMB800–900 (US$100–110). Then further provincial government grants (from the Xinjiang Government) meant customers were receiving systems for as little as RMB100–200 (roughly US$20–30). Furthermore, the project could rely on local government office support to sometimes buy the systems on behalf of the population, and then collect the money from the rural customer base.

The project was ultimately successful in meeting its highly ambitious sales targets. This was no small achievement, and 25 per cent of the unelectrified population in Xinjiang now have a solar system for some modicum of more convenient light. Moreover, the target was achieved with far less subsidy than was used in, say, the case of South Africa. Even if you assume the Government bore the full cost of a RMB2000 system, that is still only US$250 per system – half as much subsidy as the grant in South Africa – and diffusion was more than twice as fast.

Figure 7.12
Customer next to small solar system (20 watt) in China

Figure 7.13
Typical solar home in China

Figure 7.14 Mobile solar system for semi-nomadic family, returning to valley for the winter

Figure 7.15 Mobile solar system for semi-nomadic family, in the highlands during spring

Figure 7.16 Family in China using solar system for home that also serves as village shop

The only criticism that should be made of the way things were done in Xinjiang is that a policymaker should ensure that such a grant is available to all local players. Unlike the Silk Road Project, where the grant was only available to the local Chinese player, it needs to be available to all to encourage competition both in the use of the grant and in developing a quality product and service.

Figure 7.17 Solar-powered television in China

Figure 7.18 Typical retail site for solar systems in China

Under a programme of heavily subsidizing smaller solar systems, a policy-maker cannot ensure that customers have enough power to run a TV, for instance. But they do have enough for the essentials – light. The next trick is to assure that a customer is receiving a high-quality product and after-sales service.

Establish an Independent Agency and Monitor

Once a grant and lines of credit are in place and being deployed in the market, it is then imperative that the deployment be monitored. Without this, customers are likely to suffer – such as those in Kenya. It is estimated that about one-third of the solar systems in Kenya are not fully operational because of a lack of enforced installation and design standards, mixed quality of components, and lack of customer awareness.[46]

Specifically, standards of product quality and service need to be set and enforced. But in terms of what to standardize, policymakers should go for a minimalist approach. This means using some accepted international standards for component testing – of modules, batteries, lights and so on – but avoiding dictating precise system configurations – for example, two or three lights or 20 or 40 watts. A solar system should always be designed by the firm selling it, not a government agency. Some households prefer to pay for only two or three lights; some prefer to pay for more. Some will only need DC output for radio and black and white TV; others will want AC output for refrigeration, colour TV and ceiling fans. A policymaker should use the grants to encourage firms to serve the precise needs of the customer, not to try to standardize one or two packaged solutions.

A policymaker also needs to monitor the quality of installation and, critically, of after-sales service. Sometimes it is felt that you need the business to finance the customer – either through a company finance scheme or through fee-for-service – for the business to have the long-term incentive to provide after-sales service.[47] But while it is true that if a company finances a customer, they need to provide service to collect their money, it is also true that a firm that has sold a system to a customer through a bank will be just as on the hook for the quality of the installation and after-sales service as if it financed it itself. If the firm does not provide a decent system, and good quality installation and service, the customer will stop paying the bank, and the bank will stop working closely with the firm to finance further customers.

That said, inevitably there are always those companies which for whatever reason – whether having access to less capital or less long-term vision – will try to cut corners at the customer's expense. So once a grant is deployed, the policymaker must set standards for product quality, installation and after-sales service, and must establish an agency to ensure these standards are met and enforced.

In some cases, government agencies have preferred to do this monitoring themselves. In Benin and Togo, for example, the rural electrification agency was given the responsibility of spot-checking installed systems and conducting regular consumer surveys to ensure customer satisfaction with the service provided.[48] But generally, as we have seen, it is better to establish an independent agency to manage the disbursement of the grant and the lines of credit, and that independent agency can also do the required monitoring of quality.

In looking for best practice, we can again look to the World Bank loan to Sri Lanka. Here the independent agency, the AU, set reasonable technical standards and required a test certificate showing that the components used by the firm – the solar module, the battery and the electronics – had passed the specific test standards. Without pre-approval of these essential components by the AU, a firm could not claim a grant for the system installed.

Furthermore, the AU had the responsibility to make sure that solar systems for which businesses claimed a grant were actually installed, and that they were being adequately maintained. If a firm was found to be deficient in terms either of the components used, the installation of the system or the after-sales service, the firm would be warned, and then black-listed in the case of repeat violations.

We can also point to Bangladesh, where the independent agency, IDCOL, set up a Technical Standards Committee whose functions were to establish and update equipment and service standards; design a quality-assurance programme; determine technical standards for equipment to be financed under the programme; review the product credentials submitted by dealers and approve the eligible equipment; and evaluate feedback from dealers and participating organizations to develop the industry standards.

In addition, IDCOL also took on the function of appointing independent organizations to conduct two types of audits. The first is a commercial audit to ensure that the participating organizations were using the grant for the designated purposes. The second, critical to the success of the overall programme, are technical audits, where it is ascertained that the equipment used is approved by the programme.

The beauty of offering the grant to the firm responsible for selling solar is that it gives a policymaker some *leverage* with which to improve standards. Any firm that does not meet these standards cannot access the grant and will be at a competitive disadvantage in the market. It is a strong incentive to improve performance for the benefit of the customer, as well as the business itself. Many firms may not even know how to improve their components or offers until the administering agency informs them. But once informed and alerted to better components and a better standard of service, an independent administering agency plays a key role in keeping the firms honest.

Summary

The central message of this chapter has been that for policymakers to accelerate solar diffusion they need to be able to see the market like an entrepreneur. When they do this, the policy decisions that follow will be almost intuitive.

From our earlier review in Part II, and from a review of contrasting case studies in this chapter, we were able to distil eight specific recommendations for policymakers. The most basic of these is that policymakers should avoid setting up parallel, government-driven markets for solar, as these discourage entrepreneurs from investing in a market infrastructure and selling directly to customers. Having made space for the entrepreneur, it is then imperative to also encourage the flow of capital from all quarters, domestic or international, and so policymakers should allow for 100 per cent foreign direct investment, and direct selling by foreign firms.

Although many policymakers may find it counter-intuitive, and not something they have done before, it is critical that they concern themselves with the margins and the profitability of the entrepreneurs in the marketplace. In line with this approach, they should avoid unduly constraining margins and raising prices with sales taxes and import duties. Then, to add an extra incentive, they should apply a grant-per-unit-installed approach, which proved highly effective in Sri Lanka, Bangladesh and China.

What is missing today in many emerging markets is not customer demand, but rather the sheer availability of the product and service close to the unelectrified customer. A grant encourages and assists entrepreneurs in building a market infrastructure to reach more of these customers. This is absolutely critical to the policymaker's objectives. However, once a grant is offered, we saw how important it was that policymakers achieve continuity. If they do not, as in the case of Sri Lanka, diffusion will take-off and then later stumble.

To then enable customers to afford a solar system, policymakers need to encourage banks and MFIs to lend for solar and arrange lines of credit to be on-lent to consumers. By encouraging and facilitating consumer finance, a government can tap into the surplus income of households that can afford to pay, and so save some of its scarce resources.

Ideally, if there are no lenders already financing solar in rural markets, policymakers can also use a small part of the grant to attract finance institutions – banks, MFIs and so on – to the market. But assuming the worst case, where they cannot, policymakers should remain wary of fee-for-service, based on its poor track record in many emerging markets. As we saw in the case of South

Africa, government-sponsored fee-for-service schemes are to be avoided, because they result in overall slower diffusion for more subsidy dollars.

Rather, in situations where there is no way to encourage more finance for the rural solar customer, policymakers should look to build and improve upon the example that comes out of Kenya and China: use the grant to encourage the sale of smaller solar systems on a 'cash' basis. Although such systems will not give the customer the ideal amount of service, it will provide the essential – light.

Finally, whatever programme a policymaker sets up to accelerate the diffusion of solar, it is critical to set minimal technical standards and ensure an independent agency monitors the use of any grants or lines of credit deployed. The beauty of the grant is actually that the independent implementing agency then has a carrot with which to incentivize the entrepreneurs to lift their game and provide a better quality product and service to the customer.

8

Solar Tomorrow:
100 Million Solar Homes

So far we have mainly considered solar's past: why it was slow to diffuse in the 1980s and 1990s, and why around the turn of the century it started to diffuse more quickly. In this chapter we turn now to consider solar's future – solar tomorrow – and the international forces at play that may or may not lead to a dramatic acceleration in solar diffusion in emerging markets.

To give ourselves a benchmark for what accelerated diffusion might look like, we can turn to the objective set by the G8 at the start of the new millennium. At the Okinawa Summit in 2000, the G8 called for the formation of a task force to assess barriers and recommend actions to accelerate the diffusion of renewable energy technologies in emerging markets. And the final communiqué at the G8 Genoa summit 2001 stated that:

> over the coming decade, concerted action by the G8, other countries, the private sector and the IFIs [international finance institutions] and other measures ... could result in ... provision of electricity from renewable sources to up to 300 million people in rural areas of developing countries.[1]

As we might imagine, these targets will not be met. But that has not stopped other initiatives, such as the World Bank's Global Village Energy Partnership (GVEP) from adopting the even more ambitious goal (though without specifying a timeframe) of ensuring that 400 million people previously unserved would have access to modern energy services.

There are roughly 1.6 billion people in emerging markets without electricity. That is the equivalent of roughly 400 million homes. If we consider that 25 per cent of these homes are able to afford a solar system on a cash or credit basis (see Chapter 7), that presents us with 100 million homes that would be eager to use solar if only someone would make the product available and affordable to them.

100 million homes is equivalent to roughly 400 million people, and thus

very much in line with the World Bank and G8 objectives. In terms of the time-frame, the G8 was willing to set the bar high at just one decade. But seeing that this target will be missed, and looking forward, it would seem prudent to allow more time: for instance until 2025.

In 2000 it was estimated that just 1 million solar systems had been sold in roughly 25 years. A quarter of a century on, is it possible that the world could see a dramatic acceleration to 100 million homes served? To address this question, we make the assumption that some 'outside' help will be required. That is to say, not each and every emerging market can be expected to engineer a self-sustaining, ever-increasing process of solar diffusion on their own, such that the aggregation of their efforts will reach these numbers. There will need to be some external assistance to accelerate the process. The question is what it will be.

Specifically, this chapter looks at four different international forces that could in theory have such an effect and asks:

1 Will the World Bank scale up their activities for a bigger impact?
2 Will other aid agencies have an effect that the World Bank will not have?
3 Will market forces achieve the same objective in the absence of aid?
4 Will the emergence of carbon trading make the difference?

The conclusion is that, overall, none of these forces as they stand today are likely to scale up solar diffusion to reach 100 million homes by 2025. And so I conclude by considering what a new initiative would need to look like to reach these levels of diffusion. This is not merely out of academic interest, but to identify a clear road map to a solar revolution in emerging markets.

A Big Push from the World Bank?

The World Bank has had tremendous success in lending for solar. We traced the roots of this success in Chapter 6, and many of our policy recommendations in Chapter 7 emanate from that effort. But the key question remains whether the World Bank can now build on this, and scale up its lending for solar so as to drive diffusion to 100 million solar homes by 2025. The fate of an earlier initiative – the Million Solar Homes Initiative (MSHI) – would suggest that, without some outside intervention, the World Bank would have little internal drive to do so.

The MSHI emerged around the time of the World Summit on Sustainable Development (WSSD) in Johannesburg in 2002. It was an initiative that came from the private sector, and was quickly adopted by the GEF. It was then, however, quashed by the World Bank.

The starting premise of the MSHI was that it took the world roughly 25 years for the first million solar home systems and lanterns to diffuse, whereas the next million should take just five years. In other words it was designed to accelerate the diffusion of solar in rural areas of emerging markets fivefold. It was to be set up as a 'challenge fund', to be managed by the World Bank, and would deploy the same formulas the World Bank had already found worked in countries such as Sri Lanka, China and Bangladesh.

The first pillar of the MSHI was a grant per unit installed to attract entrepreneurs into the rural markets to build the market infrastructure for solar. The grant per unit installed would be set at US$150 per unit for a 50-watt system – slightly higher than the existing World Bank programmes in order to drive diffusion more quickly. This would mean $150 million in grant funding across 1 million systems over a five-year period. In a very promising gesture, the then head of the GEF agreed at the World Summit on Sustainable Development in Johannesburg in 2002 that his institution was committed to injecting US$60 million of the required grant funding provided other donors came on board.

The second pillar of the MSHI was lines of credit for consumer finance. It assumed that the average price of a system was US$500 and that the customer paid roughly 10 per cent as down payment – meaning US$450 needed to be financed. It further assumed that the grant of US$150 brought down the price of a system by around US$100 (with the private sector keeping US$50 of the grant to support gross margins and the development of a market infrastructure). This therefore left US$350 per system that needed to be financed, or US$350 million over five years as a line of credit for consumer finance. As this finance could be provided to customers at largely commercial rates, it was proposed that the World Bank would provide the funds either through its International Bank for Reconstruction and Development (IBRD) wing or its International Development Asssociation (IDA) wing, as it had done in other countries already.

The third pillar of the MSHI was that those countries which came forward to take this money would, in exchange, agree to certain policies in the marketplace:

1   that an independent agency (for instance a private-sector bank) would disburse the grants and monitor compliance;
2   that no other government agencies would intervene directly in the markets to sell solar at lower subsidized prices; and
3   that all import duties on complete solar systems and taxes would be reduced, and eventually eliminated.

Thus to achieve a further 1 million connections to solar in rural areas over five years (between 2002 and 2007), the MSHI sought $150 million as grants per unit installed, $350 million as consumer finance and policy reform in exchange for significant funding. It was meant to be a straightforward initiative and to drive change. But the World Bank felt it was not necessary.

As the author was personally involved in developing this initiative, it is perhaps best to let another participant in the process tell the story of its fate within the World Bank:

> With the support of Phil Watts, Shell's Chairman at the time, who had personally called World Bank James Wolfensohn to suggest the idea, [I was] invited to several meetings in Washington in the spring of 2003 to explore the breakthrough solar-electrification proposal with officials at the GEF, the IFC and the World Bank. Before you could say 'three-ring circus', a dozen consultants were hired, 'expert working meetings' were convened, analysis was undertaken by World Bank contractors, thick reports were generated and recommendations were made. ... It didn't take more than two months ... to kill [the] Million Homes Initiative – even though James Wolfensohn thought it was a good idea – and it remains deader than roadkill.[2]

Instead of the MSHI, the World Bank lent support for the Global Village Energy Partnership (GVEP). As indicated earlier, GVEP's long-term goals are to ensure that 400 million people previously unserved will have access to modern energy services. By when, however, is not clear, as it does not set interim targets for people served along the way by which to measure progress. Nor it is clear exactly clear *how* it will do this.

The specific services GVEP intends to offer are development of energy action plans in national or local poverty reduction strategies, capacity development among entrepreneurs, policymakers and consumer organizations, funding facilitation with local, bilateral and multilateral financiers, knowledge management to share information on innovative approaches, and results and impact monitoring and evaluation.[3] But the GVEP clearly lacks the sort of clear, explicit strategy that will be required to entice businesses into serving the currently unserved rural masses. It is not a convincing road map and the results are so far hard to identify.

By not supporting the MSHI, the World Bank sent a clear message that it preferred to continue with business-as-usual. As we have seen, this business-as-usual is not without merit, but it would not seem to be in line with the ambitions of the G8, which after all, represents most of the World Bank's largest shareholders.

To reach its target of 300 million homes by 2010, the G8's communiqué in 2001 envisaged a key role for what it called 'Multilateral Development Bodies' (MDBs) such as the World Bank and GEF:

> We call on MDBs and national development assistance agencies to adopt
> an innovative approach and to develop market-based financing mecha-
> nisms for renewable energy. We urge the GEF to continue supporting
> environmental protection on a global scale and fostering good practices
> to promote efficient energy use and the development of renewable
> energy sources in the developing world.[4]

Certainly the case of solar shows that the World Bank has innovated so as to
drive forward diffusion of a key source of renewable energy. But according to
business-as-usual, the numbers served will be far from the G8's vision of 300
million people by 2010.

In 2005 the World Bank said it had a portfolio that included 60 MW of PV
projects that would lead to 1.2 million installations in households and facilities
in 30 emerging markets, touching the lives of some 6 million people.[5] The best
estimate is that by mid 2008, the results are 1 million installations, touching the
lives of 5 million people.[6] This is very much in line with the Bank's target set in
2005, but it is far from both the G8 target and the slightly higher target set by
the GVEP.

We therefore have to conclude that according to business-as-usual, the
World Bank will not drive diffusion to 100 million solar homes by 2025. But to
what extent can the other bilateral aid agencies pick up where the World Bank
leaves off?

Will bilateral aid agencies step into the breach?

Bilateral aid agencies were among the earliest supporters of solar in the emerging markets. This support has continued over time, and if anything has grown.
Examples include the 9 million euro Netherlands aid packages to the
Philippines for 15,100 solar home systems and the 23 million euro package (of
which 13.8m was grant) for western China for 78,770 solar home systems,
supplied by Shell Solar;[7] AusAid (an Australian aid agency) support for 38,000
solar home systems in Indonesia supplied by BP Solar in Australia, and
Spanish aid support for 2 MW of photovoltaics to be installed in 100 villages,
representing the equivalent of 150,000 homes in the Philippines, again
supplied by BP Solar, but this time from Spain;[8] or the GTZ (a German aid
agency)/KFW (the German Development Bank) participation under the
Chinese Government's 'Brightness Programme', where KFW initiated two
projects with a joint grant of 10.2 million euros for the installation of solar
powered mini-grids in 100 villages in Yunan and another 70 villages in
Xinjiang.[9]

Bilateral aid projects can happen in a variety of ways. For instance, in the
Dutch-supported projects in the Philippines and China, sales of solar are

supported with a grant which subsidizes the price in the marketplace. But in the case of Spanish aid to the Philippines, the support takes the form of a $48 million soft loan to the Government: 50 per cent of these funds will be loaned for 10 years just below market rates; the other 50 per cent will come from the Spanish Development Aid Fund as a 30-year loan, with a 10-year grace period and at an interest rate of less than 1 per cent.[10] The Philippines Government can then use this money to subsidize the price of solar in the marketplace.

While helping to increase the use of solar, there are four specific ways in which these kinds of bilateral aid projects are not ideally suited to accelerating solar diffusion. First, most of these bilateral aid programmes are 'tied aid'. For instance, only German companies (with Chinese partners) could supply the mini-grid projects sponsored by GTZ/KFW.[11] The problem with tied aid is that emerging markets may not receive the best product at the best prices, and it conflicts with OECD recommendations for the use of aid. Second, bilateral aid projects tend to pick only one successful supplier to work with. The grant is given to that supplier alone, and existing players in the market may be damaged. Third, bilateral aid projects typically allow big suppliers of equipment to sell into the country from abroad, without demanding an investment in a local market infrastructure – for example, rural technicians and salespeople to keep selling, installing and maintaining systems long after the project is complete. And fourth, rather than encourage local finance institutions to make loans available to solar customers, bilateral aid projects tend to heavily subsidize retail prices in an effort to make solar affordable. This tends to leave little basis for ongoing, sustainable sales once the project ends.

An example of a bilateral aid project not laying the foundations for ongoing, accelerated diffusion is again the GTZ/KFW mini-grid projects in China. Here consultants found that things had largely been done in reverse order. First, the mini-grids were installed prior to a clear understanding of who owned the systems: was it the communities, or the municipalities, or the implementing companies? Second, they were deployed before there were more trained technicians on the ground who could maintain and oversee their proper functioning. And third, the mini-grids were in before setting a tariff (a price) for the rural consumers to pay.[12]

There is something much more appealing about the World Bank's approach of a grant per unit installed being made available at the country level, where only companies incorporated and active in the local market can participate. First, this ensures a more competitive process which lets the consumer (rather than a government agency) decide which firm has the best reach, the best prices and the best service. Second, this approach is more likely to build a sustainable market infrastructure, since firms can only gain direct access to the grant by *investing* in a country – specifically by training and employing in-country staff to sell, install and service their products. And third, this approach tends to build more local institutional capacity – to disburse the grant, oversee quality and manage local policy conflicts (as in the cases of Sri Lanka, Bangladesh and China). Such institutional capacity is not built when the grant is passed directly to a company to implement a project.

To their credit, GTZ and KFW did follow the World Bank's approach in Bangladesh. World Bank/GEF funds supported the first 70,000 solar systems installed. The next 128,000 systems were funded by a combination of the GTZ (28,000 systems) and KFW (95,000 systems).[13] Total funding for these 128,000 systems was 4.65 million euros. By investing this money through IDCOL, and using the structure put in place under the World Bank's Bangladesh project, this bilateral support was more likely to support diffusion by encouraging local competition between multiple players, encouraging the creation of a local market infrastructure for ongoing sales and support, supporting an expansion in the provision of finance to customers to purchase solar systems, and building local institutional capacity, in this case IDCOL.

That said, we have to conclude from our review of bilateral aid initiatives in the solar sector that they will not drive diffusion to 100 million homes by 2025. Where aid agencies use the formula developed by the World Bank, or actually work through the latter, they are likely to be more effective in accelerating diffusion, but we are still left with the conclusion that the World Bank is not moving quickly enough towards the targets. So is it possible that the targets can be met without aid? That the growth of the global solar industry will naturally propel solar diffusion in the emerging markets through economies of scale in manufacturing and declining costs of the solar modules?

Will Market Forces Deliver?

Solar in emerging markets sits within a broader global solar industry, where the majority of demand comes from the industrialized markets. These markets have historically been led by Germany and Japan, but now a host of industrialized countries have announced policies to support solar. Could it be that the growth of industrialized markets will help to drive down the price of solar, such that diffusion is advanced in the emerging markets as well? To answer this question, we first examine the growth of the German and Japanese markets.

Interest in solar technology was strong in Germany throughout the 1980s and early 1990s. When the political landscape changed, and the red-green coalition came to power, the scene was set for a revolutionary set of solar policies.

The 100,000 roofs programme in Germany officially began in 1999, when the German Parliament introduced a new feed-in tariff for solar installations. From 1 April 2000, households and other owners of solar systems were able to sell the electricity they generated from solar to the national grid for a premium price of US$0.45 per kWh.[14] This now meant customers could earn more each month from selling solar electricity to the utility than they paid for conventional electricity. The difference provided customers with a return on their investment, and an incentive to buy solar.

The German Government also provided low-interest, long-term loans of 10 years at 2 per cent interest to help households afford the up-front price of a typical 3 kW system (roughly 20,000 euros). This was similar to the long-term lines of credit used by the World Bank in emerging markets. Some German states also instituted their own subsidy on top of the feed-in tariff. The result of all this was that while in 1997 the total amount of solar installed in Germany was 41.9 MW, by 2000 this installed base had tripled to 113.8 MW and by 2003 it had tripled again to 385 MW.[15]

Instead of developing a feed-in tariff for solar, the Japanese Government provided a capital subsidy to reduce the price of a solar system. During the 1990s the budget for this programme steadily increased until it reached 18 billion yen. Although the Japanese utilities were paying much less than in Germany – US$0.15–0.19 per kWh – for electricity from solar, the capital subsidies had their effect.[16] By 2001, Japan led the world, with over 50,000 solar systems installed and 350 MW. This was more than Germany reached two years later in 2003.[17] Seeking to propel this growth further, Japan's Government set a target of 4600 MW of installed capacity from solar by 2010 – more than a tenfold increase from 2001.[18]

While systems sold both in industrialized countries and in emerging markets are often for household applications, the obvious difference is the size. In 2003, the average system size in Germany was 7.4 kW.[19] By contrast, in Sri Lanka, the average system sold in 2003 was only 45–50 watts – more than 100 times less. This difference explains why industrialized markets, like Germany and Japan, are now the driving force behind global demand and production.

To give a sense of their meteoric rise to prominence, as early as in 2000, the solar markets in Japan and Germany alone were responsible for 40 per cent of global PV installations.[20] And since then, other industrialized countries have entered the fray. France, Italy and Spain have introduced their own feed-in tariffs for solar, and the US has also improved the federal incentives for solar.[21] Needless to say, the entry of new players, combined with the continued growth in the German and Japanese markets, has led to incredible growth in production (Figure 8.1).

So what has all this growth meant for the emerging markets? First of all, it's worth noting that it has meant a big opportunity for some entrepreneurs in some emerging markets who manufacture solar mainly for export to the industrialized markets. For example, China has seen a phenomenal growth in its

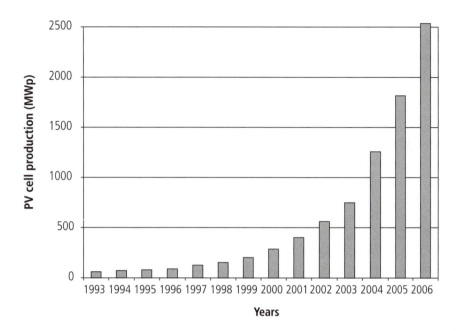

Figure 8.1 Enormous recent growth in global PV production

Source: Inglin[22]

solar industry, manufacturing and exporting solar modules to Europe and America.[23]

But more relevant to our study, this surge in demand in the industrialized world led to an increase in the price of a solar module. In 2002 the wholesale price of a solar module in Japan was US$2.5 per watt, but by 2005, the price had risen to close to $3.5 per watt.[24] By 2006, you were lucky if you could buy a solar module for $4 per watt on a wholesale basis in emerging markets.[25]

Of course, these price increases were not ideal for solar diffusion in the emerging markets. It meant that firms selling solar needed to increase their retail price to consumers. For example, in Sri Lanka, various market leaders increased the retail system price by 50 per cent between 2003 and 2005, partly due to a reduction in the World Bank grant, but primarily due to the rising price of solar modules. Yet, as we have seen in earlier chapters, despite these increases, diffusion surged ahead.[26]

The point is this: where a strong market infrastructure exists in tandem with consumer finance, increases in the price of a solar system do not have a big effect on diffusion. The reason for this is that the full effect of any price increase is moderated by consumer finance. Provided loans are available, then solar customers are only paying 10–15 per cent of the system price on day one, with the rest spread out over a three- to five-year loan. Price increases do not help diffusion, but they also do not necessarily stop it in its tracks where finance is available.

That said, if we are to look forward, what will happen to the price of solar modules as industrialized countries surge ahead, and what will this mean for emerging markets? Between 2007 and 2010, the price of a silicon-based solar panel is expected to fall from $3.66 per watt to $2.14 per watt.[27] Moreover, if we apply the historical maxim that for every doubling of installed PV capacity, the cost of PV technology drops by 20 per cent, then prices could drop to as low as $1.5 per watt for silicon-based panels by 2012.

This represents more than a 50 per cent drop from 2007 wholesale prices. But in line with our earlier findings, such a drop is unlikely to have the determining impact on solar diffusion in emerging markets. These expected reductions in the price of a solar module will only lead to a 20–25 per cent decline in the retail system price – for example an average 50-watt, five-light system can be expected to fall from US$600 to US$450–475.

Solar is already competitive with alternatives such as kerosene and battery charging in many unelectrified markets. While a 20–25 per cent decline in system prices can further help this competitiveness, it does not address the two core barriers to diffusion: consumer finance and a market infrastructure. Consumer finance can have a much bigger impact on affordability than 20–25 per cent price reductions, because it effectively reduces the up-front cost to the customer by 85–90 per cent, that is from US$600 to less than US$100.

Similarly, we cannot expect that a decline in system prices will naturally create a market infrastructure. It is true that lower module prices should mean bigger margins for those selling solar, which in turn should provide an incentive to build a market infrastructure to reach the rural customer base. But first of all, this process is likely to happen gradually, and so it will take time for other would-be entrants to the market to see the potential. Second, it is possible that any increase in margins can be bid away by the entry of new participants and thus competition in the marketplace. In the absence of any additional incentive, it is unlikely that entrepreneurs will build the required market infrastructure as quickly as is required to meet the 2025 objectives.

Many policymakers feel that the key to diffusion of solar in their emerging markets is a reduction in the price of a solar module. For instance, as the Minister of New and Renewable Energy in India recently said:

> My Ministry has promoted over 1 million PV systems in the country so far. These systems are highly reliable and popular among the people. There is a huge demand for these systems, particularly in rural areas where no reliable alternatives are available. The biggest constraint with PV is its high cost, which needs to be brought down.[28]

But our analysis suggests otherwise, and it is important that policymakers internalize this message: *waiting for the cost of the solar module to come down is simply not sufficient as a policy to enhance the diffusion of solar in rural areas of emerging markets.*

To reach the levels we seek by 2025 will require some kind of institutional intervention to incentivize entrepreneurs to build the rural market infrastructure, and to put in place lines of credit that reach the rural customer base. Could it be that by tweaking existing market forces – for example through carbon trading – these twin objectives can be achieved?

Can Carbon Trading Accelerate Solar Diffusion?

When customers in emerging markets buy solar systems, they reduce emissions of carbon dioxide (CO_2) that would have otherwise been generated. In the case of an unelectrified home or business, those customers displace kerosene for lighting, the charging of batteries or diesel generators that would have otherwise been used. Under carbon trading arrangements that we will go on to discuss, it is possible to turn those carbon savings into a commodity that can be bought and sold.

Of course, this might seem a little odd. After all, compared to other commodity markets, where actual goods are bought and sold, in the carbon market the commodity being bought and sold does not exist: it is the certified absence of carbon dioxide that is being traded. But as strange as it might seem, there are buyers for these carbon savings. As early as 2005, the year the Kyoto Protocol came into force, industrialized countries were already investing US$2.7 billion to cut greenhouse gas emissions in emerging markets by around 374m tonnes of CO_2 equivalent – about half of Texas's annual emissions.[29]

In theory, carbon trading provides a potential boon for solar in emerging markets. In line with the interests of this book, it can for instance be used by entrepreneurs to help them build out the market infrastructure to reach more customers. In practice, however, there are *seven* significant hurdles that any entrepreneur will need to overcome to access these new resources. We will review these obstacles in detail. But before doing so, it is useful to understand how the carbon trading market came into existence, and how it works in practice.

Carbon trading has its theoretical foundations in a concept called 'joint implementation' (JI) that was introduced at the Rio Earth Summit in 1992. Specifically, the United Nations Framework Convention on Climate Change (UNFCCC) said that the countries listed in Annex I (a list of largely industrialized countries) may implement 'policies and measures jointly with the other Parties and may assist other Parties in contributing to the objective of the

Convention'.[30] So if an industrialized country found it more cost-effective to jointly reduce emissions in cooperation with another country, it could do so as a way of meeting its commitments under the UNFCCC.[31]

This introduction of greater flexibility in ways and means of meeting one's commitments under the UNFCCC had its detractors. It was seen by some as a means of industrialized countries shirking their responsibilities 'at home'. Yet if global climate change was a global problem, with global causes, then it made sense for countries to be able to find the lowest-cost means of mitigating emissions of greenhouse gases. Moreover, JI laid the theoretical foundation for the Clean Development Mechanism (CDM), which would, in turn, provide a regulatory framework for trading in carbon emission reductions.

The CDM was initially conceived by the Brazilians as more of a punitive fund. For example, if an industrialized country failed to meet its commitments, it would need to pay into a fund on a US$-per-tonne basis for the greenhouse gas emissions that it failed to reduce. These funds would then be redistributed to emerging markets for their own clean development. However, in the final days of negotiating the Kyoto Protocol, this concept was essentially turned on its head.[32]

Arguing that its trading scheme to reduce sulphur dioxide had been successful at home, the US insisted that the Kyoto Protocol include the possibility of a market in emission reductions.[33] So instead of the Brazilian's concept of a punitive fund, the CDM, as enshrined in Article 12 of the Kyoto Protocol, would become a clearly articulated mechanism by which industrialized countries could meet their climate change commitments by investing in emission reductions in emerging markets. Here it is worth returning to the original text of the Kyoto Protocol, where Articles 12.1 and 12.2 read:

> A clean development mechanism is hereby defined. The purpose of the clean development mechanism shall be to assist Parties not included in Annex I [the emerging markets] in achieving sustainable development and in contributing to the ultimate objective of the Convention, and to assist Parties included in Annex I [the industrialized countries] in achieving compliance with their quantified emission limitation and reduction commitments.[34]

The text in Article 12 then goes on to explain how this would happen in practice, and it is important for our understanding of carbon trading to review this in more detail. First, it was clear that the CDM would need to be governed and regulated for it to work. As such, the Parties to the Protocol called for the establishment of an Executive Board (EB) that would report to the Conference of the Parties to the UNFCCC. The EB would, among other things, be responsible for overseeing the creation of 'certified emission reductions' (CERs). The creation of CERs 'may involve private and/or public entities, and is subject to whatever guidance may be provided by the executive board of the clean development mechanism'. Importantly, such reductions must be 'real' and 'measurable', with 'long-term benefits related to the mitigation of climate change'. Moreover, 'they must be *additional* [emphasis added] to any that would occur in the absence of the certified project activity'.[35]

By enabling industrialized countries to meet their national objectives by investing in projects in the emerging markets that create CERs, the Kyoto Protocol and the CDM had created a potentially powerful incentive for renewable energy diffusion in the emerging markets. Once businesses or governments have a *cost* of implementing mandatory commitments at home, CERs from an emerging market that help meet these commitments immediately take on a *value* at the international level. In turn, once you give a value (for example US$ price) to a CER, then you immediately create an incentive for increased investment in renewable energy businesses or projects that deliver such emission reductions.

That is the theory. But in practice, as mentioned earlier, an entrepreneur has to overcome seven key hurdles to be able to put CERs to work for a solar business in the emerging markets.[36]

1	Establish ownership of the emission reductions
2	Bear the transaction costs
3	Designate the project as a programme of activities
4	Establish a viable and cost-effective monitoring mechanism
5	Generate enough scale to justify the time and expense
6	Meet the additionality criteria
7	Establish a viable price per CER

The first hurdle is the 'ownership issue'. It is not possible to create a CDM project for each individual household or enterprise which buys a solar system. Somehow these emission reductions need to be bundled, and owned by an entity that can then sell them. The firm that has sold the systems could do this, but in many cases, the firm has transferred ownership to the customer. Therefore how can they then own the CERs and trade them?

While not straightforward, this is, however, possible. A firm that is selling, installing and servicing solar systems *can* become the vehicle for bundling emission reductions and creating and owning CERs. It can do this because under a CDM project the CO_2 reductions are actually the sovereign property of the country government, and so if the country approves the project wherein the business is undertaking this function, then it becomes permissible. But this must nonetheless be achieved in practice prior to the business being able to trade in the carbon savings.

Second is the issue of 'transaction' costs. Regardless of the size of a CDM project, there are several sets of fixed and up-front costs to create the CERs: the cost of the project design document (PDD), which establishes how much CO_2 will be reduced for each solar system installed; the costs of validation, to validate the methodology for calculating the emission reductions and the chosen method of monitoring; the ongoing verification costs on the ground, to verify that the emission reductions claimed have actually occurred; and the fee for registering the project with the CDM – a variable fee associated with the number of CERs to be produced, but still an up-front cost. As has been recognized, and is applicable to solar:

> Due to these relatively large fixed costs, many small activities that have the potential to reduce greenhouse gas emissions cannot be implemented cost-effectively, even when taking into consideration the CER revenues.[37]

The CDM did try to address this issue by setting different, and in theory more simplified, rules for projects under 15 MW, but the overall conclusion remained that:

> projects using 'pico-scale' measures or technologies cannot absorb the high cost of project development, validation, monitoring and verification required even under the simplified small-scale CDM project rules. ... Only by creating flexible rules for aggregating and bundling a significant number of units could these measures or technologies become commercially viable as CDM projects.[38]

Third, under its original rules and guidelines, the CDM was not well set up to handle ongoing sales of a decentralized technology. Under old rules, an entrepreneur would need to incur all the transaction costs, each and every year, to establish what are called CER vintages – CERs pertaining to a particular year. This is difficult for an entrepreneur selling decentralized solar systems, for instance, because in the early years, there are less cumulative systems, and so less ability to meet the annual transaction costs.

However, in 2007 the EB to the CDM proposed a new approach called a 'programme of activities' (PoA), under which there would be one approved baseline and monitoring methodology (only one PDD) for the entire project duration. Once registered and approved by the CDM, a programme will have a maximum lifetime of 28 years and a crediting lifetime of a maximum of 21 years.

This is potentially highly beneficial to solar, as well as other decentralized renewable energy and energy-efficient technologies. The World Bank's carbon finance unit is, for instance, considering a PoA to increase the market penetration of more energy-efficient air-conditioners in Ghana.[39] This PoA proposes to monitor the increased market penetration of energy-efficient air-conditioners in Ghana beyond the historical trend, and use random sampling to establish the actual operational hours of these units. Over seven years, this project is expected to offset more than 3 million tonnes of CO_2 that would have otherwise been created.[40]

Equally, we can point to projects which support the sale of biogas installations to farmers for electricity and cooking purposes.[41] Or to compact fluorescent lights (CFL) projects, or to improved HCFC chillers in India, or to solar systems – basically, in any case where it a question of selling a decentralized technology (for example individual-scale systems to individual homes and businesses), then a PoA will make a lot of sense for an entrepreneur. But the reality today is that the PoA approach is new and still largely untested. While it retains a potential to assist solar diffusion, there are still other hurdles to overcome.

Fourth, given the decentralized nature of solar, there is the tricky issue of setting up a monitoring mechanism that gives sufficient assurance to the CDM that emission reductions have occurred, without imposing too much cost on the entrepreneur. Of course, it is quite right that the CDM might want to know that customers are actually using their systems to the extent the business suggests, but the methodological requirements can be rigorous. In the case of CFL projects, this has actually been tackled by 'recording' the hours of use with a meter. But this adds further costs. Instead, monitoring can also be based on 'reported' hours of use, but this raises the issue of what is reliable reporting, and establishing a methodology for reliable reporting.

Fifth, even assuming that a PoA and reliable monitoring mechanism can be established for lower transaction costs, it is still a question of generating enough CERs to make it all worthwhile. Solar photovoltaic systems do not displace as much CO_2, relative to their cost, as other decentralized renewable energy technologies. For example, a study in Sri Lanka found that while a solar PV system will reduce 0.93 tonnes of CO_2 per annum per US$1000 invested, the same US$1000 invested in a solar thermal water-heating system in India will reduce 4.29 tonnes of CO_2 per annum.[42] This does not make solar photovoltaics in rural areas of emerging markets less worthy for meeting climate change objectives, as by establishing this technology *today*, it can be scaled up later to avert much larger future emissions when consumption in rural households increases. Moreover, the application of solar in rural areas has considerable social benefits that also have a value. But it does mean that an entrepreneur must have sufficient scale to justify the time and expense of creating the CDM project.

Sixth, assuming that an entrepreneur can compensate for less CO_2 saved by installing many more solar systems under a PoA approach, and that it is still worthwhile to go ahead, even then there is the thorny issue of 'additionality'. Recall that the Kyoto Protocol made it clear that any reductions much be 'additional' to any that would occur in the absence of the certified project activity. But demonstrating additionality is not always straightforward.[43]

In the case of CFLs in Honduras, for example, when customers were asked whether they would have bought CFLs without incentives from the project, they said yes. This implied there was *not* additionality. There was therefore no basis for the CERs, as customers would have bought anyway. This though is when it becomes tricky, because it could be that the survey responses were influenced by 'individual pride' or 'culture'.[44]

In the case of solar, it can probably be shown that without the CERs and the money from them, invested by an entrepreneur in a market infrastructure, the customer would not have been able to buy a solar system. That said, this is something that must be shown and, given the rather subjective nature of additionality, this is not a straightforward process.

Seventh, and finally, is the 'price'. To take on the transaction costs, the burden of developing the PoA, setting up a monitoring mechanism and so on, a business needs to know that it is all worthwhile. Here the price of the CER becomes critical. Some analysts contend that a price of US$10 per CER for solar installations is needed 'to make CDM participation worthwhile'.[45] This is positive, as the price for a CER was on average US$10.70 per CER in 2007.[46] But that is the *retail* price of a CER, and entrepreneurs will not get this full amount if they hire a broker to help them manage the paperwork and find them a buyer.

That said, there is a potential for entrepreneurs in the solar sector to earn more per CER. While the average price per CER is US$10.70, some projects are getting as high as US$24.[47] Moreover, as countries get closer to the deadlines for their agreed commitments, so the demand for CERs is likely to increase, and so too will the average price.

European countries such as Germany, France and the UK are close to meeting their commitments under Kyoto. But Japan, for instance, is running at 24 per cent above 1990 emission levels, compared to their commitment to reduce emissions by 6 per cent below 1990 levels. Other big emitters, such as Canada, are also finding it 'impossible to meet their targets'. And of course the US has not signed on to Kyoto, but when it does, it will need to catch up quickly. In short, the rich countries that ratified Kyoto (not including the US) are expected to produce roughly 3.5 billion tonnes of CO_2 more than what they agreed by 2012 – 'so the prospect for sellers is good'.[48]

Looking further ahead, the last Intergovernmental Panel on Climate Change (IPCC) report, which called for an energy 'revolution', estimated that to bring global CO_2 emissions by 2030 back down to 2000 levels will require a cost of US$50–100 per tonne.[49] That is 5 to 10 times higher than the average price of a CER today. Assuming that the other kinks in the CER trading process are resolved, such price levels would give entrepreneurs a strong incentive to establish a market infrastructure for solar. It would also provide entrepreneurs with the funds to simultaneously incentivize more solar financing. But of course, the only way for CERs to take on this kind of value is for key emitters, such as the US, to accept a mandatory cap on emissions, and then have trading of CERs to facilitate compliance.

Ironically, it was the US that lobbied for the CDM to be included in the Kyoto Protocol and thereby created the mechanism for the development and trading of CERs. But without a mandatory cap in the US, there has not been sufficient incentive to buy CERs at higher prices to meet binding emission targets. Demand remains low compared to what it would otherwise be, the price of CERs remains correspondingly low and entrepreneurs do not have sufficient additional incentive to build the market infrastructures for solar.

This directly links the prospects for solar in emerging markets with the politics of climate change in the US. We may not intuitively or initially see this link, but thanks to the onset of carbon trading, there is a very real and very direct connection between the unelectrified household getting power in their home through solar and the US and other big emitters setting mandatory caps on emissions.

But until such time that the kinks are ironed out in the CDM process, and the world accepts a new radically higher price of carbon, solar in emerging markets is not an ideal candidate for carbon trading. Therefore, we can conclude that while it retains enormous potential, carbon trading is unlikely to propel the world to 100 million solar homes by 2025. It would seem that the only way these targets can be met is through increased intervention in the solar markets – specifically, through the establishment of a dedicated fund.

100 Million Solar Homes Fund

The 100 Million Solar Homes Fund ('the Fund') would take the same approach as the Million Solar Homes Initiative (MSHI) discussed earlier. But it would do so at a much larger scale.

We have seen in earlier chapters how important a market infrastructure is to solar diffusion. Furthermore, we saw how a grant per unit installed provided an excellent incentive for firms to build this market infrastructure in countries like Sri Lanka, Bangladesh and China, leading to a rapid increase in diffusion. The grant per unit installed therefore becomes the first pillar on which the Fund would rest.

The Fund would use a straight grant of US$150 per unit installed. This is equivalent to roughly 25 per cent of the retail price of an average 50-watt, five-light system. It would be channelled to the firm responsible for invoicing the final customer – in other words the final step in the retail chain. It would be up to this firm to decide how much of the grant it retained to build the market infrastructure for solar in remote rural areas, and how much it passed on to the customer as lower prices. For instance, a firm selling a 50-watt, five-light system for US$600 may pass on US$100 to the customer as a price reduction, and retain US$50 per unit to help fund its expansion to reach the rural customer base. The residual retail price of US$500 would then need to be financed (a point to which we return below).

Obviously, not all rural homes can afford a US$500 system. But with a straight grant per unit installed, there would also be an incentive for firms to offer smaller systems for very low prices. For example, imagine a firm had a small one- or two-light solar system priced at US$101. It could in theory retain US$50 to help build its market infrastructure to reach remote rural customers and still pass on US$100 to the customer. A poor family would now pay only US$1 for a basic solar system. This would serve to reach the poorest of the poor, who would never be creditworthy but who still need the bare essential that is light.

This grant of US$150 per system installed is not fixed in stone. It could be less in cases where there is already a well-developed market infrastructure, or where the solar systems being offered are significantly smaller and lower cost. But it might also need to be more in some cases where the market conditions are particularly challenging. It could also decline over time, as we saw in the case of Bangladesh. But it is not clear that a grant can ever be eliminated entirely if the aim is to reach unelectrified homes in the most remote parts of emerging markets.

Taking an average of US$150 per system across 100 million systems, the total grant requirement is US$15 billion. This is not a trivial amount of money, but consider that if the Fund started operations in 2010, it would be spread over 15 years, making the sum a more manageable US$1 billion per annum. Also, much of the grant requirement would come in the later years, in line with the gradual ramp-up in global diffusion. Finally, emerging market governments would be encouraged to contribute to the grants made available to their country. As we saw in Chapter 7, complementary grants from governments in Sri Lanka and China proved quite effective.

But a market infrastructure for solar needs to be complemented by accessible consumer finance in order for solar diffusion to take off. Therefore, the second pillar of the Fund would be a large line of credit to be lent to financial institutions on the ground that are willing to finance solar users. Such financial institutions may be private- or public-sector banks, they may be microfinance players, or they may even be companies or NGOs willing both to build a market infrastructure and to finance solar consumers.

Take the earlier case where a firm uses US$100 of grant to reduce the retail price from US$600 to US$500. Now imagine that a customer can take advantage of a finance facility where they pay a 10 per cent down payment – US$50. This would leave a residual amount of US$450 per system that needs to be financed, or US$45 billion for 100 million homes over 15 years. Again, this is not an insignificant amount of money. But consider that the average tenure of the loan would be three years. This would mean that, on a very rough basis, the solar loans could be cycled five times between 2010 and 2025. Therefore the Fund would need a line of credit of roughly US$10 billion. Still not an insignificant amount of money, but by no means insurmountable given that this money would be on-lent on a commercial basis, which means it could also attract private-sector investment over time. Moreover, as with the grant, the majority of the funds would be required in later years.

The third and final pillar on which the Fund would rest is 'policy'. We have seen that the right policies can make or break a solar market. There would be no point in deploying significant funds into an emerging market if the policies were not conducive to accelerating diffusion. Key policies to be negotiated and agreed would be non-intervention by government agencies in creating a parallel market for solar, the elimination of import duties and taxes on solar, allowing for foreign investment and direct retailing in the solar sector, and the establishment of an 'independent agency' (ideally private-sector) to disburse the funds and monitor performance. These policies will not always be easy to achieve, and the Fund would have to be flexible to ensure that the programme did not become bogged down in ideology. But it would be an essential pillar of the Fund nonetheless.

Finally, there is the question of who would manage the Fund. We saw earlier in the chapter that the World Bank was not supportive of the Million Solar Homes Initiative (MSHI). So we can imagine that it will not be that excited about the prospects of trying to reach 100 million solar homes by 2025. But if the Fund is to be established, then its natural home is in the World Bank. Above all other global institutions, the World Bank has demonstrated the capacity to accelerate the diffusion of solar on a sustainable basis. It also has the reach, the financial resources and the skill set to manage and execute such a Fund.

That said, given the earlier reaction of the World Bank to the MSHI, such a Fund would need a nudge from the shareholders of the Bank to make it happen. This is not inconceivable, as solar is a technology that has captivated the imagination of governments in the industrialized countries and emerging markets alike. But for it to come into existence, such a Fund will need outside political champions. We will return to this theme in the final chapter, as the case of solar is a microcosm for how the World Bank's lending in the energy sector should evolve.

A hundred million solar homes by 2025 is by no means a fantasy: 25 per cent penetration of the total base of unelectrified households is possible in roughly 15 years with the right combination of well-managed grants, lines of credit and limited policy reforms. This will not only improve the lives of new solar users, but it will encourage thousands of entrepreneurs and create millions of jobs in rural areas of emerging markets, where skilled employment opportunities are scarce. Moreover, it will build on a solid track record of success in terms of what it takes to rapidly accelerate solar diffusion. It is an initiative waiting for political champions to seize, and in so doing, bring light to close to half a billion people throughout the emerging markets.

Summary

I started out by asking whether there were any international forces that might dramatically accelerate diffusion towards 100 million solar homes by 2025. Through a review of the existing World Bank approach, the existing bilateral aid approach, the potential for declining price of solar modules and the emergence of carbon trading, the conclusion was reached that none of these forces would deliver these numbers.

Instead, I proposed an alternative: a fund which will have the specific mission of delivering 100 million solar homes by 2025. These targets would rest on three strong, tried and tested pillars. First, a grant per unit installed to encourage firms to build the market infrastructure for solar, and reach out to remote, rural, unelectrified populations. Second, a line of credit that would be on-lent to local finance institutions to make it easier for customers to afford a solar system. And third, limited policy reforms to ensure that, once deployed, the grant and line of credit would have their maximum impact on diffusion. With such an approach, the world could reach 25 per cent of the unelectrified population by 2025, not only providing them with basic essentials such as electric light, but spurring entrepreneurship, innovation and job creation in places where it is needed most.

Accelerating a Renewable Energy Future

At the outset we asked two essential questions about solar. First, why was a technology with such enormous potential so slow to diffuse in emerging markets throughout the 1980s and 1990s? And second, why at just the point when many were starting to give up on solar, did diffusion pick up in some emerging markets so quickly at the turn of the new century? We asked these questions not just because they were relevant to solar, but because through answering them, we could shine a light on the much bigger picture of renewable energy diffusion.

We now return to these questions, and summarize our solar findings in the first part of this concluding chapter. The second part then returns to diffusion research and the analytical framework developed in Chapter 2. Here I show how the framework can be used to explain the diffusion of a range of renewable energy and energy-efficient innovations. In the third and final part, I identify five 'big picture' lessons from *Selling Solar* for the challenge of accelerating a renewable energy future in emerging markets.

Solar Findings

Solar in the emerging markets started as a twinkle in the eye of its early propagators – a vision of solar on the rooftops of millions of homes, providing essential light, displacing fossil fuels, and establishing a new technology in a new setting as a beacon of hope and a guard against future growth in emissions. It was terribly compelling. But as with many innovations, the hopes and aspirations initially outran the reality.

A review of theories on innovation diffusion showed that solar technology was by no means alone. The history of technology diffusion is filled with cases of slower than expected diffusion. From these theories we distilled four essential barriers, and put them forward as questions that might help explain solar's slower than expected progress:

1   Is it attractive?
2   Is it competitive?
3   Is it affordable?
4   Is it available?

These are not the only questions that might be asked to explain the barriers to diffusion. But their relevance was shown in the case of solar diffusion, and they are broadly applicable. We will return to them again in the second part of this chapter.

Applying these questions to solar diffusion in emerging markets, we saw that by the mid 1990s a consensus had formed around the key barriers. The main barriers to diffusion were *not* the costs of solar or its relative attractiveness in the eyes of rural customers, as some analysts felt then (and some still feel today). Rather, the analysts of this market had squarely arrived at two main barriers to diffusion: the absence of finance (customer loans) to make it more affordable and the absence of a market infrastructure (sales points, locally available inventory, sales people and technicians) to make it more available.

This then answered our first question on why solar was slower to diffuse than expected. But, in examining the second question of why solar diffusion accelerated in the early part of the new century, we found it was not enough to just refer to 'overcoming' these barriers. We also needed to be able to explain *who* did it and *how*. These are the essential questions of agency, and, as it turned out, solar initially had the wrong agents backing its corner in emerging markets.

First, foreign donor agencies jumped in to try to propel solar through demonstration projects. But they parachuted in solar projects with little basis to sustain them. Then utilities dipped their toe into the solar business, only to decide later it was not for them. Government agencies in emerging markets also got involved with heavy subsidies and direct distribution, but found this led to limited diffusion and high rates of technology failure. All the while, the barriers to accelerated solar diffusion remained firmly in place.

As a result, observers of the market began to call for solar to 'go commercial'. Commercial sales of solar offered an opportunity for this promising technology to get away from one-off donor projects or under-funded government programmes, and establish a self-sustaining mechanism for diffusion. And, as if on queue, those already engaged in the business as not-for-profit entities set up commercial solar outfits, NGOs entered the market and started to sell solar like a business, and early entrepreneurs started trying to scale up their activities.

Selling Solar has profiled three different sets of entrepreneurs in India, Indonesia and Sri Lanka. All of them were attempting to pioneer a solar revolution in their local markets. Some were more driven by profit than others. But all were driven by a desire to sell solar in very large volumes. Although big, established businesses would later enter this solar market, the early pioneers were singular individuals with a vision not shared by many related industries. The solar module manufacturers were largely uninterested in directly developing the rural markets for solar in the early to mid 1990s. Electricity utilities, which in theory could reach millions of unelectrified homes easier than most, did not see an easy fit with their existing operations. And consumer durable suppliers and their dealers simply did not see the potential.

The market was wide open for these entrepreneurs to seize, and they knew it. But all the profiled entrepreneurs struggled to raise sufficient resources to realize their visions. They were starved for capital in the early stages of their growth, which inhibited their ability to unlock the market, and frustrated their plans to kick-start large-scale diffusion of solar.

In addition, the entrepreneurs brought different capacities to the business. Those that brought more solar experience had less to learn. But none of them brought all the answers. All of them had to learn a critical lesson or two the hard way – through learning by doing. Some had a second chance; others did not. But they all served as an inspiration to other firms and policymaking institutions that followed their lead.

The two entrepreneurs in India set out to sell solar on a commercial basis in a country where solar was largely controlled by government agencies that heavily subsidized and distributed it. It was not a conducive environment in which to start up. But they picked the right state in south India, where government programmes were weaker, and started selling solar directly to power-starved populations in rural areas.

Initially they struggled without sufficient resources. They were unable to effectively participate under the World Bank solar programme in India, and were delayed in receiving funds due to government restrictions on foreign ownership. Nonetheless, they succeeded in convincing one of India's largest government-owned banks to start lending for solar. With customers able to access loans, demand for solar grew rapidly in their local market. Initially, they were unable to capitalize on this demand due to a continued lack of resources. But once they had successfully raised more equity capital, their sales grew rapidly, and started to serve as an example to others. They demonstrated that, despite the strength of the government programmes in India, it was indeed possible to sell solar commercially in rural areas.

Their model attracted smaller local competitors, as well as bigger businesses like Shell Solar. More competition meant that more capital was now being ploughed into an effective market infrastructure, and more banks were encouraged to start lending for solar. Seeing this, UNEP judged that the time was ripe to enter with a low-interest loan scheme. With easy access to solar products, and now easy access to low-interest loans, rural demand for solar jumped, and so did the rate of diffusion. Over ten years, the private sector sold an estimated 100,000 solar systems in the state of Karnataka, roughly 15 times the rate of diffusion achieved through government channels in other states in India.

Our second case study profiled an entrepreneur in Indonesia, who came to the market intent on growing a big business. He wanted to sell solar in rural Indonesia like Coca-Cola. He had experience in the country selling solar to the Government, but his ambition now was to sell solar directly to the millions of unelectrified homes, independent of government support.

He knew that providing customers with finance was essential to realizing his vision. Unable to identify any banks that were willing to offer loans to the unelectrified rural customer base, he did it himself. He set up a four-year loan scheme that sparked a strong demand for solar. Then, to meet this demand, he rolled out an extensive market infrastructure of more than 40 service outlets, with trained salespeople, technicians and administrators. Having overcome the twin barriers of affordability and availability, sales grew rapidly. In just two years he sold an unprecedented 8000 solar systems.

But without sufficient capital, his business was always on a knife-edge. The more he sold, the more his consumer finance scheme depleted his capital reserves. He was able to find temporary relief with long-term supplier credits, but in the end, when the Asian economic crisis hit at the end of 1997, his business was too fragile, and it folded.

The entrepreneur's legacy, however, endured. Largely based on his example, the World Bank developed a new approach to supporting solar. It first developed this approach in Indonesia, where it had a limited impact due to the onset of the economic crisis. It then replicated the approach in Sri Lanka to much greater effect.

In Sri Lanka, we reviewed a case of three entrepreneurs smitten by the solar vision, jumping into a market they knew little about, but making up for their lack of experience with enthusiasm and drive. Needless to say, there was a lot to learn. They would try many different approaches to kick-starting the market: doing their own manufacturing, setting up roaming demo teams, tying up with a large consumer goods retailer, trying to do their own finance and trying to work with the largest bank on the island. And they did this with considerable resourcefulness, until they arrived at a crunch point of insufficient funds to continue.

At this point, two of the founding entrepreneurs decided to step down for the sake of the business, leaving the third to carry on. The company was renamed, and the debts were paid off with an outside investment. The remaining entrepreneur would prove to be immensely committed. He ploughed in his own resources, and continued to pursue the vision of bringing solar to the unelectrified masses in Sri Lanka. It was not easy – like the other profiled entrepreneurs, he was continually short of funds. He had to be resourceful and stay afloat by winning a few larger projects in addition to his smaller-scale retail sales. Key among his efforts was successfully lobbying the World Bank to launch a solar project in Sri Lanka, which it eventually did at the end of 1997.

With a World Bank project now in place, other firms followed the entre-preneur's lead. Shell Solar entered the Sri Lankan market by acquiring the entrepreneur's firm, and the entrepreneur remained to run the new company. With sufficient resources now in place, he set about rapidly rolling out a market infrastructure into corners of the country he already knew well. And with this burgeoning infrastructure he was able to convince Sri Lanka's largest microfinance company to step out of the solar sales business and focus instead on aggressively expanding its solar lending business. With both the product and the finance now widely available to rural unelectrified customers, solar sales grew quickly. This in turn attracted other firms and banks to the market, and diffusion rapidly accelerated from about 500 systems per annum in 1999 to 18,500 in 2003 alone. By the end of 2006, 14 firms were selling solar, four banks were financing solar and more than 100,000 solar systems had been sold since the launch of the World Bank project at the end of 1997.

Like the profiled entrepreneurs, the World Bank had to learn by doing. The Bank did not have a ready template it could pull off the shelf, as solar was different to the other energy-sector projects it typically funded: large fossil-fuel power plants or hydro-power stations and large-scale transmission and distri-bution networks. So not surprisingly, when it first got into the solar game in India, the World Bank stumbled. The solar component of its Indian renewable energy project did not accelerate solar diffusion in rural markets as anticipated. Finance did not reach the rural customer, and entrepreneurs on the ground were not sufficiently incentivized or supported to build a market infrastructure for the technology.

To the credit of the World Bank (and its staff), it learned from the India project. The Bank had earlier established the Asia Alternative Energy Unit (ASTAE), which served as an advisory group and centre of excellence for renewable energy projects. ASTAE was able to act as a bridge, and transfer the learning from India to the next solar project in Indonesia. Here the World Bank developed an innovative policy proposal to channel grants (from the GEF) directly to firms selling solar, as a way to incentivize and support them in building a market infrastructure for solar. It also set up lines of credit to on-lend to solar customers, and established an independent agency to monitor the project. The Bank did not know it at the time, but it had established a winning formula for promoting solar diffusion in emerging markets.

Although the project in Indonesia was to be derailed by the Asian economic crisis, the template was successful in Sri Lanka (125,000 systems installed by mid 2008). The World Bank would then take this model and replicate it with even greater success in China (500,000 systems by mid 2008) and Bangladesh (211,000 systems by mid 2008). Along the way it would keep innovating and learning what worked best. It is a testimony to what the World Bank can achieve with the right staff, the right focus and the right resources (a point we shall return to later in this chapter).

These case studies help to answer the second question we posed at the outset of the book: Why did solar diffusion accelerate in several emerging markets at the turn of the century? As we have seen, it was not a sudden break-through in R&D, or a radical decline in the price of solar modules that prompted an acceleration in diffusion. Solar was already competitive in rural areas of emerging markets. Instead, diffusion only accelerated once a market infrastructure had been developed to make solar and after-sales services widely available, and finance channels were in place to make it widely affordable. But this of course begs the question of how did this happen? The answer lies in the efforts of pioneering entrepreneurs up to a decade prior to a 'take-off' in solar diffusion.

Consumed by a vision, these early entrepreneurs set up shop, struggled through the lean years, figured out how to elicit a rural demand for solar, and service it on a small scale. During these years they learned valuable lessons, and developed the capacities they would need to grow their solar enterprises.

In doing so, they also served as an example to others. Competitors, sensing that these entrepreneurs had hit upon a high-potential market, followed their lead. So did policymaking institutions, such as the World Bank, which saw in these small-scale operations the basis for much larger-scale diffusion. But the competitors and the policymakers also had a lot to learn about what worked and what did not. Nobody had all the answers on day one.

And during this time, investors sat it out, either ignoring the process because it was too small and too risky, or watching cautiously from the side-lines. Only a few were willing to put their toe in to test the market. It was only once the capacities had been developed not just in the pioneering entrepreneurs, but in the firms that followed, and more effective policies were in place, that investors and the competing firms, committed more resources to the solar market.

Once the learning (capacity) had been established across a range of firms, more capital (resources) was invested in serving the market, and the right incentives (policy) had been put in place, solar diffusion was poised to accelerate. To elicit customer demand for solar and service it, entrepreneurs and competing firms built a market infrastructure that reached deep into rural areas, making solar products and essential after-sales service available on the doorsteps of thousands of rural households. In parallel, consumer finance channels were opened through banks, microfinance institutions and sometimes the same entities that were selling solar. As a result, customers were now able to access long-term loans to make solar more affordable. This combination of increased availability and affordability of solar led to a 'take-off' in its diffusion.

Referring back to the diffusion framework proposed in Chapter 2, the case of solar stands as a clear example of how capacities, resources, and policies can come together to take the diffusion of a renewable energy technology to new heights. But as we have seen, this process fundamentally took *time*. Even after solar was competitive with the alternatives, it did not automatically and rapidly diffuse. It took time for entrepreneurs and the competing firms to develop the required capacities, for investors and firms to commit the required resources, and for policymakers to identify the right set of incentives to support the process. We might call this the 'lag effect' in solar diffusion, and it suggests that we must not be made complacent by hopes that once a renewable energy technology is competitive, it will rapidly diffuse – a theme I will return to later in this chapter.

With the essential questions answered, *Selling Solar* then turned overtly prescriptive. Our reviews of case studies of entrepreneurship and policy formation in Part II provided us with a guiding principle for policymakers in Part III: to successfully accelerate solar diffusion, policymakers must be able to *see* the solar market like an entrepreneur. In practice, this led to eight policy recommendations to accelerate the diffusion of solar in emerging markets.

Policy Recommendations

1   Do not create parallel government-driven markets
2   Make foreign direct investment and direct selling easy
3   Do not apply import duties and sales taxes
4   Deploy a grant per unit installed on a consistent basis
5   Facilitate lines of credit to rural finance institutions
6   If there is no rural finance, do not do fee-for-service
7   If there is no rural finance, target smaller system sales instead
8   Establish an independent agency and monitor

Our findings showed that policymakers should not create parallel, subsidy-driven markets for solar (as in India or the Philippines), which will crowd out entrepreneurs. Similarly, policymakers should avoid taxing solar through sales taxes and import duties – this applies to the entire solar system as well as the solar module. After all, there is little point in subsidizing kerosene, which unelectrified households use for lighting, and taxing solar, which is a superior source of energy for electric light.

Following the World Bank's lead, policymakers were advised to use a grant per unit installed (roughly 25 per cent of the retail price) to incentivize entrepreneurs to build a market infrastructure for solar, and to help support them in a difficult setting. They were also advised to put in place lines of credit, and ensure that this credit reaches the intended financial institutions, which can in turn make it widely available to a customer base waiting for solar loans.

In the unlikely event that policymakers cannot identify or entice *any* finance institutions to lend for solar in rural areas, they were strongly advised not to run fee-for-service programmes. Fee-for-service may seem ideal, since customers pay a low up-front fee to rent a solar system and receive guaranteed service (including battery replacement) in exchange for a monthly fee. But when a customer does not have an ownership incentive to care for the system, fee-for-service can be a very high-cost business model and thus a difficult one for entrepreneurs to profitably execute. To compensate for these high costs, governments have offered lavish subsidies. But as we saw in South Africa, this then leads to a highly politicized environment. Prescribing a high-cost business model in a politically charged setting is guaranteed to deliver a low rate of solar diffusion.

Instead, in the absence of loans for solar customers, policymakers were encouraged to promote the sale of smaller solar systems on a cash basis. The review of solar diffusion in Kenya and China showed this to be an effective route to rapid diffusion. Although smaller solar systems do not deliver the full amount of power that customers ideally want, they do provide essential light. And they provide it in a way that is more affordable to the customer, and easier for entrepreneurs to profitably execute.

To then administer grants and lines of credit, policymakers should identify an *independent* agency, for example a private-sector bank, as in the case of DFCC in Sri Lanka. This agency will be responsible for setting standards, disbursing funds, and monitoring the quality of products, installations and after-sales service. There will always be firms that try to cut corners, and an independent agency is the best way to regulate this.

Finally, having seen the enormous potential for rapid diffusion of solar in emerging markets, and having seen that through the early activities of entrepreneurs, and the right set of policies, a process of self-sustaining commercial sales of solar can be set in motion to the benefit of thousands of unelectrified households, *Selling Solar* turned its attention to the future.

In 2001, the G8 set a target of reaching 300 million unelectrified people in emerging markets with renewables by 2010. This deadline will obviously be missed. But since the time the G8 set this target, solar has started to diffuse rapidly in some emerging markets and started to fulfil its enormous potential. In light of these new developments, the G8 target is worth another try.

Specifically, in line with the G8 target, we set the goal as 100 million solar homes by 2025.[1] Reaching 100 million solar homes would be the equivalent of providing power to 400 million people, or 25 per cent of the world's current unelectrified population. It represents a staggering hundred-fold increase in cumulative solar diffusion between 2000 and 2025. Based on the scale of this challenge, it seems natural to assume that emerging markets will not be able to reach these numbers without some outside assistance. In which case, what prevailing international forces might help them get there?

Selling Solar considered the impact of four prevailing international forces on solar diffusion in emerging markets:

1   World Bank solar projects;
2   bilateral aid initiatives;
3   future price reductions of solar modules; and
4   the emergence of carbon trading.

After a careful review, none were found to be up to the challenge. World Bank projects are likely to reach only 1 million solar homes by 2010. Replication is not happening fast enough within the World Bank. So instead, can we rely on bilateral aid agencies to step in? The answer here, again, is unfortunately no. Aid agency programmes suffer from being largely 'tied-aid', stop-and-start programmes, with little basis for sustainable solar sales once the programme finishes.

Is it possible then that market forces can pick up where multilateral and bilateral agencies leave off? Will strong demand for solar in industrialized countries, and the strong growth in production this creates, lead to economies of scale that reduce the price of solar modules, and thus naturally enhance diffusion in the rural areas of markets? Our findings again indicated no. Future reductions in the price of solar modules will not lead to a significant decline in the average retail price of a solar system delivered and installed in a rural customer's home. It will still take expanded access to consumer finance to make solar widely affordable to millions in emerging markets.

Finally, could the emergence of carbon trading assist? Here we noted that entrepreneurs selling solar in emerging markets can in theory benefit from the sale of CERs. But in reality there are seven significant hurdles (described in Chapter 8) that any entrepreneur will need to successfully breach before this potential can be realized. Given the existing kinks in the carbon trading system, and the burden it presently places on entrepreneurs, it is unlikely to take us to our target.

Thus this book concludes that the only way to reach 100 million solar homes by 2025 is with the establishment of a dedicated challenge fund ('the

Fund'). The Fund should rest on three tried-and-tested pillars for supporting solar diffusion:

1   It should use a grant per unit installed to incentivize firms to build a market infrastructure for solar that reaches deep into emerging markets.
2   It should use a line of credit to encourage and enable local finance institutions to offer solar loans.
3   It should seek limited policy changes to ensure these funds have maximum impact in accelerating solar diffusion.

We further suggested that the Fund could be managed by the World Bank. Why the World Bank? Primarily because the Bank has the best existing reach to emerging markets of any international institution, has highly trained staff well attuned to emerging market conditions, and can effectively raise, manage and disburse the required funds to client countries. Moreover, the Fund would use the same formula innovated by the World Bank itself.

With such a Fund in place, 100 million solar homes by 2025 is attainable. It will need political champions to make it a reality. But it will also create a tremendous legacy for those who support its establishment: improving quality of life for families in 100 million homes (roughly half a billion people); propelling entrepreneurship, technological innovation and economic growth; and leading to millions of skilled jobs in the parts of the world that need it most. It remains an opportunity waiting to be seized, much like solar in emerging markets was once waiting for the entrepreneurs.

Having summarized the findings of the book for solar diffusion, we now turn to the lessons for other renewable energy technologies in emerging markets. The theories explored and developed in Chapter 2 can be used to explain and expedite the diffusion of a range of renewable energy innovations and other complementary technologies.

Wider Relevance of the Diffusion Framework

Solar is but one of the renewable energy technologies that emerging markets can choose from to lessen and eventually eliminate their dependence on fossil fuels. Others include, for example, wind turbines, hydro installations, biomass power units, solar thermal concentrators and geothermal units. In addition, energy-efficient and other clean-energy innovations are a natural complement to renewable energy, either because they reduce the amount of energy needed in the first place or they help put renewable energy to use in a meaningful way for customers. Examples might include energy-efficient lights such as CFLs or LEDs, appliances such as energy-efficient fans, fridges and pumps, smart meters to inform customers about their power consumption, or fuel cells, electric vehicles and low-emission cooking stoves. Assuming a willingness to encourage their wider use, the key questions remain: What is limiting the diffusion of these innovations today? How can emerging markets expedite their diffusion tomorrow?

We can think of a range of actors that would like these questions answered: politicians and government officials in emerging markets who are intent on reducing the amount spent on imported fossil fuels; international agencies and officials who are helping emerging markets introduce renewables into their energy mix; entrepreneurs and larger firms that are engaged in selling renewable energy and other related innovations and want to sell more; investors who would like to know which technologies and which entrepreneurs and companies to back; environmental activists who would like to see a reduction in local pollution with immediate health impacts, as well as the emergence of a more sustainable development pattern; and students who have taken up the challenge of explaining the diffusion of an innovation and hope to make a contribution to the policy dialogue. But, very often, those with a stake in the accelerated diffusion of renewables in emerging markets do not have the right tools. Where should they begin to look to identify the barriers to diffusion? Who will surmount these barriers? And how will they do it? The diffusion framework developed in Chapter 2 is intended to help those interested in diffusion answer these pivotal questions (Figure 2.4).

This diffusion framework (repeated, for the sake of convenience, as Figure 9.1 overleaf) is of particular relevance to a technological innovation in its early stages of diffusion.[2] At this point, it is more a question of 'someone' bringing the innovation to market, and trying to make it relevant to a wider customer base. This gives pioneering entrepreneurs a special and pivotal role to play. Later in the technology's life cycle, the role of the early entrepreneurs is obviously of less relevance, except from a historical perspective. Because many renewable-energy, energy-efficient and clean-energy innovations are still in the early stages of diffusion, the framework is of particular relevance to these technologies.

How then to use the framework? First, select the innovation in question. It could be micro wind turbines; it could be high-efficiency LED lights; it could be solar thermal water heaters. Then demarcate the geographical territory of interest. This could be a country; it could be a state within a country; it could even be at the district or sub-district level. Then within that geography, try to identify the pioneering entrepreneurs – those most responsible for the early introduction of the product. These will be the key units of analysis.

Once the innovation, the geography and the entrepreneurs have been selected, proceed to analyse the existing barriers to diffusion. Here, a word of caution. There is a knee-jerk reaction to assume the main barrier to diffusion is always

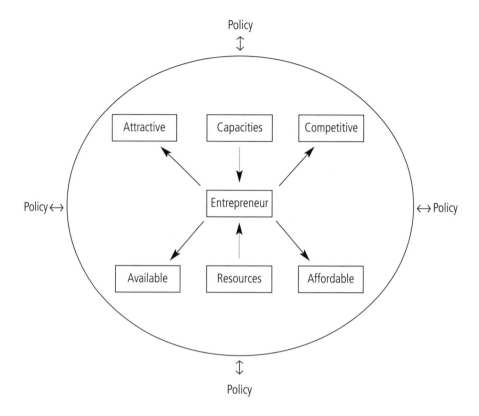

Figure 9.1 An integrated analytical framework for explaining innovation diffusion

the 'price' of an innovation: if the innovation could just be made cheaper then diffusion would accelerate. But as we saw in the case of solar, this can lead to flawed analysis. Many were writing off solar as too costly for rural markets even though it was more cost-effective than the alternatives over its lifetime and was starting to be sold by entrepreneurs on a commercial basis. In line with this view, the sceptics were advocating more R&D as the precursor to diffusion. But as we saw, the actual precursor to diffusion was not more R&D, but rather the introduction of finance to make solar affordable, and a market infrastructure to make the product and services more available.

Turning first to the barriers to diffusion, the diffusion framework suggests we ask four essential questions pertaining to the innovation in question:

1   Is it attractive?
2   Is it competitive?
3   Is it affordable?
4   Is it available?

Is it attractive?

When we ask if an innovation is attractive, it is a simplified way of asking how customers *perceive* the innovation. Therefore the analyst's first objective is to get inside the mind of the customer to understand their initial reactions to the innovation and their satisfaction after purchase. This will help to establish the relative attractiveness of the product. If it is not attractive, then the innovation may not yet be ready for market. But if it is attractive, the key is to understand how the early customers first heard about the innovation, and what helped them overcome their uncertainties and decide to buy it. Analysts should particularly look out for the role of referencing (word of mouth), opinion leaders, change agents and social norms. Any process that helps accentuate the perceived benefits of the innovation and reduce uncertainty will be critical to diffusion. For instance, in the case of solar we saw that customers appreciated the benefits of solar over kerosene lighting, and that referencing of existing solar users was critical to diffusion. But this only applied if the solar system was coupled with reliable after-sales service. Without service, diffusion was more likely to be hampered by negative perceptions that solar did not work.

Is it competitive?

By contrast, the question of whether an innovation is competitive or not is intended to be totally objective (devoid of customer perception). First, identify the alternatives to the innovation that customers presently use, and compare the competitiveness of the innovation in terms of both economic gain and functionality. In the case of renewable energy and energy-efficient technology, it will be essential to look at the life-cycle costs of the technology, and not just the up-front costs. A cost/benefit analysis of the innovation compared to different substitutes over 5, 10 and 20 years will be a particularly useful tool. If the innovation is competitive on a life-cycle basis, then there is a solid basis for its diffusion, all else being equal. If not, then it is likely that, without significantly superior functionality, it will require further development and reductions in cost for diffusion to accelerate.

Is it affordable?

As we saw in the case of solar, even if an innovation is competitive, it will not rapidly diffuse if it is not affordable. Here, rather than consider the innovation in an objective economic sense, the analyst needs to relate the price of an innovation to the very specific disposable income of the target customers, and consider whether they have the purchasing power to afford it. For example, although green revolution agricultural technology was competitive in terms of enhanced profitability per acre, it was not initially affordable to most farmers in emerging markets. Renewable energy innovations like solar will also tend to fall into this category. Although these innovations can save the customer money over time due to lower running costs, they tend to have higher up-front costs, which can put them out of reach for many customers in many parts of emerging markets. Once that is understood, then the analyst can properly assess the strategies for making an innovation more affordable. As in the case of solar, is finance the solution to greater affordability? Or can an innovation be radically redesigned for substantially lower costs?

Is *it available?*

Finally, if an innovation is attractive, competitive and affordable but not easily available, then diffusion will suffer. Here it is important to assess the extent to which an innovation is infrastructure-constrained, meaning the extent to which it relies on a supporting infrastructure for its diffusion. If an innovation can use a pre-existing infrastructure, then it may be able to diffuse more rapidly. But if an innovation needs a new infrastructure, then its diffusion will be tied to how quickly this can be built. For instance, in the case of solar, diffusion was initially limited by the absence of sales points, locally available inventory, salespeople, and technicians who could provide both installation and after-sales services. Only once this market infrastructure was built did diffusion accelerate.

The entrepreneur

Having reviewed the barriers to diffusion, the next challenge is to look more closely at how they are overcome. This brings us to the role of the entrepreneur. As we saw in the case of solar, to explain the acceleration of diffusion without reference to the pioneering entrepreneurs would have been meaningless. Similarly, entrepreneurs today are toiling throughout the renewable energy and energy-efficiency sectors to bring new innovations to market. In order to explain innovation diffusion, the analyst needs to be able to account for what empowers these agents to make their impact on diffusion.

Entrepreneurs often play a central role in bringing an innovation to market and trying to make it attractive, competitive, affordable and available enough that thousands if not millions of customers will buy it. The analyst's job is to understand how exactly they achieve this. This is the essence of *agency* – the ability to effect change. And specifically, to understand entrepreneurs' ability to effect change, I recommended looking at their capacities and resources.

Capacities

By 'capacities' we mean the prior experience entrepreneurs bring to their businesses, and the key lessons they have learned along the way. Both of these inform business strategy, and influence the entrepreneur's effectiveness in overcoming barriers to diffusion. In the case of solar, we identified the core barriers to diffusion as the lack of consumer finance and the lack of a market infrastructure. Entrepreneurs had to learn the hard way how to tackle these barriers, and each brought different sets of capacities to the task. In India and Sri Lanka, for example, both entrepreneurs tried to finance customers themselves, but neither of them had experience in this activity, and learned that this was difficult to do. Ultimately, they learned it was better to focus on building a market infrastructure and let the banks or microfinance institutions take on the role of financing customers. This lesson proved key to their being able to stay in business and drive forward the diffusion process in their respective countries.

Resources

By 'resources' we mean capital. Without capital, even the most effective entrepreneur is unlikely to affect diffusion. Of course, the amount of capital that needs to be raised will depend on the barriers identified and the entrepreneurs' strategies for surmounting them. If the innovation is not yet competitive, then the entrepreneur's capital requirements are likely to be higher – to finance R&D, for example. And if the innovation is already competitive but it is not yet widely available, the capital required may be less, albeit still sufficient to enable an entrepreneur to build a market infrastructure.

In addition to the amount of capital required, analysts need to explore the avenues through which entrepreneurs have been trying to access capital and the reasons for success or failure in doing so. In *Selling Solar*, all the profiled entrepreneurs had insufficient capital to realize their objectives, and solar diffusion suffered as a result. There was initially no 'investor fit', as most investors were unfamiliar with rural solar markets and the risks were perceived to be too high relative to the returns.

However, at some point investors' perceptions changed. We saw in Sri Lanka for example, that the entrepreneur was able to use World Bank policies to attract a sizeable investment by Shell Solar. Once he had put this investment to work in the market, it encouraged further investment by competing firms, and an unprecedented expansion in the market infrastructure and finance channels for solar.

Overall, *Selling Solar* showed that capital, in line with the theories in Chapter 2, is critical to an entrepreneur's ability to influence the diffusion process, and any analysis of renewable energy in emerging markets will fall short without considering the factors affecting its flow. The challenge for the analyst is to 'get inside' the mind of potential investors, and understand what determines the decision to invest, or not to invest, in the entrepreneurial ventures in question.

Policy

In a final step, the analyst needs to turn from considering the entrepreneurs to considering the more structural features of the environment in which they are working. In the case of energy (an essential commodity for life), the entrepreneur's environment tends to be heavily regulated. This in turn gives policy a prominent role to play when considering the diffusion of renewables and energy-efficient technologies.

Here the analyst needs to examine the specific policies that facilitate or impede the entrepreneur from selling more of the innovation in question. Again, the policy of concern will depend on the barriers to diffusion the analyst has identified earlier. If the main barrier is the absence of a market infrastructure, then perhaps the main policy hindrances are taxes (import duties and sales taxes) that are squeezing the entrepreneurs' margins and limiting the extent to which they can raise further capital to profitably expand. We saw in the case of solar that the entrepreneurs in India faced high import duties and high taxes, both of which limited their margins and made expansion difficult. On a more positive note, the policy of putting in place lines of credit for solar, which banks and microfinance agencies could on-lend to solar customers, proved critical to the acceleration in solar diffusion.

Conclusions

By now the framework will have helped the analyst draw three sets of conclusions:

1   It will have helped isolate the key barriers to diffusion of the innovation in question.
2   It will have shed light on how and why entrepreneurs are able, or not able, to effectively surmount these barriers.
3   It will have identified which policies facilitate or hinder entrepreneurs in the overall diffusion process.

Finally, while the diffusion framework is good at explaining diffusion that has already accelerated, it can also be applied to innovations that have not yet taken off. Applying it in such instances can help to understand precisely why entrepreneurs in the marketplace are not yet able to effect change. Moreover, applying it in this context can also have some predictive value. The conclusions should tell the analyst whether or not an innovation is poised for rapid diffusion and, if so, what it will take for this to happen and when this might occur. This is obviously of interest to many people with a stake in diffusion, not least the interested investor or business person.

Many emerging markets desperately need energy to lift their populations out of poverty and fuel their economic growth. Renewable-energy and energy-efficient innovations can provide this energy in a way that helps to lessen (and one day eliminate) their dependence on fossil fuels. Many entities and individuals have a stake in this process, including emerging-market governments, international organizations, businesses, investors, activists, students and concerned citizens. The diffusion framework developed in *Selling Solar* is intended to provide these interested parties with a tool they can apply to the diffusion of other renewable energy and energy-efficient innovations. The lessons and prescriptions that flow from such analysis will ideally help emerging markets accelerate their transition to a renewable energy future.

Accelerating a Renewable Energy Future

As promised at the outset, the story of *Selling Solar* offers some 'big picture' lessons. Specifically, five lessons can be distilled to accelerate a renewable energy future. These lessons are primarily intended for policymakers with an interest in renewable energy in emerging markets. But it would not hurt for policymakers in industrialized countries to absorb these lessons as well.

Lesson 1: Entrepreneurs are central to diffusion, so support them
Entrepreneurial ventures are never easy. But entrepreneurs in the renewable energy sector of emerging markets are operating in a particularly challenging environment. Policy needs to start from this premise.

Some parts of emerging markets lack the essentials that many entrepreneurs in industrialized countries take for granted: easy access to reliable market data, customers with bank accounts, direct debit and credit cards, relatively low rates of interest, easier means of communication and reaching customers, and so on. This tends to mean more challenges for entrepreneurs in emerging markets (not to ignore the opportunities), and higher perceptions of risk by investors.

In addition, there is the challenge of working specifically in the energy sector. This sector tends to be highly regulated and state controlled. It has changed over the years, with the onset of privatization and de-bundling of utilities. But in many emerging markets, it remains a politically sensitive area, seen, for instance, in the popular backlash against removing subsidies for diesel, LPG or kerosene. In this sense, renewable energy entrepreneurs in emerging markets have their work cut out for them: politicians are under pressure to deliver cheap energy to the masses, while entrepreneurs are trying to innovate with renewable energy products that inherently have higher up-front costs but lower running costs. We saw in the case of South Africa, just how politicized support for solar became.

Yet despite these difficult conditions, *Selling Solar* has shown that pioneering entrepreneurs can create markets for renewable energy where before none existed. Even when existing policies were not conducive, entrepreneurs set up shop and demonstrated that customers were willing to pay commercial prices for solar. It was only on the back of this effort that policymakers started to think about how to scale up this promising new approach.

So the first lesson for accelerating a renewable energy future is that policymakers need to learn how to attract, support and retain entrepreneurs in this challenging sector. The trick, as we have discussed earlier, is to be able to 'see' the renewable energy market in question like an entrepreneur. If this can be achieved, then largely the right policies for accelerated diffusion will follow.

This may sound simple, but it is amazing how often policymakers fail to do it. This is largely because 'business' has for a long time been viewed as part of the problem, rather than the solution – perceived as working against the interests of local societies rather than with them. It also has to do with the different mindsets with which firms and policymakers approach a problem. One needs to make money from making or selling a product or service; the other simply wants a societal problem solved, and may not understand or have time for understanding what it will take for an entrepreneur to make money doing it. But to accelerate the diffusion of renewable energy technologies, it is imperative that analysts and policymakers learn to devise policies that incentivize entrepreneurs to deliver the solutions they seek.

In the case of solar, policies that helped accelerate diffusion were lower import duties, a grant per unit sold channelled directly to firms and lines of credit to be on-lent as solar loans. These were all things that either helped entrepreneurs reduce costs and improve margins, or helped them sell more solar – all of which ultimately contributed to profitable sales and diffusion in this sector. Policies that did not work were those that restricted foreign direct investment, unnecessarily increased the costs or capital intensity of doing business – such as fee-for-service in South Africa – or crowded out the entrepreneur by setting up parallel, heavily subsidized government programmes – such as those in India or the Philippines.

These sorts of policy conclusions may not initially appeal to some readers. For instance, eliminating import duties and encouraging foreign direct investment may smack of 'globalization' and corporate agendas that do not advance the interests of the poor. But as *Selling Solar* has shown, the lower the barriers to trade and investment in the renewable energy sector in emerging markets, the faster these essential technologies will diffuse. Similarly, the idea of channelling grants to firms participating in a renewable energy market may not sound that palatable either. But again, as *Selling Solar* has shown, if you want more entrepreneurs to enter a difficult sector, and remain there under difficult conditions, to deliver the renewable energy solutions that you seek, do not be afraid to incentivize them *directly*.

It will be entrepreneurs, and the firms that follow them, that lead emerging markets towards a renewable energy future. But it is policymakers who need to lead entrepreneurs by the nose with the right set of incentives. Learning how to 'see' a renewable energy market like an entrepreneur, and design policies that support and encourage pioneering entrepreneurs, will be one of policy-makers' main challenges when it comes to accelerating the diffusion of renewable energy in emerging markets.

Lesson 2: Big business is not the panacea

A movement of academics and activists is urging businesses to target the 'bottom of the pyramid' as a way of addressing chronic poverty:[3] not to write off the poorer 3 billion people in emerging markets, but to treat them as a huge untapped source of future growth. This applies to energy just as much as to mobile phones, computing and so on. But within this movement there tends to be a preoccupation with larger corporations, rather than the entrepreneurial start-ups. Is it right that we should be more preoccupied with attracting big business when it comes to accelerating renewable energy diffusion in emerging markets?

If we look at solar diffusion in emerging markets, we can see that it was actually the entrepreneur, the consummate 'outsider' that pioneered the market. This is very much in line with the theories of innovation and diffusion discussed in Chapter 2. The existing industries, the established players that could in theory have propagated this innovation, decided to stay on the side-lines when faced with the opportunity to participate. This included utilities, PV module manufacturers and consumer goods companies. They did not see the same opportunity that the entrepreneurs saw in this market in the early stages, nor did they have the will or the drive to try to create it.

But is there not some point in the diffusion process when it helps if big business comes behind the innovation and promotes it? In the case of solar, we saw that when larger firms entered with more resources and a different set of capacities – such as Shell Solar – they could help accelerate diffusion. They did this by investing more, by building a stronger market infrastructure, by holding more inventory, by weathering accounts-receivable challenges more easily, and by bringing new management tools and the power of their brand to the business.

However, we should also take note that, in the case of solar, big business did not demonstrate the same staying power as entrepreneurs. For instance, Shell Solar chose to exit the solar business in emerging markets about six years after entering it. By contrast, several of the entrepreneurs profiled in this book are still at it – still working to drive diffusion onwards more than one, some-times two, decades later. In contrast to big businesses, entrepreneurs tend to be rather single-minded individuals who, in Schumpeterian style, do not quit that easily. This is critical generally, but it is particularly critical to trying to sell renewable energy in emerging market conditions which can be very difficult at times, and which might prompt a larger corporation to pull out.

Big businesses tend to have multiple divisions and multiple streams of revenue. If their solar business is not working out, for example, but the others are, then it is easy to exit the solar business. But a solar entrepreneur cannot relax if his solar division is doing poorly, because he only has one division, one line of business. This focus means an entrepreneur will tend to develop a better understanding of the market, more determination to find a way through and a greater propensity to take risks. Furthermore, big businesses are often founded on policies that restrict quick decision-making, and are encumbered with political machinations that dilute focus. For all these reasons, big businesses are unlikely to prove the ideal vehicles for renewable energy diffusion in emerging markets.

We might note that in the broader, global solar market, this has already played out. Many of the present market leaders in the solar PV industry were mere entrepreneurial start-ups five or six years ago.[4] But they invested aggressively, grew rapidly, went public to raise more capital and have since gone on to dominate the space. At the same time the larger energy companies, such as BP and Shell, which were in the top five of the solar industry when these entrepreneurs were just beginning, have either been eclipsed or have exited.

There is still a lot of excitement around the potential for large corporations to transform the world's energy infrastructure.[5] But whether larger companies have the staying power to accelerate renewable energy diffusion in emerging markets over the longer term is questionable. It is easier to imagine if a large corporation can see its way clear to setting up a completely independent unit, branding it differently, funding it like an investor and treating it like a start-up. This would give employees the freedom and focus they need to develop and grow the business, and the corporation the distance it needs to be patient with the progress. But in the absence of this, it is likely that the entrepreneur will remain the stronger vehicle for accelerating the diffusion of renewable energy in emerging markets.

Lesson 3: Focus on finance

In *Selling Solar*, we have seen that there were two critical forms of finance necessary for diffusion: consumer finance for customers who wanted to buy solar systems and venture finance for entrepreneurs who were selling them. Both kinds of finance will be critical to the diffusion of renewable energy in emerging markets.

When customers buy a solar system, they are essentially buying at least 20 years of power, up-front, on day one. So the up-front costs tend to be high relative to the running costs. The running costs are of course relatively low because the fuel, sunlight, is free. Many other renewable energy and energy-efficient technologies fit this description – solar thermal water heaters, small wind turbines, micro-hydro generators, LED lights, energy-efficient fans and so on tend to have higher up-front costs and lower running costs than conventional technologies. It is a beautiful concept, but it makes for a lousy price structure for entrepreneurs trying to sell the innovation. Now add to this the fact that entrepreneurs in emerging markets are selling to customers that generally have little purchasing power, and you start to see why financing the customer becomes so critical to the future of renewable energy diffusion in emerging markets.

This point was made rather well in a small, probably little-read article published in the *Financial Times* in December 1996. In an editorial entitled 'High price of a green machine', the *Financial Times* quoted a producer of environmental technologies who described his products as 'nice to have, but ugly to pay for'. Because of this, he prescribed that companies like his have to be 'creative in cracking open markets. This will mean helping clients devise longer-term payback mechanisms for companies to recoup their investments.' And with specific reference to the emerging markets, he cautioned that:

> Even when there is a demand for products in, for example, some of the richer, faster-growing economies of Asia, financing remains a problem. If you want to go to Asia, you have to bring the money with you. You have to do everything.[6]

The experiences of this businessman with needing to arrange finance in order to sell an environmental technology in emerging markets are very similar to the experiences of the profiled entrepreneurs in *Selling Solar*, as they will be to those of any entrepreneur trying to sell renewable energy technologies in emerging markets.

Financing the user is so critical that it bears repeating. Concentrating on making this and that improvement to a technology, so as to reduce the costs by a few percentage points, without focusing on how to make it more affordable through financing, will not significantly drive renewable energy diffusion in emerging markets. Many like to focus on the costs of a technology to the detriment of focusing on how to make it more affordable. *Selling Solar* demonstrates how this kind of thinking can miss an opportunity waiting to happen.

But if financing the user is essential, we also saw that such finance will not occur without an entrepreneur on the ground making the product widely available. There is a 'symbiotic relationship' between an entrepreneurial venture being well capitalized and being able to arrange finance for the consumer. Indeed, of these two forms of finance – venture finance and consumer finance – if anything, venture finance must come first. Consumer finance for renewable energy systems will only materialize where entrepreneurs are actively selling in the market and building a reliable market infrastructure that can promise a financial institution a steady stream of creditworthy customers, strong warranties, and high-quality installation and after-sales service. And entrepreneurs can only do this at a meaningful scale with sufficient capital.

For instance, it was only when the entrepreneur profiled in Sri Lanka had sufficient capital at his disposal that he could convince the country's largest microfinance entity to expand their lending to solar customers. Similarly, it was only because the entrepreneur in Indonesia could bring more capital to the business than other profiled entrepreneurs that he could pioneer his own 'in-house' consumer finance scheme and build such an extensive market infrastructure to serve it. Capital is very much the life-blood of the entrepreneurial ventures we reviewed, and in this sense it was also the life-blood of solar diffusion. This finding will prove to be broadly applicable to the accelerated diffusion of renewable energy in emerging markets.

In this regard, it is encouraging to note that venture capital has started to flow to renewable energy ventures in a way that ten to twenty years ago, when solar entrepreneurs in emerging markets were struggling along, was hardly imaginable. In the US, for example, venture capitalists put US$727 million into 39 alternative-energy start-ups in 2006, compared with just US$195 million in 2005.[7] But this is not just happening in industrialized countries. The surging growth of China, India and other emerging markets, coupled with surging demand for energy, has encouraged venture capitalists to look more closely at funding renewable energy start-ups in emerging markets. This bodes well for accelerated diffusion, provided policymakers can also bring in the right set of policies to support, complement and enhance the flow of funding.

And again, there would appear to be a positive trend. For as more money enters a sector, so policymakers tend to listen and observe a little more intently. This has certainly happened in industrialized countries, where the 'tech barons' of Silicon Valley have started to lobby for energy policies that will stimulate renewable energy markets.[8] And this they are doing because they have a direct stake in the outcome of these policies through their investments in renewable energy start-ups. It is a universal process that as more companies become invested in manufacturing or selling a technology, so they will lobby for policies that help support the technology in question. And policymakers will tend to listen more intently, because more money and more jobs are now on the line. It suggests that over time an increase in the flow of new venture finance could help encourage a more suitable set of policies for solar and other renewable energy technologies in emerging markets.

Lesson 4: Re-energize the World Bank

The case of solar in emerging markets has clearly shown how effective the World Bank can be in helping to accelerate the diffusion of renewable energy.

As we saw, when the World Bank entered the solar sector, it had very little prior knowledge it could draw on. Like the profiled entrepreneurs, it was a question of learning by doing. This, however, it did to quite some effect: learning the lessons in India, it developed a strong project in Indonesia that, although thwarted by the Asian economic crisis, was replicated in Sri Lanka. Here it took hold and led to the diffusion of 125,000 solar systems by mid 2008 (representing 7 per cent of unelectrified households). Then the World Bank replicated again in Bangladesh (211,000 systems by mid 2008) and China (500,000 systems by mid 2008). It is an impressive track record, and shows the potential for the World Bank to take the lead in helping emerging markets transition to a new, renewable energy infrastructure.

Why focus on the World Bank? First of all, the World Bank has the 'reach', with an infrastructure of offices and staff that extends into virtually every emerging market. Second, it has highly trained, highly skilled staff, who, if properly focused on key targets and winning strategies in the renewable energy sector, will be able to deliver unprecedented levels of diffusion. Third, it has the funding: not only does it have long-term debt capital (some of it at very low rates of interest) for lines of credit for users of renewable energy technologies, but it has access to GEF grants. The World Bank is the ideal global institution to help emerging markets accelerate a renewable energy future.

But we have also seen, in the case of solar and the Bank's rejection of the Million Solar Homes Initiative (MSHI) proposed in 2002, that there is a reluctance in the organization to seize bold targets pertaining to renewable energy and organize its staff and resources around meeting them. Partly, this is due to the inherent conservatism of a large global bureaucracy. Partly, it is because most World Bank professionals are economists, who still think that solar and other renewable energy technologies do not compete, who do not think it is their job to 'pick' winning technologies, and who focus more on economic growth regardless of the energy technologies deployed. But a major reason for the Bank's reluctance is that it remains primarily a poverty-alleviating organization.

It is true that many of the world's poorest will be hit hardest by climate change, but *Selling Solar* has shown that the World Bank's poverty-alleviating mission can dilute the impact of its renewable energy activities. For example, to ensure smooth passage of the Bank's second follow-on solar project in Sri Lanka, Bank staff decided to target GEF grants at only smaller solar systems, ostensibly for poverty-alleviating reasons. But GEF grants are intended for global environmental benefits, not poverty alleviation. This shift in policy from the first to the second solar project compromised the entire industry by leading more affluent solar customers towards smaller systems, and thus smaller margins for the supplying firm and less satisfaction for the user. If anything, from a global environment perspective, you want a financially strong solar industry on the ground, and you want customers to be buying bigger solar systems, so that their entire needs are eventually met with solar, their satisfaction levels are very high, and they recommend similar systems to their family and friends.

At the 2008 World Economic Forum in Davos, Switzerland, the UK Prime Minister recognized this tension in the World Bank and called for it to be overcome:

> I can't see why we should not move immediately to the World Bank becoming a World Bank for the environment as well as development. ... We need a global carbon market and we need a climate change agreement ... and we need an institution that is global and can provide funds for the developing countries that want to introduce alternative sources of energy.[9]

For its part, when it comes to addressing climate change through renewable energy and energy-efficiency projects, the World Bank feels it is on track. It issued a press release towards the end of 2007 that proclaimed it had significantly exceeded the targets it agreed to at the Bonn Renewable Energy Conference in 2004. Its Bonn goal was US$913 million of new renewable energy and energy-efficiency projects between 2004 and 2007, and in the end it actually doubled this, delivering US$1.8 billion. Moreover, it said this represented an increase from 12 per cent in the early 1990s to 25 per cent of the World Bank's total energy-sector lending.[10]

While on the face of it, these are impressive results, they go nowhere near the amount of lending required by the climate crisis and opportunities for renewable energy in emerging markets. The paradigm shift towards renewable energy that one Bank employee referred to in the early 1990s is *still* going on. It's just not clear that the world can afford to wait any longer.

In light of the Bank's demonstrated success in the solar sector, and in generally increasing its lending for renewables and energy efficiency, it is time for the majority of the World Bank's shareholders to mandate that 100 per cent of all its energy-sector lending be for renewable energy and energy-efficiency projects. Projects like the 4000 MW complex of coal-fired power plants, called the 'Ultra-Mega Complex' in Gujarat, India, would simply be off the table.[11] There is no reason why such projects under normal economic conditions cannot be financed by the private sector, independent of World Bank assistance. And if they cannot, then the question should be raised whether a public-sector organization like the World Bank should be financing them in the first place.

Moreover, the Bank will also need to consider some internal restructuring. When it comes to renewable energy, the Bank needs to approach diffusion like a business: select the renewable-energy technologies with the potential for immediate deployment, select the attractive segments where there is a demand, select the strategies that have been show to work, and then allocate and drive resources towards ambitious targets, as agreed between senior management and the Bank's Board.

The suggestion that the World Bank house and manage a Fund to target 100 million solar homes by 2025 falls precisely into this category of new initiatives. Solar has already shown it is a winning technology in unelectrified areas of emerging markets. Moreover, the World Bank has also identified winning policies to help drive its diffusion forward. The key task now is to roll out a much larger programme that would meet much more ambitious targets than, for instance, 1 million solar connections by 2010 (the current World Bank trajectory). The new targets would instead call for 100 million solar connections by 2025, representing 25 per cent of today's unelectrified population and equivalent to a hundredfold increase in cumulative solar installations in emerging markets between the years 2000 and 2025. There would be annual targets to be met towards this goal, there would be a dedicated team for consistency and retained learning, and there would be a clear motivating mission and objective for all involved.

In addition to solar, for instance, you could imagine other parallel divisions that were dedicated to achieving 100,000 MW of wind energy capacity (the total current installed capacity globally) in emerging markets by 2025, or the diffusion of 100 million biogas digesters for smokeless cooking by 2025. Similar targets could be set for solar water heating, micro-hydro stations, geothermal units, bio-fuels and so on, and separate divisions, each with a separate executive and dedicated team, would be tasked with delivering the numbers in conjunction with client countries.[12]

World Bank staff will say their job is to respond to client needs, and not to push solutions on them. But the reality is that, through its negotiations for each project, it is always advocating the technologies or the approaches that are deemed best. When it comes to renewable energy, and accelerating its diffusion, the World Bank would make this implicit approach more explicit. It would become a mission-driven organization, making new technologies and approaches known to its client countries, sharing best practice and the best technological solutions known across geographical boundaries and continents, and actively encouraging the uptake and diffusion of renewable energy. There is no question that its client countries, and their populations, want these solutions. But they may not fully know about their potential, know how to deploy them, know how to accelerate their diffusion, or have the necessary funds. The World Bank would be the source both of this knowledge and of this funding.

This is not how the World Bank works today in the energy sector. But if it is to fulfil its nascent role of helping to tackle climate change, it will have to consider how to dramatically accelerate the diffusion of renewable energy across the emerging markets. In turn, it will need to reform and re-energize itself to properly address this challenge. Some politicians, such as the former President of France, have suggested the need for an independent global institution to tackle global environmental challenges.[13] But when it comes to emerging markets, one already exists – the World Bank.

Lesson 5: Don't wait for R&D; develop the markets now

Where the electricity grid is either not present or extremely unreliable, solar is competitive now. Indeed, it has been competitive for at least one, getting close to two decades. But, as with any technology, there is a period of time when the issue is not so much the competitiveness of the product as the success of entrepreneurs in making it relevant to customers and selling it.

Most people like to conclude that when an innovation is economically competitive with the substitute technologies, it will just diffuse – that the economic benefits of the innovation will mean that it just sells itself. And so the inverse is also concluded – for as long as there is not more R&D, followed by a breakthrough that leads to lower costs, diffusion will remain limited:

> For all the enthusiasm about harvesting sunlight, some of the most ardent experts and investors in solar technologies say that moving this energy source from niche to mainstream – in 2007 it provided less than 0.01 per cent of US electricity supply – is unlikely without any technology breakthroughs. And given the current scale of research in private and government laboratories, that is not expected to happen anytime soon.[14]

But this ignores that one of the best ways of attracting money to R&D, and the best minds to a technological breakthrough, is by using policy to stimulate the market first. It is only with the stimulus provided by Japan, Germany, and now the US and other markets that solar has attracted so much private capital to invest in improved efficiencies of cells, new generations of solar modules and improvements in manufacturing techniques. Moreover, by building the market infrastructure for sales, installation and service *now*, it ensures that when a breakthrough is made, there are already the channels in place for that breakthrough technology to more easily reach the waiting customer base, enabling diffusion to happen much more quickly.

We saw how some analysts, after studying the potential for solar in emerging markets, concluded that efforts to promote PV markets were premature, and that funding should instead go to R&D and manufacturing to bring down the costs before trying to stimulate local markets. This study, however, has arrived at precisely the opposite conclusion.

As we have seen, although solar had higher up-front costs than the alternatives, it was already cost-effective over its lifetime, was preferred by customers over the alternatives – such as kerosene lanterns and battery charging – and, provided that consumer finance was available, customers were willing to buy it in ever-increasing numbers. Accelerating its diffusion was not about returning to the laboratory to figure out how to further reduce the cost of the solar module. Instead, accelerating solar diffusion was reliant on entrepreneurs entering the market, learning how to sell solar effectively, learning how to arrange consumer finance in a way they could manage, learning how to extend their distribution channels without over-extending their cash position, and learning how to raise the capital they needed for expansion. In parallel, policymakers had to learn which types of policies worked best to help promote and stimulate the solar markets, and which ones did not. All of this took learning by doing, and fundamentally it took *time* to figure it out. Earlier in this Chapter, I referred to this as the 'lag effect' associated with solar diffusion.

Had the World Bank and other policymakers taken the opposite approach, and diverted all the funds just to R&D and improved manufacturing of solar modules, as we have shown, it would not have made a significant difference to the retail price of an installed solar system in a rural unelectrified home. Moreover, imagine how much further behind we would be if the world had just waited. Entrepreneurs in emerging markets like Sri Lanka, India, Bangladesh and China would still be selling in relatively small numbers, there would just be a few of them, most customers would not know about the product, banks would still be wary of lending for it, salespeople and technicians would not have been trained in how to sell and install it, and policymakers would not yet have started to learn which policies work and which don't work in support of the technology. Instead, thanks to early action, thriving solar industries now exist selling solar to eager consumers, people understand the technology and are more aware of it, salespeople and businesses overall are better at selling it, banks have learned how to finance it, policymakers have figured out how best to stimulate the market further, and diffusion has already ramped up significantly.

Today, prominent analysts have recognized the urgency of helping emerging markets accelerate the diffusion of renewable energy technologies:

> What is needed, [Jeffrey] Sachs and others say, is the development of radically low carbon technologies. ... And time is critical, they say, as China, India and other developing nations march headlong into the modern world of cars and electricity consumption on their way to becoming the dominant producers of greenhouse gases for decades to come.[15]

And yet these analysts continue to arrive at the wrong answer for how to accelerate the process. In the same article Sachs maintains that, for renewable energy technologies to take hold, it will require a commitment approaching the scale of the Manhattan Project, 'a major overhaul in energy technology', financed by 'large-scale public funding for research, development and demonstration projects'. But if anything, *Selling Solar* has taught us that the *last* priority for emerging markets is actually more R&D and demonstration projects. Instead, the central message is to develop policies that incentivize entrepreneurs to sell the renewable energy technologies that exist today. If we keep downplaying the technologies that already exist, rather than supporting entrepreneurs to make them immediately relevant and available to customers, we are likely to wait too long.

Summary

When it comes to deploying renewable energy technologies to address climate change, we are in a race against time. Unfortunately, the history of technology diffusion suggests that time is not on our side. Technological innovations rarely diffuse at the rate their propagators and enthusiastic supporters hope for. That is why theories of innovation diffusion, which explain the time it takes for an innovation to gain widespread use in a society, are so relevant to meeting today's challenge of climate change.

There is a tendency among analysts and onlookers of renewable energy markets to concentrate on the 'price competitiveness' of these technologies relative to existing, conventional alternatives. If only it was less expensive than the alternatives, it would naturally diffuse. This, in turn, makes them predisposed to recommending policies for more R&D to accelerate diffusion. But the case of solar in emerging markets has shown how such analyses can be flawed.

Of course, there is no way for a fully installed solar system to have the same up-front price as a kerosene lantern. When you buy a solar system, you are not only buying the energy delivery system, but you are also buying the fuel for the next 20-plus years. This means the only way to compare the competitiveness of renewables like solar against fossil-based alternatives is on a life-cycle basis. When doing this, we saw that by the mid-1990s, solar was already competitive in the rural markets in comparison with what unelectrified customers were otherwise using. It was not the price of solar holding it back, it was something else.

Those who have studied the diffusion of innovations have long recognized that even after an innovation is competitive with the technological alternatives, it does not sell itself. As we have seen through a review of diffusion research, and application of the diffusion framework, there are a host of barriers other than the price competitiveness of an innovation that can hinder its diffusion. In the case of solar, these barriers included the absence of consumer finance to make the up-front cost more affordable for rural customers and the absence of a market infrastructure to make the product and related services more available.

Therefore, it was not more R&D or a technological breakthrough that led to an acceleration in solar diffusion in emerging markets. Rather, it was entrepreneurs recognizing the competitiveness of this new energy innovation, and stepping into the rural marketplace to start selling it. Once they did so, there was inevitably a lag effect, during which entrepreneurs were trying to learn how to sell solar in a commercially viable and sustainable manner, and trying to raise the resources their businesses required. This lag effect lasted throughout most of the 1990s, during which time solar diffused at a very slow rate. But through their actions, these pioneers sent signals to both new market entrants and policymakers that there was enormous potential in rural solar markets. In turn, new entrants helped to build the essential market infrastructure for solar and put in place more financing for solar consumers, and policymakers put in place further incentives to expedite this process, with the net result that several of the emerging markets profiled in this book are now in the midst of a solar revolution.

The story of *Selling Solar* serves as a wake-up call in two ways. First, no longer should we be made complacent by analysts who focus only on the price competitiveness of renewable energy. Instead, we need to dig deeper and identify the full range of factors that inhibit the diffusion of renewable energy innovations today. It may be that even 'competitive' technologies will 'lag' in their diffusion due to barriers other than price, and therefore any policies intended to support diffusion need to be targeted at these other barriers. [16]

Second, even in cases where a renewable energy innovation is not yet competitive, *Selling Solar* suggests that policymakers should avoid the temptation of targeting their spending on R&D and waiting for a technological breakthrough. A competitive innovation that is still not attractive to customers, affordable through finance, or widely available simply will not diffuse. Instead, the lessons of *Selling Solar* are that policymakers should use policies to encourage entrepreneurs to start selling and deploying the renewable energy technologies that are already at their disposal *today*. Entrepreneurs will have a lot to learn to address the full range of barriers to diffusion, such as how to raise capital, how to package the innovation in an attractive way for customers, how to build a market infrastructure for it, and how to work with finance partners. But having acted early, the policymaker has achieved two things: first, he has created a burgeoning market that will encourage more flow of capital towards R&D and manufacturing-at-scale than government programmes could otherwise achieve; and second, by the time these technologies are competitive in their own right, the early entrepreneurs and the firms that follow them will have already addressed the other barriers to diffusion, so that the newly competitive technologies will be able to diffuse that much more quickly.

In the end, there is no viable solution to climate change without making a wholesale shift to renewable energy technologies. This applies to both industrialized countries as well as emerging markets. But in emerging markets, the challenges are immense. By sheer force of will, some entrepreneurs will prevail. They always have done. But some entrepreneurs is not enough. If the goal is an unprecedented acceleration in the diffusion of renewable energy technologies in emerging markets, then policymakers need to encourage thousands of entrepreneurs to start selling these solutions *today*. They need to urgently orchestrate a crescendo of commercial interest, frenzied learning and a deluge of capital flows to the renewables sector. *Selling Solar* illustrates how policymakers who can 'see' a market like an entrepreneur will be best able to achieve this, and will be most successful in accelerating a renewable energy future.

Notes

Prologue

1   For the statistics quoted in this paragraph, see US Department of Energy (2005), p3.
2   Of course, all renewables will have their role to play. But it is important to note that without large-scale diffusion of solar, we will not have a renewable-based solution to the climate crisis. And in case the reader was wondering about the nuclear option, to deliver 10 TW of nuclear power would require the addition of one gigawatt (1 GW) of nuclear plant somewhere in the world every other day for the next 50 years: a trajectory with which the many would not be comfortable.
3   Roberts (2004), p162.
4   See *The Economist* (2006b). The statistics on cars that follow come from the same article.
5   Adiga (2006).
6   This article was originally written for *The Observer* newspaper in the UK. It is a sign of the growing awareness in emerging markets of the dangers of climate change that I read it in the local *Deccan Herald*, which publishes in Karnataka, India. See McKie (2007).
7   Kanter and Bennhold (2007).
8   Bradsher (2007b).
9   Moore (1995).
10 Kanter and Bennhold (2007).
11 Roberts (2004).
12 Yardley (2007).
13 Watt (2007).
14 But there is no question that, as we turn to technology for solutions, we must tread carefully. Technology can also backfire. Consider the case of bio-fuels, which are deemed a more environmentally benign alternative to oil. It was recently reported that 'rising demand for palm oil in Europe brought about the clearing of huge tracts of Southeast Asia rainforest and the overuse of chemical fertilizer there. Worse still, the scientists said space for the expanding palm plantations was often created by draining and burning peat, which sent huge amounts of carbon emissions into the atmosphere. Factoring in these emissions, Indonesia quickly became the world's third largest producer of carbon emissions that scientists believe are responsible for global warming.' See Rosenthal (2007).
15 Kanter and Cowell (2007).
16 Anderson (1992), p16.
17 Sang-Hun (2007).
18 President Abdul Kalam made this call at the South Asian Conference on Renewable Energy, where he said, 'For true energy independence, a major shift in the structure of energy sources form fossil to renewable energy sources is mandated.' See Yee (2006).
19 Planning Commission (2006), pxiii.
20 See, for instance, Prins and Stamp (1991); Lenssen (1992); Johansson et al (1993).
21 Bradsher (2007b), p4.

Acknowledgements

1   Prins (1992).
2   Northrop et al (1996).

Chapter 1

1   Indeed Standard Oil (S.O., then Esso, now Exxon) built its business on the back of kerosene for lighting.
2   Nye (1990), p304.
3   IEA (2002).
4   Gunaratne (1996a), p3.
5   For a general overview of these costs, see Rady (1993); Lovejoy (1992); Foley (1995); Cabraal et al (1996). For the specific cost estimates in western China, the Amazon and the Himalayas, see Flavin and O'Meara (1997).
6   Ranganathan (1993), pp142–151.
7   See Lovejoy (1992); World Bank (1996a).
8   IFC (1995), p6.
9   Bradsher (2007a).
10   Of course, other renewables also have a role to play, but they require that the local resource be present, such as running streams for micro-hydro or a good wind regime for small wind turbines. While some rural communities have access to these resources, many do not, whereas virtually all have access to sunlight for most of the year.
11   World Bank/UNDP (1989), p13. These findings have not stopped other emerging markets from continuing to deploy solar mini-grids. For instance, China recently rolled out hundreds of them, without first resolving the more thorny issues of who owns them, who will run them, who will maintain them, who will train communities to run and maintain them, who will collect the money from them, and who will pay for them. Not surprisingly, 20 years after the Pakistan experience, people are again questioning the sustainability of this approach. See Hirshman (2003), p25.
12   Solar water heaters are also enormously popular in some emerging markets. For instance, it is not well known that China has roughly 60 per cent of the global solar water-heater market. More than 30 million Chinese families already use a solar water heater, and over the last six years the market has grown sixfold. This is another case of incredibly successful diffusion in the solar sector, deserving of further research. See Perlin (2008).
13   Appliances running on grid electricity use AC current, largely because when you transport electricity from large dams, coal-fired power plants and so on, you need to transport it as AC power so as not to have efficiency losses. Of course, if your source of power is now directly overhead on your roof, in theory you could use DC power (since you don't need to transport it), but the problem here is that you will find it hard to run the full range of appliances on DC power.
14   In the solar industry a module is measured by the watts it produces at peak sunshine conditions. This is called a watt peak. The typical solar home system sold throughout the 1990s and early 2000s has been 50-watt peak (Wp). In typical conditions this provides about 200 watt hours of power – or roughly 20 per cent of one unit of power (a kWh) that a person using grid electricity will see on their electricity bill.
15   *The Economist* (1995), p26.
16   Halpert (1996).
17   Foley (1993), p195.
18   The first quote is from Foley (1993), p195; the second is from Foley (1995), p53.

19 For these statistics on Sri Lanka, see GEF (1998), p2, which was based on World Bank documentation; see, for instance, World Bank (1997), p2.

20 Van der Plas (1994).

21 Acker and Kammen (1996), p82.

22 For the World Bank's estimate, see Cabraal (2000). The GEF initially estimated that between 500,000 and 1 million solar home systems were in use by 2000: see Martinot et al (2000). However, the same author, E. Martinot, later clarified that, by the year 2000, 1.1 million households were estimated to be using either a solar home system or a solar lantern: see Martinot et al (2002), p312.

23 IEA (2002).

24 Wade (1996), p1.

25 Correspondence from the local administrator of the Sri Lanka project (30 January 2007) confirms that, under the World Bank's Energy Services Delivery Project (end 1997 to end 2002), 20,953 solar systems were installed. Under the follow-on project, Renewable Energy for Rural Economic Development (end 2002 to end 2006), 80,598 systems were installed. We can extrapolate from this that 100,000 solar systems were installed between 2000 and the end of 2006, in addition to the 6000 installed from the early 1980s to the end of 1999.

26 Rogers and Shoemaker (1971), p12.

27 Although this point was made in relation to understanding the diffusion of solar thermal systems in the US, it nonetheless demonstrates the applicability of the literature to solar applications and renewable energy innovations. For quote see Warkov and Meyer (1982), p13.

28 Rogers (1995), p7.

29 Giddens (1984), p14.

Chapter 2

1 This categorization of perspectives builds on the highly influential work of Brown (1981). Brown's work received widespread support from others in the discipline: see Leuthold (1982); Jones (1982); Penn (1984); Villeneuve (1982); Heertje (1983).

2 Many have recognized that diffusion research has been historically divided along the lines of academic disciplines, and that future research needs to concentrate on identifying the complementarities between the different perspectives: see Kelly and Kranzberg (1978); Leuthold (1982); Jones (1982); Deshpande (1983); Heertje (1983). Brown shares this point of view: 'Let us then go on with the task of exploring the complementarities between paradigms and working towards including all in a comprehensive model ... rather than arguing which is best' (Brown (1981), p191). Ten years later, the same point was still being made by Jain et al (1991, p90). However, in an article co-authored by the author, it is proposed that management literature on entrepreneurship may help to provide the unifying glue (see Miller and Garnsey, 2000). This book tries to put a more unified approach to work in explaining the diffusion of solar in emerging markets.

3 Brown actually calls this perspective the adoption perspective (Brown, 1981). But since all four perspectives are fundamentally concerned with adoption, which after all is the precursor to diffusion, this study prefers to use the term communication perspective, as used by Rahm (1993). The communication perspective is most closely associated with Rogers (1995). According to Agarwal, Rogers's work quite literally provides the basis for the vast majority of diffusion studies in the world (see Agarwal, 1983).

4 Rogers (1995), p34.

5 These findings by Ryan and Gross (1943, p22) on the importance of communication between early and later adopters would ultimately provide the foundations for the commu-

nication perspective, and would be widely applied and refined by other disciplines such as marketing (see Bass, 1969) and geography (see Hagerstrand, 1967). It has more recently been applied to the adoption of high-technology products emanating out of technology hubs like silicon valley (Moore, 1991).

6   Rogers and Shoemaker (1971).

7   Rogers (1983).

8   Long-standing sources on the influence of opinion leaders includes Tarde (1969); Stone (1952); Weimann (1994); Rogers (1995). The final quote on the 'law of the few' comes from the more recent work by Gladwell (2000).

9   Fliegel and Kivlin (1966).

10   Ryan and Gross (1943).

11   Rogers (1995), p243.

12   Rogers (1995), p213.

13   Havens and Rogers (1961), p414.

14   Rogers (1995).

15   Rogers and Shoemaker (1971), p227.

16   Foster (1973), p177.

17   Rosenberg (1994), p6.

18   Griliches (1957), p516. It is also worth noting that 20 years later, the same study was conducted again, using more complete data, and the conclusions proved to be 'supportive of Griliches's findings of a close association between the variability in the rates of diffusion across states on the one hand, and yield per acre and acres per farm on the other' (see Dixon, 1980, p1460).

19   Iowa Agricultural Extension Service (1955), p6.

20   Griliches (1957), p522. This conclusion set off a flurry of correspondence between the two camps (see Havens and Rogers, 1961; Griliches, 1962), resulting in a concession by Griliches that sociological variables still mattered: 'Let me say that in general I see little point in pitting one factor against another as the explanation of the rate of adoption. The world is just too complicated for such an approach to be fruitful. Thus I regret some of my own previous "all or none" remarks quoted by Havens and Rogers. If one broadens my "profitability approach" to allow for differences in the amount of information available to different individuals, differences in risk preferences and similar variables, one can bring it as close to the sociological approach as one would want to.' (Griliches, 1962, p330).

21   Mansfield (1961). However, later work by Mansfield is also interpreted as including sociological variables such as uncertainty and the rate at which uncertainty is reduced (see Rossini and Bozeman, 1977).

22   Rosenberg (1972), p6.

23   Rosenberg (1972), p12.

24   Hughes (1976), p425.

25   Sahal (1981), p4.

26   Bryant (1976), p446.

27   Hughes (1979).

28   Rosenberg (1972), p6.

29   Hayami (1970), p134.

30   Bass (1980), p52.

31   Rogers (1995), p213.

32   Rosenberg (1972).

33   Jain et al (1991), p90.

34   Hughes (1979), p148.

35   Hughes (1979), p148.

36   Roy (1994).

37 Agarwal (1983), p363.

38 Gotsch (1972).

39 Roy (1994), p31.

40 *Financial Times* (1996).

41 Roling (1982).

42 Rogers (1995).

43 Havens and Flinn (1975).

44 Fliegel and Kivlin (1966), p248.

45 For the example of the radio, see McNeil (1996). For the example of the water filters, see Tancred (2002).

46 Brown (1981), p50

47 Brown (1981), p507

48 Simon and Sebastian (1987), p460. Because 'limitations in production capacity or difficulties encountered in setting up distribution systems' (Jain et al, 1991, p83) can create a stream of *waiting adopters*, some analysts recommend that the Bass model (Bass, 1980), which reflects the economic history perspective, actually be refined to include supply-side restrictions.

49 Brown (1981), p7.

50 Brown (1981), p50.

51 Brown (1981), p104.

52 For the example of cable television, see Sieling et al (1975). For the example of high-yielding varieties of seeds, see Edesses and Polak (1993). For the example of using India's existing railway infrastructure to deliver internet and telephony, see Crampton (2000).

53 Brown (1981), p52.

54 Brown (1981), p31.

55 Brown (1981), pxiv.

56 See Penn (1984), p317. More generally, Brown is also praised for introducing business concepts such as market segmentation, pricing and target marketing to diffusion research (see Villeneuve, 1982; Deshpande, 1983).

57 This is recognized in one review of Brown's work as an omission: 'On the one hand [Brown] expresses the view ... that individual behaviour does not represent free will so much as choices within a constraint set and that it is government and private institutions which establish and control the constraints. On the other hand, Brown also believes very much in entrepreneurship. Paradoxically, the free will of entrepreneurs does not appear to be constrained as much as that of other individuals' (Villeneuve, 1982, p392). Thus the reviewer concludes that 'we also need to have a conceptualization of the relationship between entrepreneurship and institutional structures'. In a similar vein, others have found that 'the structural characteristics of the industry offering the innovation affect the speed of diffusion and the total market potential realized' (Robertson and Gatignon, 1986, p4). The analytical framework developed in this book attempts to provide some link between entrepreneurs, their structural environment and rates of diffusion.

58 Brown (1981) p60.

59 For quotes, see Robertson and Gatignon (1986), p2 and p6 respectively.

60 Wilkins (1970), p166.

61 Rosenberg (1994).

62 Nelson (1995), p68.

63 Schumpeter (1947), p223.

64 Schumpeter (1947), p224.

65 Knight (1921).

66 Drucker (1985).

67 Packard (1995).

68 Schumpeter (1947), p224.

69   Drucker (1985), p19.
70   Drucker (1985), p20.
71   Rothwell and Zegveld (1982).
72   Utterback (1994).
73   Utterback (1994), p73.
74   Utterback (1994), p74.
75   Porter (1990), p46.
76   This definition builds on the perspectives of Schumpeter and Drucker, but it is provided by Garnsey (1996 and 1998).
77   Schumpeter (1928), p385.
78   Robertson and Gatignon (1986), p4.
79   Utterback (1994), p8.
80   Porter (1990), although it is also clear that Porter's view is more nuanced, as he has also concluded that a 'stress on resources must complement, not substitute, for stress on market positions' (Porter, 1991).
81   Giddens (1984), p177.
82   Penrose (1995), pxiii.
83   Muzyka (1997).
84   Penrose (1995), p39.
85   Porter (1990), p49.
86   Schumpeter (1947), p224.
87   See Kenney (1986).
88   For first quote, see Schumpeter (1928), p379. For the second quote see same article, p384. Schumpeter reaffirms these views in later writing: 'Entrepreneurial performance involves, on the one hand, the ability to perceive new opportunities that cannot be proved at the moment at which action has to be taken, and, on the other hand, will power adequate to break down the resistance that the social environment offers to change' (1947, p229).
89   Drucker (1985), p26.
90   Smilor and Feeser (1991), p170.
91   Penrose (1995); Garnsey (1996 and 1998).
92   Smilor and Feeser (1991).
93   Mintzberg (1989), p124.
94   Garnsey (1996 and 1998).
95   Grant (1991). Many larger corporations can bring this full range of resources to the task of innovation diffusion. This in theory means they can have a larger impact on diffusion than their smaller rivals. The reality, however, is that for reasons discussed earlier, larger established corporations often miss the opportunity to seize upon an innovation.
96   Schumpeter (1928), p381.
97   Rothwell and Zegveld (1982).
98   Roberts (1991).
99   Smilor and Feeser (1991), p167.
100 Schumpeter (1928), p384.
101 See, for instance, Kelly (1997); Mason and Rogers (1996); Muzyka and Birley (1997).
102 Hughes (1979).
103 Mason and Rogers (1996), p2.
104 Kane (1997), p22.
105 Kenney (1986).
106 Zake (1995).
107 Mead (1995), p86.
108 See, for instance, Steel (1995); Soedjede (1995); Aleke-Dondo (1995).
109 Rosenberg (1972). Institutional change is broader than policy change, but it includes the latter.

110 Brown lists various types of institutional occurrences, among which he includes political changes that affect relative factor prices (1981, p194).

111 This example is also developed by Walton (1971).

112 Utterback (1994).

113 Rahm (1993).

114 See, for instance, Rosenberg (1972).

115 Brown (1981), p189.

Chapter 3

1   See, for instance, Foley (1995); Cabraal et al (1996).

2   Huacuz (1991).

3   Gunaratne (1996a), p3.

4   Gunaratne (1996a), p3.

5   Acker and Kammen (1996).

6   For a critical analysis of solar in emerging markets, see Erickson and Chapman (1995) (for quote see p1136). The abbreviation of 'kWh' stands for kilowatt hour: 1000 watts of energy supplied over an hour; it is a standard measurement of power delivery and consumption.

7   Erickson and Chapman (1995), p1136.

8   Acker and Kammen (1996), p100.

9   Acker and Kammen (1996), pp98–101

10 Acker and Kammen (1996), pp100–101.

11 Hankins (1993).

12 Interview with Programmes Coordinator of Enersol Associates, Washington, DC, 3 November 1995.

13 Acker and Kammen (1996), p97.

14 Hankins (1993), p37.

15 Acker and Kammen (1996), p96.

16 Hankins (1993), p63.

17 Presentation by representative of Condumex Energias Alternas, Conference on Decentralized Electrification in Developing Countries, Marrakech, Morocco, 13–17 November 1995.

18 Interview with Programmes Coordinator of Enersol Associates, Washington, DC, 3 November 1995

19 Hankins (1993), p119. Hankins offers an excellent portrayal of early aid projects in the solar sector and the impact these had on local perceptions of solar technology.

20 Wade (1996).

21 Today, this single component makes up roughly 30 per cent of the installed retail price of a 50-watt solar system with 4–5 lights (US$600). The batteries, wires, brackets and other accessories all put together are also roughly 25 per cent of the price and are pretty standard technologies with little scope for cost reductions. The electronics and lights have a little more scope for cost reduction, but these represent only 10 per cent of the price of a system. The rest is transportation, installation, sales commission and supplier margin.

22 US Department of Energy (1995).

23 Ahmed (1994), p47.

24 Drennen et al (1996), p12.

25 Ahmed (1994), p7.

26 Cabraal et al (1996).

27 Erickson and Chapman (1995), p1132.

28 Acker and Kammen (1996).

29 Erickson and Chapman's calculations in Table 3.3 assume a discount rate of 10 per cent and a lifetime of 10 years.

30   Erickson and Chapman (1995), pp1137–1138
31   For typical load of rural customers in emerging markets, see World Bank (1996a).
32   Miller and Hope's analysis used data from 1996.
33   Erickson and Chapman (1995).
34   Cabraal et al (1996).
35   Cabraal et al (1996), p19.
36   Foley (1995), p45; assuming a discount rate of 10 per cent and a lifetime of 10 years.
37   Cabraal et al (1996).
38   Miller and Hope (2000).
39   Acker and Kammen (1996).
40   Covell and Hansen (1995).
41   Foley (1995), p64.
42   Hankins (1993).
43   GTZ (1995).
44   Northrop et al (1996), p8.
45   Foley (1995), p67.
46   That said, smaller solar systems can be designed and sold for much lower power requirements (at much lower prices), for instance just one or two basic lights.
47   UNDP (1995), p45.
48   GTZ (1995), p136.
49   Cabraal et al (1996), pxi.
50   Of course, an alternative is to use a much smaller panel, limited electronics and low-wattage CFL or LED lights to arrive at a much cheaper product. But this is comparing apples and oranges, since it will not have power for radio and TV as well. Nonetheless, we will return to this approach in Chapter 7 as an alternative for policymakers to consider when no consumer finance channels are available to support solar diffusion.
51   Cabraal et al (1996).
52   Northrop et al (1996), p8
53   Huacuz (1991).
54   Hankins (1995), p19.
55   Barozzi and Guidi (1993), p2.
56   Cabraal et al (1996), p47.
57   Stone (1994), p20
58   Hansen and Martin (1990), p138.
59   Enersol Associates (1995).
60   Presentation by representative of Condumex Energias Alternas, Conference on Decentralized Rural Electrification in Developing Countries, Marrakech, Morocco, 13–17 November 1995.
61   See Hankins (1993).
62   Wade (1996), p8.
63   Liebenthal et al (1994).
64   Hill et al (1994).
65   Cabraal et al (1996), p66.
66   Martinot et al (2002), p316.
67   Hill et al (1994), p1.

Chapter 4

1   As a source for all interview material in this chapter, and for further quotes from relevant interviews, see the author's PhD thesis: Miller (1998).

2   Interview with Project Manager of NREL (National Renewable Energy Laboratory), 5 October 1995, Golden, CO.

3   See Huacuz (1991); Foley (1995).

4   Foley (1995), p72.

5   Gunaratne (1996b).

6   Ebisch (1995).

7   Hankins (1993), p12.

8   Foley (1993), p195. It was largely as a result of these early failed initiatives by aid agencies that those watching the progress of solar in emerging markets started to call its promise into question. As Foley wrote, 'The photovoltaic community must accept that the adoption of solar electric generation for development applications has been disappointing. Despite the obvious benefits, the take-up has been slow and sporadic. Really widespread use still looks as far away today as it was five years ago. It must be time to reassess the situation and evaluate whether we misinterpreted the potential or merely failed to capitalize on it.'

9   Liebenthal et al (1994), p13.

10   See too Covell and Hansen (1995), who came to similar conclusions.

11   Hirshman (2003).

12   More recent estimates were that approximately 2737 homes had received a solar home system and 3169 had received a battery for a battery-charging facility under the Government's scheme by 2003. Since 2000, the Department of Energy (DoE) has stepped in with an ambitious target of electrifying all villages, called *baranguays*, by 2006. The name of this project is O'Ilaw, and by 2003 an additional 5010 homes had received a connection to either an independent solar system or a centralized solar battery charger. This means that by 2003, a total of only 11,000 homes had received a connection to solar, and many of these were not in working condition (Philippines National Electrification Administration, 2002; World Bank, 2003).

13   Sastry (1994).

14   World Bank (1993a).

15   World Bank (1992a).

16   ECN (1996), p8.

17   Interview with former adviser to MNES, 3 January 1996, New York.

18   ECN (1995).

19   Interview with MD of PV manufacturer, 22 February 1996, Hyderabad, India.

20   Interview with former adviser to MNES, 3 January 1996, New York.

21   Interview with MNES consultant, 23 February 1996, Hyderabad, India.

22   TERI (1995b); see also TERI (1995a). Project reports by the World Bank came to similar conclusions (1993a and 1993b).

23   The Indian Government's programmes did scale up in the second half of the 1990s. By 2000, MNES said that their PV programme had managed to distribute 278,000 solar lanterns and 117,000 solar home systems (see Sastry, 2000). This means that over nearly two decades only roughly 13,900 lanterns and 5850 solar home systems were distributed each year by MNES throughout all of India, for a total penetration of still only 0.4 per cent of unelectrified homes.

24   Prabhakara is a former Secretary of MNES.

25   Interview with PV adviser of MNES, 11 March 1996, New Delhi.

26   Interview with Principal Scientific Officer of MNES, 29 February 1996, New Delhi.

27   Interview with PV adviser of MNES, 11 March 1996, New Delhi.

28   GTZ (1995), p142.

29   Cabraal et al (1996), pxiii.

30   Hankins (1993).

31   Hankins and Best (1994), p63.

32   For this general consensus, see Hankins and Wambutura (1994); Covell and Hansen (1995); GTZ (1995); Hankins (1995); Sanghvi (1995); Jechoutek (1995); Cabraal et al (1996).
33   Interview with NGO director, 10 December 1996, Washington, DC.
34   Interview with NGO director, 10 December 1996, Washington, DC.
35   Specifically, the NGO director set up what are called 'revolving credit funds'. Under this arrangement, customers pay for their systems on a financed basis – for example over 3 years. The funds collected from monthly customer payments are held aside by a local administrator, and then used to pay for new systems for later customers who also want to buy. Yet while such funds clearly demonstrated that people were willing to pay for solar on commercial terms, if they are not administered properly, and if the costs of this administration are not built in, as a World Bank analyst of this market once commented, they will quickly 'revolve down to zero'.
36   Before he set up a commercial company, he would go on to launch pilot electrification projects in 11 developing countries over seven years.
37   Article written by director of a solar NGO in 2000. In line with respecting the anonymity of the profiled entrepreneurs, this source is not quoted in full.
38   Article written by director of a solar NGO in year 2000. In line with respecting the anonymity of the profiled entrepreneurs, this source is not quoted in full.
39   Interview with Programmes Coordinator of Enersol Associates, Washington, DC, 3 November 1995.
40   Erickson and Chapman (1995).
41   ECN (1995).
42   Interview with Karnataka dealer to PV manufacturer, 5 June 1996, Bangalore, India.
43   Interview with marketing manager and general manager of PV manufacturer, 21 February 1996. Hyderabad, India.
44   World Bank (1996b).
45   Presentation by representative of Condumex Energias Alternas, Conference on Decentralized Electrification in the Developing World, ADEME (France)/UN Commission on Sustainable Development, 13–17 November 1995, Marrakech, Morocco.
46   See Southerland (1995); Marshall (1995).
47   Interestingly, this has a historical precedent: entrepreneurs played a prominent role in the extension of the rural grid throughout the Western world in the early 20th century. See, for instance, Hughes (1979); Nye (1990); Coopersmith (1992).

Chapter 5

1   Quotes from the entrepreneur in Indonesia come from the author's doctoral field work in Indonesia and PhD thesis; see Miller (1998).
2   Quotes from the American entrepreneur come from a combination of the author's PhD thesis and the entrepreneur's own memoirs. Quotes from the Indian entrepreneur come from the author's doctoral field work in India and PhD thesis; see Miller (1998).
3   Consultant's report, as quoted in Miller (1998).
4   This is as per the recollection of the American entrepreneur. The Indian entrepreneur recalled 40 homes.
5   Interview with DGM of Syndicate Bank, 22 February 1996, Hyderabad, India. Subsequent quotes from the DGM come from this interview, unless referenced otherwise.
6   Interview with economist at Syndicate Bank's headquarters, 29 May 1996, Manipal, India. Another colleague was even more emphatic when he said, 'The management of [the DGM] is the sole reason the scheme was launched. It is a personal, individual initiative. It was [the DGM] alone who convinced the Chairman and he has been the one to guide the formulation of the scheme.' Interview with agricultural development officer at Zonal Office, 8 June 1996, Hyderabad, India.

7　As the chairman of the Syndicate Bank explained, 'From the beginning [the bank] chose to function in rural areas. We are the only bank to have developed like this. ... By contrast, most banks migrate from the cities to the rural areas.' (from interview with chairman at Syndicate Bank headquarters, 21 March 1996, Manipal, India). This point was affirmed by an assistant manager within the bank: 'The very foundations of Syndicate Bank were built on rural banking. T. A. Pai [the founder] built this philosophy into the veins of the bank.' (from interview with assistant general manager at Syndicate Bank's headquarters, 29 May 1996, Manipal, India).

8　It is claimed the Syndicate Bank was the first commercial bank to lend for solar in the developing world; see Eckhart et al (2003).

9　The senior manager was clear there was more money for consumer finance than the entrepreneurs could then put to work: 'What [the enterprise] now needs is more people to expand the network. [We] are doing two districts under the scheme, and [Rs 400,000] has been dispensed so far, although the deposit is more. We have substantial funds to do more branches, but [the enterprise] has a limited network. There is certainly more money – [1–1.5 million] rupees can be used for solar.' (interview with senior manager of rural development bank, 7 April 1996, Dharwad, India).

10　Interview with agricultural development officer of Syndicate Bank, 8 June 1996, Hyderabad, India.

11　Interview with DGM of Syndicate Bank, 22 February 1996, Hyderabad, India. He had also learned this lesson from promoting pumping sets for irrigation: 'When we started financing pumping sets – oil, diesel, electric pumping sets – at that time there were no people supplying them. We were convinced it could work to increase [agricultural] production, but there were no suppliers of pump sets. Even manufacturers were not that interested. We did a market survey and set about encouraging them to expand production and new people to come in with manufacturing, supply and service.'

12　Interview with DGM of Syndicate Bank, Hyderabad, India, 8 June 1996.

13　Private discussion with DGM of Syndicate Bank, 30 June 1996, Mundurti, India.

14　From simulations of the enterprise's cash flow, it is clear that the Indian entrepreneur was probably right. The interest burden would have been too much at this point. For cash-flow simulations, see Miller (1998) or Miller and Hope (2000).

15　This VC firm specialized in software investments around Bangalore, often referred to as India's equivalent to Silicon Valley. It is plausible to imagine that expectations of such high returns were influenced by returns in India's IT industry at the time.

16　Interview with managing director of IREDA, 22 June 1996, New Delhi.

17　Consultant's report, as quoted in Miller (1998).

18　The strong results of the UNEP project in Karnataka suggest that if consumer finance were to be introduced in Kenya, for instance, where there is already a strong prevailing market infrastructure, we would see an equally strong (if not greater) surge in diffusion.

19　There was talk of the Indian Government continuing this scheme and transferring the existing MNES capital subsidy to an interest-rate subsidy instead. But as of today, this has yet to happen in India.

20　MNRE does not track private-sector sales of solar systems in India; it only tracks sales through the Government channel (as described in Chapter 4). However, it is possible to arrive at a close estimate. As of the end of 2007, the entrepreneurs in question had sold and installed more than 50,000 systems. Shell Solar had sold and installed an estimated 35,000 systems, mainly in Karnataka, before exiting towards the end of 2007. The rest of the local industry sold PV systems mainly to the Government channel in Karnataka. But under the UNEP programme, TATA BP dealers and other participants delivered roughly 25 per cent of the volume – equivalent to a further 5000 systems sold through private channels. This adds up to a total of 90,000 systems. To account for the final 10,000 we can easily envisage that various private dealers in Karnataka, with extensive networks, would have sold 10,000 systems between 1995 and 2007.

21 Email correspondence with consultancy responsible for implementation of UNEP project (Crestar), 25 May 2007. For an interim report on the UNEP project, with good background information, see UNEP (2004).

22 Macalister (2007), Hirshman (2007).

23 The quotes from the entrepreneur in Indonesia come from the author's doctoral field work in Indonesia and PhD thesis: see Miller (1998).

24 Recall the discussion in Chapter 2 about the advantage entrepreneurs have when they spin out of a similar, well-run business in the same sector.

25 However, the number of service centres is somewhat deceiving, because one service centre might cover several sub-districts. While there were 46 service centres, it was estimated that the entrepreneur was actually serving between 50 and 60 sub-districts.

26 The entrepreneur's business plan (1995), which is not referenced in the interest of anonymity. As a source, the reader can refer to the author's PhD thesis (Miller, 1998).

27 Miller (1998). These were the entrepreneur's prices as of mid 1996, before the economic crisis in Indonesia. Please bear in mind that these prices use the historical rate of the Indonesian rupiah (Rp) of Rp 2330 to the US dollar.

28 For a detailed analysis of the enterprise's cash-flow position, see Miller (1998); Miller and Hope (2000), p97.

29 The entrepreneur did not plan to retain margins at this level. He was focused on growing volume, and so planned to reduce his margins over time as his volumes improved. As he said, 'With more scale, you can afford to lower your margin and earn the same amount – ultimately reducing the cost to the customer and expanding the use of solar.'

30 The display unit on the wall was unique in Indonesia at this time. The entrepreneur's firm had started using it, and others soon followed suit. It enabled the battery to be enclosed, and to fix the unit on the wall like a consumer durable.

31 Correspondence from consultant to the World Bank Solar Home System Project in Indonesia, addressed to the project's task manager and technical adviser, 14 September 1995.

32 A simulation of the enterprise's cash flow shows that, without supplier credits, the entrepreneur would not have been able to sustain his consumer finance scheme, and the business would have collapsed a lot earlier – after only nine months. See Miller (1998).

33 As detailed in correspondence between the entrepreneur and World Bank staff from 1993 to 1996.

34 Assuming that competition forced the entrepreneur to pass on 50 per cent of the grant, and he retained the other 50 per cent, the author's financial projections suggest the entrepreneur could have sold 20,000 systems over three years and would have still been in a strong financial position for further expansion. See Miller and Hope (2000), p97.

35 The quotes of the entrepreneurs in Sri Lanka come from an article written on their experience. It is not referenced in line with maintaining the anonymity of all the entrepreneurs referred to in this book.

36 The entrepreneur recalled how, in one of the earlier meetings to lobby the World Bank, he was accompanied by the American entrepreneur profiled in the India case study. Some of the American entrepreneur's earliest work was in Sri Lanka, when he was director of the solar NGO described earlier.

37 Key to SEEDS entering the market when it did was that the managing director did not feel his organization was doing a good job of selling, installing and servicing solar. He did not see this as their core strength. But it was ultimately the entrepreneur who had to convince the managing director to follow his instinct and focus on just financing solar (and leave the selling to him). This was not necessarily an easy sell, as SEEDS's reputation and pride was at stake. And SEEDS had many doubts about whether the entrepreneur could deliver the busi-

ness and guarantee the right level of service to its customers. But once the entrepreneur could show the investment by Shell Solar, he was able to coax SEEDS into this new partnership and formalize the arrangement.

38 Eckhart et al quote the managing director of SEEDS as concluding that 50 per cent of people in Sri Lanka can afford a solar system with reasonable credit. Assuming he meant the unelectrified household base of 1.4 million, this translates into a market size of 700,000. See Eckhart et al (2003), p12.

39 Finucane (2005).

40 See Martinot et al (2001), p49. For a similar explanation, see also Martinot et al (2002), p329.

41 Cabraal and Fitzgerald (2001), p7.

Chapter 6

1 World Bank (1975).

2 Lovejoy (1992). Indeed, an internal report within the World Bank concluded that there were considerable limitations to mini-grids powered by diesel generators. See *Solar Industry Journal* (1991).

3 Bosshard (1993).

4 Morse (1992).

5 Interview with former renewable energy specialist in World Bank, 11 December 1996, Washington, DC.

6 Johansson et al (1993), p61. See also Office of Technology Assessment (1992).

7 World Bank (1993b), p92.

8 Interview with World Bank member of staff (ASTAE), World Bank, 19 July 1994, Washington, DC.

9 Interview with World Bank member of staff (Energy and Industry Division), World Bank, 20 July 1994, Washington, DC.

10 Van der Plas (1994).

11 Anderson and Ahmed (1994) and (1995); Ahmed (1994).

12 12 per cent was the benchmark to use funds from the International Development Association (IDA). The IDA is a line of credit within the World Bank for poorer countries.

13 World Bank (1992a and 1992b).

14 Background information provided by former renewable energy specialist at the World Bank, who participated as a consultant in the project design phase, 11 December 1996, Washington, DC.

15 In 1992 the Indian Government took the decision to upgrade the Department of Non-Conventional Energy Sources (DNES) to a ministry: the Ministry of Non-Conventional Energy Sources (MNES). This was later changed to the Ministry of New and Renewable Energy (MNRE).

16 World Bank (1993a), 5.3:3.

17 Interview with World Bank member of staff (India Desk), World Bank, 2 October 1995, Washington, DC.

18 World Bank (1993a), px.

19 World Bank (1993a), pp1–2.

20 World Bank (1992b), p3.

21 Interview with World Bank member of staff (ASTAE), World Bank, 16 December 1996, Washington, DC.

22 IREDA (1987), p1.

23 Interview with PV adviser of MNES, 11 March 1996, New Delhi.

24 Deviah (1995).

25   Interview with World Bank member of staff (India Desk), World Bank, 11 December 1996, Washington, DC.

26   Hassing and Mendis (1992), p30.

27   Interview with managing director of IREDA, 22 June 1996, New Delhi.

28   Interview with assistant to managing director of IREDA, 26 June 1996, New Delhi.

29   World Bank (1996b).

30   Interview with World Bank member of staff (India Desk), World Bank, 2 October 1995, Washington, DC.

31   Interview with World Bank member of staff (India Desk), World Bank, 11 December 1996, Washington, DC.

32   Interview with World Bank member of staff (ASTAE), World Bank, 16 December 1996, Washington, DC.

33   Hassing and Mendis (1992), p30.

34   Interview with World Bank member of staff (India Desk), World Bank, 11 December 1996, Washington, DC. By 'the Indian enterprise' is meant the enterprise launched by the American and Indian entrepreneurs profiled in Chapter 5.

35   The Bank had in part selected IREDA due to its 'satisfactory collection rate' (see World Bank, 1992a, p27). Yet perversely, the security requirements to ensure this collection rate effectively precluded many entrepreneurial start-ups.

36   Interview with former renewable energy specialist within the World Bank, and independent consultant to the World Bank's project in India, 11 December 1996, Washington, DC.

37   Hassing and Mendis (1992), p22.

38   World Bank (1993a), pxiii.

39   Interview with assistant to managing director of IREDA, New Delhi, 1 March 1996.

40   The incentive of 100 per cent accelerated depreciation was attractive to profitable companies, who could use it to reduce their tax liability to the Government. This, combined with a 2.5 per cent interest loan from IREDA (repayable over ten years), made PV installations very attractive to corporate clients.

41   Interview with World Bank member of staff (ASTAE), World Bank, 16 December 1996, Washington, DC.

42   Interview with World Bank member of staff (Indonesia Desk), World Bank, 17 December 1996, Washington, DC.

43   For more details on this project, see World Bank (1995a and 1996c); *World Bank News* (1997).

44   Interview with World Bank member of staff (Indonesia Desk), World Bank, 17 December 1996, Washington, DC.

45   Interview with World Bank member of staff (Indonesia Desk), World Bank, 17 December 1996, Washington, DC.

46   Interview with World Bank member of staff (ASTAE), World Bank, 16 December 1996, Washington, DC.

47   Interview with World Bank member of staff (Indonesia Desk), World Bank, 17 December 1996, Washington, DC.

48   Interview with consultant to Indonesia project, World Bank, 6 October 1998, Washington, DC.

49   Martinot et al (2001).

50   Martinot et al (2001), p49.

51   World Bank, *Republic of Sri Lanka; Energy Services Delivery Project*, Annex 5, 1.

52   World Bank (1999).

53   However, under RERED, the World Bank added a catch to the continuation of the grant. It would now be gradually targeted at smaller solar systems. This had a distorting effect on the market which I discuss in more detail in Chapter 7.

54   Finucane (2005).

55   See website for RERED: www.energyservices.lk/statistics/details_shs1.htm.

56   Hirshman (2003).

57   Cabraal (2000).

58   World Bank (2008).

59   Email correspondence, 21 June 2007.

60   Martinot et al (2000), p27.

61   Eckhart et al (2003), p13.

62   Martinot et al (2000), p27.

63   Loans by NGOs for solar are often mislabelled as 'microfinance'. See, for instance, Bernhard (2007). But microfinance is different from financing solar customers. The key characteristic of microfinance is that it is given without any collateral to facilitate the poorest accessing it – peer pressure is used as 'social collateral', whereas in the case of financing solar, there is often a hefty down payment and the asset is the collateral (in some cases banks ask for additional security). Moreover, microfinance tends to be short term, to boost a small business, while solar finance benefits from being longer term. That said, the skills attained in doing microfinance are very relevant to entering solar financing. It is, for instance, interesting to note that, while some explain Grameen Bank's success by the interesting group loans and social collateral they use, others explain it by the strength of their adherence organizational procedures (see Jain, 1996). Bringing that strength to solar for the management of finance has been a boon to solar diffusion in Bangladesh.

64   IDCOL (2008).

65   IDCOL (2008).

66   Like other World Bank projects, this project has a line of credit to finance solar consumers. It is managed by the Development Bank of the Philippines. In addition there are considerable subsidies and incentives. The subsidy from the Philippines Government, which must be passed on to the customer, is US$160 for 20–30-watt systems and US$80 for 30–50-watt systems. In addition, firms selling solar are eligible for a GEF grant of $2.5 per watt for 10–50-watt systems, $1.5 per watt for 50–100-watt systems and $1.5 per watt for community facilities above $450 per system. The GEF grant can be retained by the firm to 'reduce market development barriers'. Both the GEF grant and the Government subsidy are to be disbursed by the Department of Energy (Philippines Department of Energy, 2006).

67   In Uganda a grant was also applied to solar systems for rural institutions such as health clinics and schools. As in China, the grant in Uganda was provided on a US dollar-per-watt basis. Particularly interesting is that eligible systems can go up to two kilowatts. The grant amounts to $2.5 per watt for systems up to 30 watts and institutional sales, $1.5 per watt for 30–50-watt systems, and $1 per watt for systems up to two kilowatts (provided the system is for commercial use).

68   Interview with lead consultant to the REEF, 12 December 1996, Washington, DC.

69   Nyerjisi (1995), p393.

70   Memorandum by lead consultant to REEF (sent to IFC officers), 2 December 1996.

71   IFC (2002).

72   Interview with energy-financing arm of American foundation, 19 December 1996, Bloomfield, New Jersey.

73   Eckhart et al (2003).

74   An example of SDF funding was money provided to SEEDS to help improve its IT infrastructure. The aim was to connect the SEEDS head office in Colombo with roughly 15 branches around Sri Lanka to improve the institution's management information system.

75   SDG (2003).

76   SDG (2003).

Chapter 7

1   World Bank (1993a).
2   Interview with PV adviser of MNES, 11 March 1996, New Delhi.
3   Interview with director of Karnataka nodal agency (MNES), 18 March 1996, Bangalore, India.
4   MNRE (2007). These numbers do not include private-sector sales, which are not tracked by MNRE.
5   For example, although the Philippines has an easy route for foreign direct investment, once invested, a foreign company is not entitled to engage in retail – including the retail of solar systems – without investing amounts that cannot yet be justified by the nascent size of the solar market.
6   Interview with director of energy technology, BPPT, 26 July 1996, Jakarta.
7   Interview with PV adviser of MNES, 11 March 1996, New Delhi.
8   Interview with PV adviser of MNES, 11 March 1996, New Delhi.
9   World Bank (1993a).
10 A detailed cash-flow analysis suggests the entrepreneurs in India could have sold four times more systems during the same period with these improved margins. See Miller and Hope (2000), p95.
11 Cabraal and Fitzgerald (2001), p5.
12 Finucane (2005), pp9–10.
13 In the consultant's original report, he uses the term 'gross profit'. For consistency sake, I have replaced this with the term 'gross margin'.
14 Finucane (2005).
15 For a discussion on how this approach was applied to GEF and World Bank solar projects, see Martinot et al (2001), p50.
16 It may be that, as a solar programme progresses, grants actually have to increase, rather than decrease, to ensure that diffusion continues. If the remaining customer base is harder to reach and has less purchasing power, grants will be the only way to ensure that businesses stay engaged and continue to offer service and reach out to those who remain unserved. This is an area for future research.
17 Interview with marketing manager and general manager of PV manufacturer, 21 February 1996, Hyderabad, India.
18 This worked well, for example, on the island of Palawan in the Philippines. Through a programme with the Malampya Natural Gas project (operating just off Palawan), a default guarantee was put in place with the Palawan Cooperative Bank to encourage it to offer financing to solar customers. Before this guarantee was in place in 2002, this cooperative bank had never lent for solar and was sceptical. But by the end of 2006, it is estimated that this bank had provided loans for more than 2000 solar customers on Palawan.
19 World Bank (2002).
20 IDCOL (2008), p2.
21 SEEDS (2008).
22 ESMAP (1999), p31.
23 Martinot et al (2002), p329.
24 Eckhart et al (2003), p12.
25 Stone (2003), p25.
26 Martinot et al (2002), p329.
27 Karottki and Banks (2000), p58
28 Martinot et al (2001), p47.
29 Martinot et al (2000), p25.
30 Yelland (2004), p9.

31 Hirshman (2004), p8.

32 Hirshman (2002).

33 Hirshman (2004), p8.

34 For the impact of devaluation, see Hirshman (2002). But it is not that South Africa was alone in facing devaluation of their currency. In many other emerging markets, such as Sri Lanka, the currency was devaluing by 10 per cent per annum. But the difference in South Africa was that, because the price to the customer was regulated by the Government, the businesses couldn't pass on the cost difference and so get started with their installations: 'The companies, taking a united stand, complained to the DME that without an increase to the subsidy, they would require a boost to the already high monthly fee to make their business plans work.' (Hirshman, 2004, p8).

35 In August 2003, the National Electricity Regulator (NER) heard that the 65 million rand allocated by the DME as subsidy was to be unilaterally reallocated by the DME from NER to Eskom to fund 'special ministerial projects' – that is, uneconomic electrification projects that had resulted from political pressures (Yelland, 2004).

36 Correspondence with the former managing director of Eskom-Shell joint venture, 19 February 2007. He acquired these numbers through telephone interviews and correspondence with heads of companies still, at that time, engaged in the fee-for-service business in South Africa.

37 In Sri Lanka, the average GEF grant over 100,000 systems was roughly US$75. But the Sri Lankan Government also applied an additional subsidy. If we assume that 50% of the 100,000 systems sold also attracted US$100 from the Sri Lankan Government, the average subsidy per system is US$$125. In Bangladesh, if we take the information provided by IDCOL (2007) on declining grants per system, the average grant over 100,000 systems was just US$64.

38 Hirshman (2004), p8.

39 Karottki and Banks (2000), p51.

40 Hirshman (2004).

41 Hankins (1993).

42 ESMAP (1999), p31.

43 Estimates of installed base of 150,000 systems and growth of 25 per cent between 1992 and 1999 come from ESMAP (1999), p8. Estimates of an installed base of 120,000 systems and growth of 10–20 per cent come from Martinot et al (2002).

44 ESMAP (1999), p6.

45 Hirshman (2003).

46 ESMAP (1999), p9.

47 For this argument, see Bernhard (2007), p26.

48 Martinot et al (2001).

Chapter 8

1 Clini and Moody-Stuart (2001), p17. This initiative received the strong backing of Tony Blair, 'who successfully persuaded his fellow leaders [in the G8] to adopt the plan' (Lean, 2000).

2 This account is provided by the American entrepreneur profiled in our India case study. For consistency in referring to the profiled entrepreneurs anonymously, this quote is not referenced.

3 GVEP (2002), p3.

4 Clini and Moody-Stuart (2001), p3.

5 Hering (2005b), p110.

6   Correspondence with World Bank staff, 9 July 2008.

7   For description of China project, see Hirshman (2003), p28.

8   Eckhart et al (2003), p15.

9   Hirshman (2003), p26.

10 Eckhart et al (2003), p15.

11 Hirshman (2003), p26. The same can be said of the Dutch, Australian and Spanish programmes mentioned earlier.

12 Hirshman (2003), p25.

13 IDCOL (2007), p1.

14 Equivalent to DM0.99/kWh at the time of introduction in 1999 (before the introduction of the euro); see Geller (2003), p59.

15 Bradford (2006), p180.

16 Over time, the amount of capital subsidy from the Japanese Government for every watt installed has declined. Whereas the programme started by giving 900 yen per watt (US$7.5 at that time), by the end of 2000 it was offering only 150 yen (US$1.2) per watt. At the same time, the price per watt installed also come down, from $30 per watt in 1993 to $8 per watt by 2000. This equates to a decline in the capital subsidy from roughly 25 per cent of the system price in 1993 to 15 per cent by 2000. Since then the subsidy has continued to decline, and the market for solar, while slowing in growth, has nonetheless been sustained. See Geller (2003), pp58–59.

17 Japan's growth was even more dramatic than that of Germany if you consider that in 1995 Japan had only 4 MW of installed solar capacity, while Germany had 20 MW.

18 Geller (2003), p59.

19 Although the average in Germany is slightly skewed, as it also includes larger commercial-scale solar installations.

20 This is all the more incredible if you consider that in 1993, Germany and Japan combined accounted for only 3 per cent of the annual installations of solar PV. See Geller (2003), p59.

21 At the time of writing, there is a 30 per cent federal tax credit on the system price, up to a maximum of US$3000, to complement additional subsidies and tax incentives offered by states such as California, New York and New Jersey (see Hering, 2005a).

22 Inglin (2008).

23 For a good overview of Chinese PV manufacturing companies, see Schmela (2005). Many of these companies have listed on the stock-markets in New York or London, and raised substantial capital for further expansion. In 2006 China's seventh richest man was the founder and CEO of a Chinese solar company listed on NASDAQ (Friedman, 2006).

24 Part of the reason for this rise was a shortage of silicon – the primary raw material from which solar PV modules are made. As this shortage starts to ease, as some project in early 2009, and as the growth in a few of the pioneering markets start to slow, such as Germany's, wholesale module prices could again start to decline. For this view, see Koot (2007).

25 In addition, it meant that the manufacturers of solar PV modules diverted their production to making the larger modules for grid-connected applications for the industrialized markets, rather than the smaller modules required for emerging markets, as overall the larger modules are more cost-effective to manufacture and are better for fully loading manufacturing plants.

26 That said, the market dipped in China in 2007, primarily due to a shortage of smaller solar modules. With Chinese solar manufacturers directing all their attention to making larger modules for export, it became hard to source smaller modules for the domestic market.

27 Barron (2008). The price of a thin-film panel is expected to fall to $1.81 per watt by 2010.

28 Muttemwar (Minister of MNRE) (2007), p5.

29 *The Economist* (2006a), p14.

30 UNFCCC (1992), p8. This treaty was opened for signature at the United Nations in New York on 20 June 1992.

31 JI would later be enshrined in the 1997 Kyoto Protocol – effectively as an amendment and addition to the UNFCCC. But it would apply only to industrialized countries, including countries from Eastern Europe.

32 Forsyth (1999), pp38–39.

33 *The Economist* (2006a). Ironically, the EU was reluctant at the time, but has since gone on to establish one of the most aggressive cap and trade schemes, the European Emissions-Trading Scheme (ETS), which targets emissions from the EU's five dirtiest industries and which has created a strong demand for emission reductions. The US has so far abandoned the Kyoto Protocol, as well as participation under the CDM – one of the mainstays of the Protocol it helped to establish.

34 UNFCCC (1997), p16.

35 UNFCCC (1997), pp16–17.

36 Instead of CERs, entrepreneurs also have the option of developing what are called Verified Emission Reductions (VERs). The main difference between a CER and a VER is that the latter does not go through the formal CDM process. But, like a CER, a VER confirms (verifies) that greenhouse gases have been reduced, and transfers a right to emit greenhouse gases to buyers (who often include companies and institutions seeking to offset their carbon footprint on a *voluntary* basis). Because an entrepreneur still needs to follow broadly the same rules and regulations (as for CERs) to create high quality VERs, because VERs tend to command a significantly lower price (than CERs), and because the market for CERs is likely to dominate as it matures, this book only considers how solar entrepreneurs can benefit from the creation of CERs. That said, the points raised in this chapter are broadly applicable to VERs as well.

37 *Joint Implementation Quarterly* (2006a). A good example would be a CFL bulb project. CFL projects in Honduras and Gambia that distributed only 300,000 CFLs and 40,000 CFLs respectively were deemed to be too small to justify the costs of creating the CERs, whereas a project in Indonesia with 12 million CFLs was quite likely to generate enough CERs to meet the costs of creating them (*Joint Implementation Quarterly*, 2006b).

38 Hering (2005b), p112.

39 The activities under this PoA will include setting new technical standards, new testing requirements, new consumer labelling and a new quality-assurance programme, all designed to spur the diffusion of more energy-efficient air-conditioners.

40 Opperman (2007).

41 *Joint Implementation Quarterly* (2006a).

42 Hering (2005b), p112. Solar PV systems mainly displace fossil fuel for lighting and entertainment, which are relatively low energy consuming compared to heating water for bathing.

43 Under the additionality discussion, we should also add that if an entrepreneur has been able to attract a grant per unit sold, then the same solar system will not be eligible for CDM funding.

44 *Joint Implementation Quarterly* (2006b).

45 Hering (2005b), p112.

46 Bradsher (2007b).

47 *The Economist* (2006a), p13.

48 *The Economist* (2006a), p13.

49 Mydans and Revkin (2007), p6.

Chapter 9

1 The G8 set a goal of reaching 300 million people over 10 years. The new target set in *Selling Solar* seeks to reach 400 million people over a slightly longer period of just over 15 years. But the two sets of targets are broadly proportional to one another.

2 For a broader application of the framework to any innovation, see Miller and Garnsey (2000).
3 See Prahalad (2005). For instance, when Prahalad considers the application of solar in India, he considers the case of a large Indian corporation – Indian Tobacco Corporation (ITC) – deploying solar-powered computers to help farmers improve their acquisition of soybeans. For a summary, see Prahalad (2004).
4 This includes present market leaders such as Q-cells, SunPower, SunTech, REC and First Solar.
5 Consider, for instance, how GE launched 'ecomagination', to worldwide applause.
6 *Financial Times* (1996).
7 According to the National Venture Capital Association; see Richtel (2007).
8 Richtel (2007).
9 *Environmental Leader* (2008).
10 Renewable Energy Focus (2007).
11 This project received approval by the IFC for funding and was signed in April 2008. Amazingly, it also qualifies for CDM benefits, because it uses a 'super-critical' coal technology that improves the efficiency of the plants.
12 Obviously you would also need to coordinate these activities to maximize efficiency, and ensure there is no conflict on the ground between the various initiatives. The Bank's in-country staff could serve this function.
13 Associated Press (2007)
14 Revkin and Wald (2007).
15 Revkin (2008), p8.
16 This lag effect could be of relevance to both economic and climate modellers concerned with climate change. If the prevailing assumption among modellers is that once renewable energy technologies are 'price competitive' they will diffuse rapidly, then these modellers' predictions about when renewables will take hold, and when emissions will be stabilized, could prove to be overly optimistic.

References

Acker, R. and Kammen, D. (1996) 'The quiet energy revolution: Analysing the dissemination of photovoltaic power systems in Kenya', *Energy Policy*, vol 24, no 1, pp81–111

Adiga, A. (2006) 'Running out of breath', *Time*, 9 October, p34

Agarwal, B. (1983) 'Diffusion of rural innovations: Some analytical issues and the case of wood-burning stoves', *World Development*, vol 11, no 4, pp359–376

Ahmed, K. (1994) 'Renewable energy technologies: A review of status and costs of selected technologies', World Bank Technical Paper Number 240, World Bank, Washington, DC

Aleke-Dondo, C. (1995) 'The changing roles of key institutions in the implementation of credit programs for small-scale enterprise development in Kenya', in P. English and G. Henault (eds) *Agents of Change: Studies on the Policy Environment for Small Enterprise in Africa*, Intermediate Technology Publications, London

Anderson, D. (1992) *The Energy Industry and Global Warming: New Roles for International Aid*, Overseas Development Institute, London

Anderson, D. and Ahmed, K. (1995) 'The case for solar energy investments', World Bank Technical Paper Number 279, World Bank, Washington, DC

Anderson, D. and Ahmed, K. (1994) *Two Proposals to Commercialize Solar Energy Use in Developing Countries*, World Bank, Washington, DC

Associated Press (2007) 'Global warming report builds support for bid for new world environmental body', www.iht.com/articles/ap/2007/02/03/europe/EU-GEN-France-Environment.php, 3 February

Barozzi, L. and Guidi, D. (1993) *Prospects for the Expansion of Solar PV Technology in the Developing World: Financial Mechanisms and Technology Transfer Optimisation*, WWF, Italy

Barron, R. (2008) 'Oversupply of silicon to be worse than expected', www.greentechmedia.com/articles, 29 May

Bass, F. (1969) 'A new product growth model for consumer durables', *Management Science*, vol 15, pp215–227

Bass, F. (1980) 'The relationship between diffusion rates, experience curves, and demand elasticities for consumer durable technological innovations', *Journal of Business*, vol 53, pp51–67

Bosshard, P. (1993) *Energy from Dante's Inferno: A Memorandum of the Berne Declaration and Greenpeace Switzerland on the Contradictory Energy Policies of the World Bank and the GEF in India*, Erklarung von Bern, Zurich, Switzerland

Bradford, T. (2006) *Solar Revolution: The Economic Transformation of the Global Energy Industry*, MIT Press, Cambridge, MA

Bradsher, K. (2007a) 'It's clean air vs. TV in poor India village', *International Herald Tribune*, 9 January, pp1, 12

Bradsher, K. (2007b) 'China knows which way wind blows', *International Herald Tribune*, 10 May, pp1, 4

Bernhard, B. (2007) 'Microcredit and renewables', *Sun and Wind Energy*, vol 4, pp20–26

Brown, L. (1981) *Innovation Diffusion*, Methuen, New York

Bryant, L. (1976) 'The development of the diesel machine', *Technology and Culture*, vol 17 pp432–446

Cabraal, A. (2000) 'Building on experience: Assuring quality in the World Bank/GEF-assisted China Renewable Energy Development Project', 16th European Photovoltaics Conference, Glasgow, 1–5 May

Cabraal, A. and Fitzgerald, K. (2001) *PV for Electrification within Restructured Power Sectors in Developing Countries*, World Bank, Washington, DC

Cabraal, A., Cosgrove-Davies, M. and Schaeffer, L. (1996) 'Best practices for photovoltaic household electrification programs', World Bank Technical Paper Number 324, World Bank, Washington, DC

Coopersmith, J. (1992) *The Electrification of Russia, 1880–1926*, Cornell University Press, Ithaca, NY

Clini, C. and Moody-Stuart, M. (2001) 'Renewable energy: Development that lasts', 2001 G8 Renewable Energy Task Force (Chairmen's Report), Okinawa Summit, July

Covell, P. and Hansen, R. (1995) *Full Cost Recovery in Photovoltaic Projects: Debunking the Myths about PV Equipment Subsidization*, Enersol Associates, Somerville, MA

Crampton, T. (2000) 'Rail network to bring India up to web speed', *International Herald Tribune*, 22 May

Deshpande, R. (1983) 'Comparative review of innovation diffusion books', *Journal of Marketing Research*, vol XX, August, pp327–335

Deviah, M. A. (1995) 'India may lose $55m WB loan', *Indian Express (Bangalore)*, 3 June

Dikshit, M. (1996) *Institutional Arrangements for Agricultural Credit*, Swiss Development Co-operation, New Delhi

Dixon, R. (1980) 'Hybrid corn revisited', *Econometrica*, vol 48, no 6, pp1451–1460

Drennen, T., Erickson, J. and Chapman, D. (1996) 'Solar power and climate change policy in developing countries', *Energy Policy*, vol 24, no 1, pp9–16

Drucker, P. (1985) *Innovation and Entrepreneurship*, Butterworth-Heinemann, Oxford, UK

Ebisch, R. (1995) 'Seeding the Brazilian market', *NREL in Review*, spring, pp2–4

Eckhart, M., Stone, J. and Rutledge, K. (2003) 'Financing PV growth', in A. Luque and S. Hegedus (eds) *Handbook of Photovoltaic Science and Engineering*, John Wiley and Sons, Hoboken, New Jersey

ECN (1995) *Market Development for Solar Home Systems*, Netherlands Energy Research Foundation, Petten, The Netherlands

ECN (1996) 'Market development of solar home systems: Minutes of meetings', TERI/Netherlands Energy Research Foundation Collaborative Research Programme, Petten, The Netherlands

The Economist (1995) 'The battle for world power', *The Economist*, 7 October, pp23–26

The Economist (2006a) 'Selling hot air', *The Economist (A Survey of Climate Change)*, 9 September, pp12–14

The Economist (2006b) 'More of everything: Does the world have enough resources to meet the growing needs of emerging economies?', *The Economist*, 16 September, pp20–24

Edesses, M. and Polak, P. (1993) *Market-Driven Product Development as a Model for Aid-Assisted International Development*, International Development Enterprises, Lakewood, CO

Enersol Associates (1995) *Enersol Update*, 22 August, Enersol Associates, Somerville, MA

Environmental Leader (2008) 'UK's Brown calls for green World Bank', *Environmental Leader*, www.environmentalleader.com, 25 January

Erickson, J. and Chapman, D. (1995) 'Photovoltaic technology: Markets, economics, and rural development', *World Development*, vol 23, no 7, pp1129–1141

ESMAP (1999) 'Implementation manual: Financing mechanisms for solar electric equipment', Final Report, December, World Bank, Washington, DC

Financial Times (1996) 'High price of a green machine', *Financial Times* editorial, 4 December

Finucane, J. (2005) 'Solar industry growth analysis, Sri Lanka', report prepared for the DFCC Bank, Sri Lanka

Flavin, C. and O'Meara, M. (1997) 'Shining examples', *World Watch*, May/June, pp32–36

Fliegel, F. and Kivlin, J. (1966) 'Attributes of innovations as factors in diffusion', *The American Journal of Sociology*, vol 72, no 3, pp235–248

Foley, G. (1993) 'Renewable energy in Third World development assistance', in T. Jackson (ed) *Renewable Energy: Prospects for Implementation*, Butterworth-Heinemann, Oxford, UK

Foley, G. (1995) 'Photovoltaic applications in rural areas of the Developing World', World Bank Technical Paper 304, World Bank, Washington, DC

Forsyth, T. (1999) *International Investment and Climate Change: Energy Technologies for Developing Countries*, The Royal Institute of International Affairs and Earthscan, London

Foster, G. (1973) *Traditional Societies and Technological Change*, Allied Publishers, Bombay, India

Friedman, T. (2006) 'China's sunshine boys', *The New York Times*, 26 December, pA29

Garnsey, E. (1996) 'A theory of the early growth of the firm', Cambridge Research Papers in Management Studies, vol 1, University of Cambridge, Cambridge, UK, pp1–26

Garnsey, E. (1998) 'A theory of the early growth of the firm', *Industrial and Corporate Change*, vol 7, no 3, pp523–556

GEF (1998) *Republic of Sri Lanka: Energy Service Delivery Project*, Global Environment Facility, Washington, DC

Geller, H. (2003) *Energy Revolution: Policies for a Sustainable Future*, Island Press, Washington, DC

Giddens, A. (1984) *The Constitution of Society*, Polity Press, Cambridge, UK

Gladwell, M. (2000) *The Tipping Point*, Abacus, London, UK

Gotsch, C. (1972) 'Technical change and the distribution of income', *The American Journal of Agricultural Economics*, vol 54, no 2, pp326–341

Grant, R. (1991) 'The resource-based theory of competitive advantage: Implications for strategy formulation', *California Management Review*, spring, pp114–135

Griliches, Z. (1957) 'Hybrid corn: An exploration in the economics of technological change', *Econometrica*, vol 25, no 4, pp501–522

Grilliches, Z. (1962) 'Profitability versus interaction: Another false dichotomy', *Rural Sociology*, vol 27, no 3, pp327–330

GTZ (1995) *Basic Electrification for Rural Households*, GTZ, Eschborn, Germany

GVEP (2002) *Global Village Energy Partnership: Harnessing Energy for Poverty Reduction (Questions and Answers)*, World Bank, Washington, DC

Gunaratne, L. (1996a) *Using the Principle of Marketing for Commercial Dissemination of Solar PV in Sri Lanka*, Gunaratne and Associates, Colombo

Gunaratne, L. (1996b) 'Funding and repayment management of PV systems in Sri Lanka', presented at the Specialised Seminar on Financing Models for Decentralised Photovoltaic Energy Systems, Jakarta, 25–28 November

Hagerstrand, T. (1967) *Innovation Diffusion as a Spatial Process*, Chicago University Press, Chicago, IL

Halpert, J. (1996) 'Harnessing the sun and selling it abroad: US solar industry in export boom', *The New York Times*, 5 June

Hankins, M. (1993) *Solar Rural Electrification in the Developing World. Four Country Case Studies: Dominican Republic, Kenya, Sri Lanka, and Zimbabwe*, Solar Electric Light Fund, Washington, DC

Hankins, M. (1995) *Solar Electric Systems for Africa*, Commonwealth Secretariat, London, UK

Hankins, M. and Best, M. (1994) 'Photovoltaic power to the people: The Kenya case', draft ESMAP document, World Bank, Washington, DC

Hankins, M. and Wambutura, J. (1994) 'Spontaneous PV electrification: Development of the home PV lighting market in rural Kenya', presented at the Workshop on the Implementation of Decentralised Rural Electrification Programmes, UNDP/GEF, Paris

Hansen, R. and Martin, J. (1990) 'Photovoltaics for rural electrification in the Dominican Republic', in *Photovoltaic Resources: Applications, Utilisations, and Assessment; A Guidebook for Policy Planners*, Unitar, New York

Hassing, P. and Mendis, M. (1992) 'Indian Renewable Energy Development Agency: Evaluation Report', Ministry for Development Co-operation, Den Haag, The Netherlands

Havens, A. and Flinn, W. (1975) 'Green revolution technology and community development: The limits of action programs', *Economic Development and Cultural Change*, no 23, pp469–481

Havens, A. and Rogers, E. (1961) 'Adoption of hybrid corn: Profitability and the interaction effect', *Rural Sociology*, vol 24, no 4, pp409–414

Hayami, Y. (1970) 'Conditions for the diffusion of agricultural technology: An Asian perspective', *Journal of Economic History*, vol 30, no 1, pp131–148

Heertje, A. (1983) 'Can we explain technical change?', in MacDonald et al (eds) *The Trouble with Technology: Explorations in the Process of Technical Change*, Frances Pinter, London

Hering, G. (2005) 'Feds back in the game – For now; Congress passes 30-percent investment tax credits', *Photon International*, September, pp44–46

Hering, G. (2005) 'Kyoto not ripe for PV: Low-hanging fruit fails to satisfy investor appetite for solar projects', *Photon International*, September, pp110–115

Hill, R. et al (1994) 'The successful implementation of photovoltaics in Developing Countries', presented at the 12th European Photovoltaic Solar Energy Conference, Amsterdam, April

Hirshman, W. (2002) 'Waiting under South African skies: Only 1270 SHS have found a rural home through interim program', *Photon International*, December, p8

Hirshman, W. (2003) 'You say you want a revolution: Massive PV push may be a long march in reverse', *Photon International*, June, pp24–28

Hirshman, W. (2004) 'No longer married to a number: A 300,000 SHS program in South Africa is cut back to uncertain levels', *Photon International*, April, pp8–9

Hirshman, W. (2007) 'Shell's solar light dims', *Photon International*, November, 2007, pp98–100

Huacuz, J. (1991) 'Rural electrification with renewable energies in Mexico: Financial, technical, social and institutional challenges', presented at the Southern African Development Community Annual Technical Seminar, Swaziland, 26–28 November

Hughes, T. (1976) 'The development phase of technological change', *Technology and Culture*, vol 17, pp423–431

Hughes, T. (1979) 'The electrification of America: The system builders', *Technology and Culture*, vol 20, pp124–161

IDCOL (2007) *IDCOL's Solar Energy Programme*, Dhaka

IDCOL (2008) 'IDCOL's Solar Energy Program (June 2008)', presentation downloaded from www.idcol.org/energyProject.php

IEA (2002) *World Energy Outlook: Energy and Poverty*, International Energy Agency, Paris

IFC (1995) *Cultivating the Green Carrot: A Market Stimulus for Photovoltaic Technology*, International Finance Corporation/GEF, Washington, DC

IFC (2002) Presentation on the IFC/GEF Photovoltaic Market Transformation Initiative, International Finance Corporation/World Bank, Washington, DC, March

Inglin, C. (2008) 'PV Growth 1993–2006' (presentation), Singapore.

Iowa Agricultural Extension Service (1955) *How Farm People Accept New Ideas*, Iowa State College, Ames, IA

IREDA (1987) *Memorandum of Association and Articles of Association of the Indian Renewable Energy Development Agency, Limited*, Indian Renewable Energy Development Agency, New Delhi

Jain, P. (1996) 'Managing credit for the rural poor: Lessons from the Grameen Bank', *World Development*, vol 24, no 1, pp79–89

Jain, D., Mahajan, V. and Muller, E. (1991) 'Innovation diffusion in the presence of supply restrictions', *Marketing Science*, vol 10, pp83–90

Jechoutek, K. (1995) 'Policy innovations, rural energy needs: A new partnership', presented at the Conference on Decentralized Electrification in the Developing World, ADEME (France)/UN Commission on Sustainable Development, Marrakech, 13–17 November

Johansson, T., Kelly, H., Reddy, A. and Williams, R. (1993) 'Renewable fuels and electricity for a growing world economy: Defining and achieving the potential', in T. Johansson, H. Kelly, A. Reddy and R. Williams (eds) *Renewable Energy: Sources for Fuels and Electricity*, Earthscan, London

Joint Implementation Quarterly (2006a) 'EB decides on programmatic CDM', *Joint Implementation Quarterly*, December, p4

Joint Implementation Quarterly (2006b) 'CFL projects under CDM?', *Joint Implementation Quarterly*, December, p8

Jones, G. (1982) 'Reviews: Brown, Lawrence: *Innovation Diffusion: A New Perspective*', *Journal of Agricultural Economics*, vol 33, no 2, pp252–253

Kane, J. (1997) 'Capital: Its the impetus behind silicon valley', *Technology Silicon Valley*, January, pp21–28

Kanter, J. and Bennhold, K. (2007) 'Spotlight on reducing emissions shifts to China and India', *International Herald Tribune*, 26 January, p4

Kanter, J. and Cowell, A. (2007) 'Big expansion is urged in emission caps system', *International Herald Tribune*, 27 January

Karottki, R. and Banks, D. (2000) 'PV power and profit? Electrifying rural South Africa', *Renewable Energy World*, January, pp51–59

Kelly, P. (1997) 'Catching the punter's eye', in S. Birley and D. Muzyka (eds) *Mastering Enterprise*, Pitman Publishing, London

Kelly, P. and Kranzberg, M. (1978) *Technological Innovation: A Critical Review of Current Knowledge*, San Francisco Press, San Francisco, CA

Kenney, M. (1986) 'Schumpeterian innovation and entrepreneurs in capitalism: A case study of the US biotechnology industry', *Research Policy*, vol 15, pp21–31

Knight, F. (1921) *Risk, Uncertainty, and Profit*, Houghton Mifflin, New York

Koot, E. (2007) 'Price decrease for solar modules might start consolidation in solar PV supply chain', www.solarplaza.com, 3 November

Lean, G. (2000) 'Blair backs solar power plan for world's poor', *The Independent*, 23 July, p4

Lenssen, N. (1992) *Empowering Development: The New Energy Equation*, Worldwatch Institute, Washington, DC

Leuthold, F. (1982) 'Book reviews: Brown, Lawrence: *Innovation Diffusion: A New Perspective*', *Rural Sociology*, 47, no 3, pp572–73

Liebenthal, A., Mathur, S. and Wade, H. (1994) 'Solar energy: Lessons from the Pacific Island experience', World Bank Technical Paper Number 244, World Bank, Washington, DC

Lovejoy, D. (1992) 'Electrification of rural areas by solar PV', *Natural Resources Forum*, May, pp101–110

Macalister, T. (2007) 'Big Oil lets sun set on renewables', *The Guardian*, www.guardian.co.uk/business/2007/dec/11/oil.bp

Mansfield, E. (1961) 'Technical change and the rate of imitation', *Econometrica*, vol 29, pp741–766

Marshall, J. (1995) 'Bechtel venture thinks small', *San Francisco Chronicle*, 17 October, pD1

Martinot, E., Ramankutty, R. and Rittner, F. (2000) *The GEF Solar PV Portfolio: Emerging Experience and Lessons*, GEF, Washington, DC

Martinot, E., Cabraal, A. and Mathur, S. (2001) 'World Bank/GEF solar home system projects: Experiences and lessons learned, 1993–2000', *Renewable and Sustainable Energy Reviews*, vol 5, pp39–57

Martinot, E., Chaurey, A., Lew, D., Moreira, J. and Wamukonya, N. (2002) 'Renewable energy markets in developing countries', *Annual Review of Energy and Environment*, vol 27, pp309–348

Mason, C. and Rogers, A. (1996) *How Private Investors Make Decisions: A Fly-on-the-Wall Investigation*, Venture Capital Report Ltd, Oxford, UK

McKie, R. (2007) 'Global warming closer than we thought', *Deccan Herald* (Bangalore), 22 January, p14

McNeil, D. (1996) 'This $40 crank-up radio lets rural Africa tune-in', *The New York Times*, 16 February

Mead, D. (1995) 'How the legal, regulatory, and tax framework affect the dynamics of enterprise growth', in P. English and G. Henault (eds) *Agents of Change: Studies on the Policy Environment for Small Enterprises in Africa*, Intermediate Technology Publications, London, UK

Miller, D. (1998) 'Agents of sustainable technological change: The case of solar electrification in the developing world', PhD thesis, University of Cambridge, Cambridge, UK

Miller, D. and Garnsey, E. (2000) 'Entrepreneurs and technology diffusion: How diffusion research can benefit from a greater understanding of entrepreneurship', *Technology in Society*, vol 22, pp445–465

Miller, D. and Hope, C. (2000) 'Learning to lend for off-grid solar power: Policy lessons from World Bank loans to India, Indonesia, and Sri Lanka', *Energy Policy*, vol 28, pp87–105

Mintzberg, H. (1989) *Mintzberg on Management: Inside Our Strange World of Organizations*, The Free Press, New York

MNRE (2007) *Estimated Medium-Term (2032) Potential and Cumulative Achievements as on 31 March 2007*, Ministry of New and Renewable Energy, New Delhi

Moore, G. (1991) *Crossing the Chasm: Marketing and Selling High-Tech Products to Mainstream Customers*, Harper Business, New York

Moore, T. (1995) 'Developing countries on a power drive', *EPRI Journal*, July–August, pp26–36

Morse, B. (1992) *Sardar Sarovar: The Report of the Independent Review*, Resources Future International, Ottawa, Canada

Muttemwar, V. (2007) 'Solar India 2007: Valedictory Address', presentation at *Solar India 2007*, Bangalore, India, 20 July

Muzyka, D. (1997) 'Spotting the market opportunity', in S. Birley and D. Muzyka (eds) *Mastering Enterprise*, Pitman Publishing, London

Muzyka, D. and Birley, S. (1997) 'What venture capitalists look for', in S. Birley and D. Muzyka (eds) *Mastering Enterprise*, Pitman Publishing, London

Mydans, S. and Revkin, A. (2007) 'UN panel endorses energy "revolution"', *International Herald Tribune*, 5–6 May, pp1, 6

Nelson, R. (1995) 'Recent evolutionary theorizing about economic change', *Journal of Economic Literature*, vol XXIII, March, pp48–90

Northrop, M., Riggs, P. and Raymond, F. (1996) 'Selling solar: Financing household solar energy in the Developing World', Pocantico Paper No 2, Rockefeller Brothers Foundation, New York

NREL (1994) 'NREL India Initiative: Phase One visit report', National Renewable Energy Laboratory, Golden, CO

Nye, D. (1990) *Electrifying America: Social Meanings of a New Technology, 1880–1940*, MIT Press, Cambridge, MA

Nyerjisy, F. (1995) 'Private investment in rural electrification: The role of the IFC's proposed Renewable Energy and Energy Efficiency Fund', presented at the Conference on Decentralized Electrification in the Developing World, ADEME (France)/UN Commission on Sustainable Development, Marrakech, Morocco, 13–17 November

Office of Technology Assessment (1992) *Fueling Development: Energy Technologies for Developing Countries*, US Government Printing Office, Washington, DC

Oppermann, K. (2007) 'CDM programs of activities in energy efficiency', paper presented at Carbon Expo, Cologne, Germany, 3 May 2007

Packard, D. (1995) *The HP Way: How Bill Hewlett and I Built Our Company*, Harper Collins, New York.

Penn, T. (1984) 'Book reviews. *Innovation Diffusion: A New Perspective*, by Lawrence A. Brown', *Technology and Culture*, vol 25, no 2, pp316–317

Penrose, E. (1995) *The Theory of the Growth of the Firm* (third edition), Oxford University Press, Oxford, UK

Perlin J, (2008) 'Solar water heaters: The workhorse of the solar industry', http://miller-mccune.com/main/article/171, 21 February

Philippines Department of Energy (2006) *Project ACCESS: Accelerating Community Electricity Services Using Solar*, Philippines Department of Energy, Manila

Philippines National Electrification Administration (2002) 'Status of Photovoltaic Installation', Philippines National Electrification Administration, Manila.

Planning Commission (2006) 'Integrated energy policy: Report of the Expert Committee', Government of India, New Delhi

Porter, M. (1990) *The Competitive Advantage of Nations*, The Free Press, New York

Porter, M. (1991) 'Towards a dynamic theory of strategy', *Strategic Management Journal*, vol 12, pp95–117

Prabhakara, B. (1996) 'The promise of renewable energy resources', presented at Regional Workshop on Solar Power Generation Using Photovoltaic Technology, Asian Development Bank, Manila, January

Prahalad, C. (2004) 'Why selling to the poor makes for good business', *Fortune*, 15 November, p32

Prahalad, C. (2005) *The Fortune at the Bottom of the Pyramid: Eradicating Poverty Through Profits*, Wharton School Publishing, Upper Saddle River, NJ

Prins, G. (1992) 'Liberated by a magic bullet', *The Guardian*, 24 July, p16

Prins, G. and Stamp, R. (1991) *Top Guns and Toxic Whales*, Earthscan, London

Rady, H. (1993) 'Renewable energy in rural areas of Developing Countries: Some recommendations for a sustainable strategy', in T. Jackson (ed) *Renewable Energy: Prospects for Implementation*, Butterworth-Heinemann, London

Rahm, D. (1993) 'US public policy and emerging technologies', *Energy Policy*, April, pp374–384

Ranganathan, V. (1993) 'Rural electrification revisited', *Energy Policy*, February, pp142–151

Renewable Energy Focus (2007) 'World Bank raises funding for renewables by two-thirds', www.renewableenergyfocus.com, 29 October, Washington, DC

Renewable Energy for Rural Economic Development Project (2007), 'Projects implemented under ESD and RERED', www.energyservices.lk/statistics/esd_rered.htm, Sri Lanka

Revkin, A. and Wald, M. (2007) 'Lack of funds leaves solar power in dark', *International Herald Tribune*, 17 July, p11

Revkin, A. (2008) 'A new focus in climate negotiations', *International Herald Tribune*, 7 April, pp1, 8

Richtel, M. (2007) 'Tech barons take on new project: Energy policy', *The New York Times*, www.nytimes.com, 29 January

Roberts, E. (1991) *Entrepreneurs in High Technology: Lessons from MIT and Beyond*, Oxford University Press, Oxford, UK

Roberts, P. (2004) *The End of Oil: On the Edge of a Perilous New World*, Houghton Miflin, New York

Robertson, T. and Gatignon, H. (1986) 'Competitive effects on technology diffusion', *Journal of Marketing*, vol 50, July, pp1–12

Rogers, E. (1983) *Diffusion of Innovations* (third edition), Free Press, New York

Rogers, E. (1995) *Diffusion of Innovations* (fourth edition), Free Press, New York

Rogers, E. and Shoemaker, F. (1971) *Communication of Innovation: A Cross Cultural Approach*, Free Press, New York

Roling, N. (1982) 'Alternative approaches in extension', in G. Jones and M. Rolls (eds) *Progress in Rural Extension and Community Development,* vol 1, Wiley Publishing, New York

Rosenberg, N. (1972) 'Factors affecting the diffusion of technology', *Explorations in Economic History*, vol 10, no 1, pp3–33

Rosenberg, N. (1994) *Exploring the Black Box*, Cambridge University Press, Cambridge, UK

Rosenthal, E. (2007) 'The push for biofuels is victimized by the law of good intentions', *International Herald Tribune*, 1 February, p1

Rossini, F. and Bozeman, B. (1977) 'National strategies for technological innovation', *Administration and Society*, vol 9, no 1, pp81–110

Rothwell, R. and Zegveld, W. (1982) *Innovation and the Small and Medium-Sized Firm*, Pinter, London

Roy, K. (1994) 'Neglected issues in technological change and rural development: An overview', in K. Roy and C. Clark (eds) *Technological Change and Rural Development in Poor Countries*, Oxford University Press, Calcutta, India

Ryan, B. and Gross, N. (1943) 'The diffusion of hybrid seed corn in two Iowa communities', *Rural Sociology*, vol 8, pp15–24

Sahal, D. (1981) *Patterns of Technological Innovation*, Addison-Wesley Publishing, Reading, MA

Sang-Hun, C. (2007) 'South Korea seeks cleaner Energy', *International Herald Tribune*, 10 May, p11

Sanghvi, A. (1995) 'Equity, subsidies, and economic viability', presented at the Conference on Decentralized Electrification in the Developing World, ADEME (France)/UN Commission on Sustainable Development, Marrakech, Morocco, 13–17 November

Sastry, E. (1994) 'Solar photovoltaic programme in India', *Urjha Bharati*, vol 5 (Special Issue on Solar Energy, Ministry of Non-Conventional Energy Sources), no 1, pp5–11

Sastry, E. (2000) *The Indian Photovoltaic Programme*, MNES, New Delhi

Schmela, M. (2005) 'Green light for solar power: China's PV industry awakens', *Photon International*, September, pp56–69

Schumpeter, J. (1928) 'The instability of capitalism', *Economic Journal*, vol 38, no 151, pp361–386

Schumpeter, J. (1947) 'The creative response to economic history', in *Essays on Entrepreneurs, Innovations, Business Cycles and the Evolution of Capitalism*, pp221–231, reprinted from the *Journal of Economic History*, November

SDG (2003) *2002/2003 Annual Review*, Solar Development Group, Arlington, VA

SEEDS (2008) 'Financing for Renewable Energy', Sarvodaya Economic Enterprise Development Services, Sri Lanka, www.seeds.lk/PDF/Funding%20for%20 Alternative%20Energy%20S

Shah et al (1993) 'India', in Ramani et al (eds) *Rural Energy Systems in the Asia-Pacific*, Asia Pacific Development Centre, Kuala Lumpur

Sieling et al (1975) 'Infrastructure growth and adoption: The diffusion of cable television within a community', in *Studies in the Diffusion of Innovation*, Ohio State University, Columbus, OH

Simon, H. and Sebastian, K. (1987) 'Diffusion and advertising: The German telephone campaign', *Management Science*, vol 33, April, pp451–466

Smilor, R. and Feeser, H. (1991) 'Chaos and entrepreneurial process: Patterns and policy implications for technology and entrepreneurship', *Journal of Business Venturing*, vol 6, pp165–172

Soedjede, D. (1995) 'Obstacles to financial innovation for small business development in the formal and informal private sectors', in P. English and G. Henault (eds) *Agents of Change: Studies on the Policy Environment for Small Enterprise in Africa*, Intermediate Technology Publications, London

Solar Industry Journal (1991) 'The limitations of diesel power', *Solar Industry Journal*, pp26–43

Southerland, D. (1995) 'Alternative Energy Unit is formed', *Washington Post*, 18 October, pC3

Steel, W. F. (1995) 'Keynote address', in P. English and G. Henault (eds) *Agents of Change:*

Studies on the Policy Environment for Small Enterprise in Africa, Intermediate Technology Publications, London

Stone, E. (1994) 'Powerful developments', *Asian Sustainable Development Prospects*, vol 1, no 4, pp17–28

Stone, J. (1952) *How Country Agricultural Agents Teach*, Michigan State University, East Lansing, MI

Stone, L. (2003) 'Bringing light to the powerless', *Solar Today*, March/April, pp24–27

Tancred, A. (2002) 'Filter to save millions from poisoning', *Financial Times*, 12 July, p10

Tarde, G. (1969) *The Laws of Imitation*, University of Chicago Press, Chicago, IL

TERI (1995a) *PV Solar Systems Survey*, Tata Energy Research Institute, New Delhi

TERI (1995b) *TERI Energy Data and Directory and Yearbook 1994–1995*, TATA Energy Research Institute, New Delhi

UNDP (1995) *UNDP Initiative for Sustainable Energy (Draft)*, United Nations Development Programme, New York

UNEP (2004) 'India Solar Loan Programme; Programme Overview and First Year Performance Report', Crestar Capital, India.

UNFCCC (1992) *United Nations Framework Convention on Climate Change: Text*, United Nations, New York

UNFCCC (1997) *The Kyoto Protocol to the Convention on Climate Change*, United Nations, New York

Utterback, J. (1994) *Mastering the Dynamics of Innovation: How Companies Can Seize Opportunities in the Face of Technological Change*, Harvard Business School Press, Boston, MA

US Department of Energy (1995) *Photovoltaic Fundamentals*, US Department of Energy, Washington, DC

US Department of Energy (2005) *Basic Research Needs for Solar Energy Utilization*, US Department of Energy, Washington, DC

Van der Plas, R. (1994) 'Solar energy answer to rural power in Africa', Financial and Private Sector Development Note No 6, World Bank, Washington, DC

Villeneuve, P. (1982) 'Books. *Innovation Diffusion: A New Perspective*, L. A. Brown', *Economic Geography*, vol 58, no 4, pp391–393

Wade, H. (1996) 'Market development of solar based rural electrification', presented at Regional Workshop on Solar Power Generation Using Photovoltaic Technology, Asian Development Bank, Manila, 20–23 February

Walton, G. (1971) 'Obstacles to technical diffusion in ocean shipping, 1665–1775', *Explorations in Economic History*, vol 8, pp123–140

Warkov, S. and Meyer, J. (1982) *Solar Diffusion and Public Incentives*, Lexington Books, Lexington, MA

Watt, N. (2007) 'Climate change: Carry on flying, says Blair', *The Hindu*, 10 January, p11

Weimann, G. (1994) *The Influentials: People Who Influence People*, State University of New York Press, Albany, NY

Wilkins, M. (1970) 'The role of private business in the international diffusion of technology', *Journal of Economic History*, vol 30, no 1, pp166–188

World Bank (1975) 'Rural electrification: Policy paper', World Bank, Washington, DC

World Bank (1992a) *Staff Appraisal Report: India Renewable Resources Development Project*, World Bank, Washington, DC

World Bank (1992b) 'GEF Memorandum and Recommendation of the Director India Country Department of the IBRD to the Regional Vice President on a proposed grant from the GEF Trust Fund to India for an alternate energy project', World Bank, Washington, DC

World Bank (1993a) *India: Pre-Investment Study of the PV Market Development Project*, vols I and II, World Bank, Washington, DC

World Bank (1993b) *The World Bank and the Environment*, World Bank, Washington, DC

World Bank (1995a) 'Proposal for review: The Indonesia Solar Home System Project (14 September)', World Bank/UNDP/GEF, Washington, DC

World Bank (1995b) *Indonesia: Market Assessment for Solar Home Systems*, World Bank, Washington, DC

World Bank (1996a) *Rural Energy and Development: Improving Energy Supplies for Two Billion People*, World Bank, Washington, DC

World Bank (1996b) *Opportunities and Barriers for Development of Rural Energy Markets in India*, World Bank, Washington, DC

World Bank (1996c) 'Staff appraisal report: Indonesia Solar Home System Project', World Bank, Washington, DC

World Bank (1997) 'Project appraisal document on a proposed credit in the amount of SDR16.9 million and a GEF Trust Fund grant in the amount of SDR4.2 million to the Democratic Socialist Republic of Sri Lanka for an energy services delivery project', World Bank, Washington, DC

World Bank (1998) 'Republic of Sri Lanka; Energy Services Delivery Project', World Bank Project Document, Washington, DC

World Bank (1999) 'Sri Lanka energy services delivery project: Draft terms of reference mid-term project status review (23 August 1999)', World Bank, Washington, DC

World Bank (2002) 'Solar credit line for rural electricity services: Draft concept for discussion – Philippines Rural Power Project' (7 February 2002), World Bank Washington, DC

World Bank (2003), 'Study of solar PV in the Philippines', World Bank Project Document, Washington, DC.

World Bank (2008) 'REDP Project PV sales achievements', World Bank Project Document, Washington, DC

World Bank News (1997) 'Solar energy to light up Indonesia: Bank to lend $44.3 million for electricity in rural areas', *World Bank News*, 30 January

World Bank/UNDP (1989) 'Pakistan: Assessment of photovoltaic programs, applications, and markets', Activity Completion Report No 103/89, Industry and Energy Department, World Bank, Washington, DC

Yardley, J. (2007) 'China says rich countries should take lead on global warming', *The New York Times*, 7 February

Yee, A. (2006) 'Alternative energy: In search of extra resources to fuel rapid growth', www.ft.com, 9 October

Yelland, C. (2004) 'Reneging on renewables?', *Energize*, January/February, pp9–10

Zake, J. (1995) 'Creating an enabling environment for the development of small-scale enterprise through tax reform', in P. English and G. Henault (eds) *Agents of Change: Studies on the Policy Environment for Small Enterprise in Africa*, Intermediate Technology Publications, London

Index

Note: Bold page numbers refer to tables and diagrams.

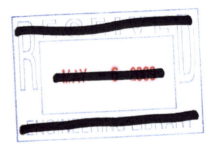